D1134534

To Rise a Trout

To Rise A Trout

Dry-Fly Fishing for Trout on Rivers and Streams

JOHN ROBERTS

The Crowood Press

First published in 1988 by
The Crowood Press Ltd
Ramsbury, Marlborough
Wiltshire SN8 2HR

Revised edition 1994

British Library Cataloguing in Publication Data

A catalogue record for this book is available from the British Library.

ISBN 1 85223 845 3

Dedication

For Tom and Luke: angling orphans

By the same author:

The Grayling Angler
The New Illustrated Dictionary of Trout Flies
A Guide to River Trout Flies
Trout on a Nymph
The World's Best Trout Flies

Typeset by Acorn Bookwork, Salisbury, Wilts

Printed and bound in Great Britain by
BPC Hazell Books Ltd
A member of
The British Printing Company Ltd

Contents

Acknowledgements

I am indebted to a number of individuals who have smoothed the path of writing *To Rise a Trout*:

Anthony Richards, who has painted the splendid picture for the dust-jacket and drawn the text illustrations from my rough artwork.

Gary LaFontaine for his generous hospitality and for guiding me round some of the trout streams of America, surely some of the most beautiful trout waters in the world; for his advice about some of the North American aspects of dry-fly fishing and providing samples and comments on his fly patterns.

Arthur Oglesby and Roy Shaw; I am fortunate to count amongst my friends two very gifted photographers, and I am pleased to record my gratitude for allowing me to use their work to supplement my own.

Many of the flies in the colour plates were tied by their creators and I am grateful to the following gentlemen for supplying examples and for commenting in detail: John Goddard, Charles Jardine, Gary LaFontaine, Lee Wulff, Roman Moser, Marjan Fratnik, Paul Marriner, Hans van Klinken, Lars-Åke Olsson, Tony Waites, Pat Russell, Gordon Mackie, Preben Torp Jacobsen and Neil Patterson. Some of the American patterns were kindly tied by Jerry Garner.

David Howden and Richard I'Anson for reading and commenting on the drafts.

Nick Bradley for tying some of the patterns in the illustrations.

Tom Saville for reading and correcting the section on fluorescent materials.

John Goddard for his permission to quote from a paper and article about binocular vision in trout, and for general comment about his fly patterns.

Dr J. V. Woolland for permission to quote from his research into trout diets.

Les Hill and Graeme Marshall, of New Zealand, for kind permission to quote from their book *Stalking Trout*.

Brian Clarke and John Goddard for generously allowing me to quote from *The Trout and The Fly*.

Nick Lyons Books, New York City, for permission to reprint sections from *A Modern Dry-Fly Code* by Vincent C. Marinaro, *Selective Trout* and *Fly Fishing Strategy* by Doug Swisher and Carl Richards, *The Trout and the Stream* by Charles E. Brooks.

Gary LaFontaine for kind permission to quote from *Caddisflies* (Nick Lyons Books).

Unwin Hyman Ltd for kind permission to quote from *A Fly On the Water* by Conrad Voss Bark.

Finally, I gratefully acknowledge the support from my publisher, John Dennis, who encouraged the germ of the idea for this book.

Introduction – A Personal Philosophy

My own dry-fly philosophy is echoed in Roderick Haig-Brown's words: 'There are times when a dry fly is poor technique, an affectation rather than an honest conviction. But there are other times, many other times, when a dry fly properly fished, will bring more action and excitement than any other method.' That just about sums it up. My biggest angling thrills come when the hatch begins and trout start to rise, when, on an exceptional day, every trout is crazed with gluttony and behaving like the town drunk who has found the keys to the distillery. No one would deny the place of the dry fly under these conditions. But more often than not during the fishing day there are few aquatic flies on the water, and in Haig-Brown's words the floating fly can be a 'poor technique, an affectation'. Because fishing the dry fly is my preferred method, the one that gives me the most enjoyment, I often use the floating fly when other anglers would be looking for a pattern packed with lead. In doing so I have learned that trout can be risen even when the river surface would suggest otherwise, and that some of those times when it has been deemed a poor technique, it can actually be very successful with the right methods and patterns.

The overriding concern for the dry-fly fisher is to present the floating fly to a trout so that when it rises to the imitation it thinks it is behaving in a rational manner, feeding on a natural food source. I believe most trout are catholic in their tastes and will, when the opportunity presents itself, eat any edible and tasty morsel that ends up in the food lane. There are times when the fly fisher must represent a diversity of un-fly-like terrestrials or use large hair wing patterns – flies to scare the traditionalist. Whether I am a privileged guest on an exclusive chalk stream or fishing an unstocked moorland beck I abide by no restrictive code (save the fishery rules); my philosophy is simply this: *If it floats and trout eat it, then fish a copy of it.*

Persuading a trout to rise in perfect faith in the surface fly is, for me, the complete and ultimate deception. The trout fisher can aspire no higher. No fishing pleasure can match the thrill of presenting a fly to a brown trout rising to a particular species of fly, in an awkward lie, on a crystal-clear stream, and then watching, as if in slow motion, the fish rising to take the artificial boldly and confidently. I make no apology for seeking the highest pleasure; after all the nonsense has been cut away that is the only reason we go fishing.

I confess I do not restrict myself wholly to the dry fly. Readers familiar with my two previous books will be aware that I have never been reluctant to fish a leaded nymph or lure (or a worm for grayling). However, my greatest pleasure of all the different techniques and tactics for brown and rainbow trout is to fish with a floating fly on a river or stream. This is no false snobbery, nor is it a belief that it is necessarily the most effective method of catching fish on every occasion, but merely a confession of pleasure in casting a fly over a surface-feeding trout, and enjoying the challenge of persuading the nonriser to change its mind. The thrill and excitement will never wane. Is the tiny dimple between the weedbeds seven-inches or twenty inches of wild brown trout? Will I be able to tempt to the surface the trout lying doggo in its lie? How do I persuade that trout that has five times followed my fly for a good look to actually take?

It seems that most of what has been written about dry-fly fishing has related to the chalk streams in England and the limestone rivers of the eastern United States and Rockies. This is a gross distortion of fly fishing practice. Less than 5 per cent of British river trout fishing takes place on chalk streams and the dry fly is widely used on all running water inhabited by trout. For many seasons I have fished a small northern freestone river. It is typical of many others throughout the British Isles; the fly life is prolific, and the brown trout and grayling rise freely for seven or eight months of the year. The hatches of Mayfly (*Ephemera danica*) would shame many chalk streams. The trout rise to all sorts of fly life and other surface food. Sometimes they rise with unqualified and undignified abandon; on other occasions they can be mercilessly selective.

Much of the content of this book relates to any river or stream wherein trout feed on the surface. Whether you fish the Test or Teviot, the Letort, Pennsylvania, or Henry's Fork, Idaho, the problem is always the same – to rise a trout to the floating fly. In this book I offer my own appraisal of some of the methods and fly patterns designed to do just that. No method or fly is foolproof, for trout sometimes conspire to thwart all that both the wise and foolish throw at them. It is my aim that by examining the theory and practice of modern dry-fly fishing the reader will be wiser in his choice of fly and its presentation. Bertrand Russell wrote: 'What men really want is not knowledge but certainty.' Fortunately, there is no certainty in any fishing, and neither I nor anyone else could offer any; my hope is that I might contribute a little to each reader's knowledge, and thereby shorten the odds on certainty.

Part One
The Trout and its Environment

The hunter and the hunted. In the last analysis this is what all the words are about – the man with the rod and line and some combination of art and science that he hopes will pass for a natural fly, and the trout, no more than a few yards away but in an alien world where man and air means death. The trout abides in an environment that is basically friendly, where food, shelter and clean, well oxygenated water are creature comforts. The type and quality of the subsurface environment controls much of the trout's behaviour and feeding habits.

If the hunter is going to have any success at all he first studies his victims and their surroundings. The trout fisher must determine just what the trout can see of the fly on the surface and of the angler and *then* assess how, why, where and when he must represent the natural fly on the water.

1 Trout Senses

It has been smugly asserted that the trout is quite a stupid creature, after all is said and done, and makes sufficient mistakes to justify fly fishing; but the marvel is that the trout, existing in an environment of almost baffling conditions, contrives very successfully to be right most of the time.

W. H. Lawrie, *Modern Trout Flies*, 1972

The trout's senses are an obvious and very necessary place to start a book about how to catch trout. If the concept is to entice a fish into believing that the construction of plumage, fur and metal we offer it is actually a living insect, while at the same time the angler remains undetected, the only successful approach to the problem will involve the fly fisher imagining himself in the trout's position below the surface. This is the only starting place; natural and artificial flies, techniques and tactics must follow later. To start at some other point is to completely miss the factors that most influence dry-fly design and formulate the angler's approach and presentation. I apologise if this first chapter is more theoretical than practical; your perseverance will be well rewarded. Skip this chapter and you may never know what the trout is thinking as it ponders your floating fly.

Much has been written of what a trout sees of the surface and the world beyond. Scientists can be very specific about some aspects of trout vision but also confess vagueness about others. Until someone teaches a trout to talk or until a believer in reincarnation who professes an earlier fishy existence can be found we shall have to be satisfied with the facts as we perceive them to be. In addition to the three senses of vision, hearing and taste, the fourth sense of smell is very strong in trout, but this has no bearing at all in fishing surface flies.

VISION

The eye is the trout's primary sensory organ. Although trout are visual feeders, they can survive well enough with only one good eye. Not only do trout feed by sight, they also use their eyes to maintain their position in a current. They do this by fixing an image on either a subsurface or a bankside object on a definite part of the retina and maintaining the image in exactly the same place by swimming against the current.

The lens of the human eye is fairly flat. The lens of a trout is a slightly elliptical sphere and considerably more powerful than that in the human eye. The trout's vision in poor light is appreciably better than man's. Within the eye there are two types of light receptor cells: rod cells, which are more effective in poor light, and are good for detecting movement, contrast and light intensity; and cone cells, which are more effective in bright light for detecting colour and fine detail. A trout's eye has more rods than the human eye and will be more sensitive to movement and contrast and work more efficiently in dim light. If that is bad news for the fly fisher trying to remain undetected on the riverbank, the good news is that because their eyes contain fewer cones than the human eye trout are less able than we are to assess fine detail and shades of colours.

Colour

Colour sensitivity in trout is a fact. Numerous experiments have confirmed that many species of fish, including brown, rainbow and brook trout, can be conditioned to respond to lights of different colours. Angling experience, which does not count for much in the eyes of the scientists, also bears out that flies and lures of different colours prompt different responses. Red is well known to be a stimulus in the animal world and this is true in relation to some species of fish. The north country grayling angler knows only too well how many of his successful fly patterns have splashes of red incorporated in their dressings. It has also been proved that trout are more sensitive to colours at the red end of the spectrum, in contrast to the human eye, which is more sensitive to the blue end of the spectrum. I have often pondered upon the success of 'Royal' patterns of fly – Royal Coachman, Royal Wulff and others – all with a broad band of red floss silk in their bodies. Despite their unnatural appearance they nevertheless prove attractive to trout. Part of the answer seems to lie in the red stimulus.

In some experiments on fish reaction to colour they proved very quick learners. I have no doubt that this is equally true of a trout learning that a particular artificial fly is to be avoided if it has once or twice been pricked or caught on it, and has been able to inspect the fly closely before taking. Much depends, of course, on how wild the trout are and whether the fishery practises a catch-and-release or a 'kill all over a size' policy. In the latter case, the likelihood is that a trout stocked at a takeable size has never been caught before and will never get the chance to become wiser.

Movement

Trout are very sensitive to movement – whether it is of natural food below the surface, or the almost imperceptible drag of an artificial fly on the surface, or the shadow of a fly rod cast across the water. Trout are always on watch for nymphs and subsurface food and must, of necessity, have high levels of movement awareness. Any unnatural movement, either on the bank or on or in the water, will alert a trout to danger. The appearance of a human form on the skyline might be enough to make a trout seek the protection of cover; when it is focusing on surface food the slightest abnormal movement of an artificial fly might deter it from feeding. The trout's eye is also ultrasensitive to contrast. The implications are obvious for any angler dressing for a fishing trip.

Direction and Angles of Vision

The reader may be aware of some of the following information, but it must be repeated here so that other aspects of what trout see of flies on the surface can be fully understood. If a trout looks straight up at 90° it will be able to see the surface, and, if the surface is not too disturbed, beyond into the air above. But there comes a point at which the line of sight will not pass through the surface at all. This point is reached at 48·5° on either side of an imaginary perpendicular line above the trout's eye. The total cone of vision through the surface is therefore 97°. The circular area within the cone at the water's surface is known as the window; outside the angle of the cone the line of sight is reflected from the undersurface by total internal reflection and this area is known as the mirror. In *The Trout*, W. E. Frost and M. E. Brown summed up the trout's view of the surface most succinctly: 'The fish lives, as it were, in a room with a ceiling made of mirrors except for a round skylight in the middle, through which the outside world is visible though distorted round the edge.' It must be strongly emphasised that, if the window ripples, the outside world beyond the surface is almost invisible except for the vaguer effects of sunlight, shadow, blurred outline and colour.

Little has been made of the circular boundary between the window and the mirror. There is no single sudden line of change where the window abruptly becomes a mirror. Rather, the two areas overlap and blend in a confused prismatic zone, known as Snell's circle, which is a mixture of both. The boundary is more sharply defined on slow-moving, unrippled, clear water than on a rougher, more turbulent river or on a wind-affected surface, where the transitional zone between window and mirror is blurred and

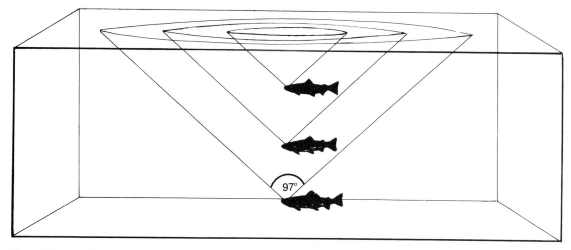

Fig 1   The size of a trout's window increases as the fish swims deeper. Its cone of vision through the window is approximately 97° irrespective of its depth.

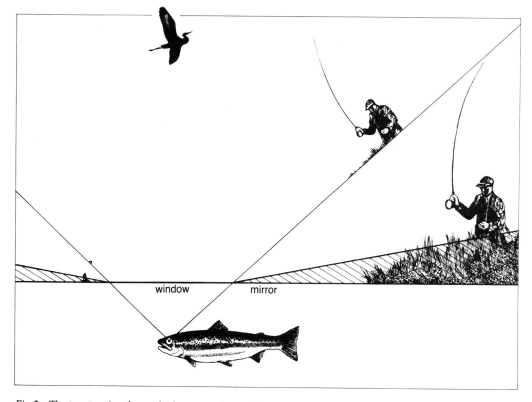

Fig 2   The trout seeing the angler has no understanding that ground level is actually much lower. Its picture of the angler is compressed because of the distorted light rays on the edge of the window. The bird overhead will appear as its true size. The shaded zones are blind areas for the fish. The undersurface here acts as a mirror reflecting the subsurface world. The wing tips of the dun on the edge of the mirror are seen by the trout on the edge of its window.

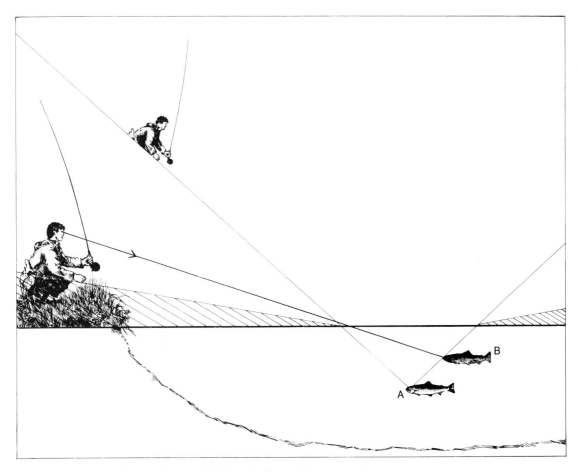

Fig 3   The effects of refraction 'bending' the line of sight mean that a trout lying
at position A appears to the angler to be at position B. The appropriate
compensation must be made when casting a fly to the fish. Similarly, the trout at
A viewing the angler has no conception of the real ground level.

disrupted by a rippled combination of window and mirror.

The 97° cone of vision that makes up the window is fixed. This means that a trout lying just under the surface has a small window compared with a trout lying much deeper (Fig 1). The deeper a fish lies, the greater will be its window, and it will see proportionately more of the world beyond. This circular window moves exactly as the fish moves across or up or down stream. It becomes smaller as the fish nears the surface and increases as the fish sinks.

Because of refraction, trout looking out through the circular window and the angler looking into the water do not see each other as they really are. Their positions will be distorted because of the refraction of light as it passes through one medium into the other. All light striking the water surface is reflected to some degree. Light striking at 90° from directly above the water will have about 95 per cent penetration. Light from lesser angles will be progressively reflected until all light striking the water surface at less than 10° is reflected. Light striking the surface at an angle greater than 10° will penetrate the surface but suffer refraction. The water surface is flat at 180° and no light of any significance striking at an angle lower than about 10°

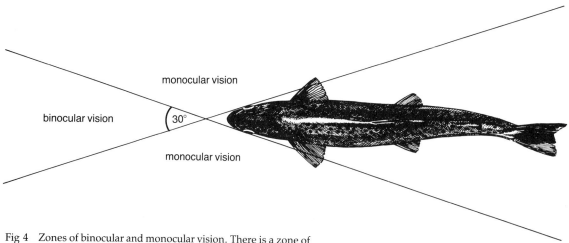

Fig 4   Zones of binocular and monocular vision. There is a zone of approximately 35° of binocular vision that extends to the front.

passes through the surface. This means that the light from a 160° arc penetrates the surface, but because of refraction it is concentrated down into the 97° cone. Objects in the air directly above a fish will be seen without distortion because there is no refraction, but objects on the very edge of the window suffer the greatest distortion because the light rays from this area are the most bent and compressed. Objects on the edge of the window appear to the trout as though they are in the air along the 97° line. The trout will have no understanding that those objects are in fact much lower (Fig 2).

Objects on a trout's horizon will appear smaller than they really are and smaller than similar objects overhead, which they will see as normal. The objects that are on the horizon will appear increasingly nearer their true size the deeper the fish swims because the size of the window is increasing and the objects will be positioned more towards its centre.

If the trout's view out of the water is sometimes distorted, so too is the angler's view into the water. The effects of refraction apply similarly. The more acute the angle of the fisherman's view, the greater the distortion, from a position directly above a fish there is no refraction, but from a position well to the side the line of sight is bent. This results in a fish appearing to lie higher in the water and slightly farther away than it actually is (Fig 3).

Zones of Binocular Vision

Whereas man is binocular – he can see things with two eyes and can assess the third dimension – trout vision is both binocular and monocular. The trout's eyes are situated laterally and are tilted slightly inwards, both forward and upward. Their position is such that there is a zone of binocular vision directly in front of the fish which extends overhead, and monocular vision at the sides (Fig 4). The binocular vision is particulary important in the feeding process as it enables distances to be assessed. In the monocular zone the trout cannot judge distances although its brain may be able to guess at distances by the size of an item in relation to other objects in view. The angle of vision of each eye is approximately 180°. This leaves a blind zone immediately to the rear. All anglers are aware that with very careful wading one can sometimes manage to get very close to trout when approaching from the rear.

Until recently the zone of binocular vision was thought only to be an area in front of the fish, but pioneering work by John Goddard, confirmed by Professor W. R. A. Muntz of Monash University, Australia, has shown that due to the upward as well as the forward tilt of the eyes the range of binocular vision is much greater than previously supposed. I am extremely grateful to John Goddard for his permission to quote from and paraphrase extracts from a paper in which he describes his experiments and findings. He regards his calculations as accurate to within a couple of degrees.

Because of the position of the eyes, which are angled inwards slightly towards the front and also overhead, the arc of binocular vision to the front was discovered to be

'approximately 35°, not as previously supposed 45°. The arc overhead was a little less and seemed to be approximately 28° (Fig 5). Due to the fact that the two arcs (or more probably elongated cones) of binocular vision overlap considerably due to the inwardly converging angles of the eyes I assumed that the overall area covered by binocular vision is approximately 130° from in front to overhead. I also assumed that the trout's binocular vision at each end of this arc would be less acute, and that its most acute vision would occur where the cones overlap, which would probably be at an angle of about 40° from the horizontal in front of the head (Fig 6). From many hundreds of subsequent personal observations of trout in their feeding lies I have noticed that most trout seem to lie at a slight angle with their head up. This in effect means that this optimum angle of acute binocular vision is probably nearer to 45° from the horizontal which would enable the trout to observe not only the mirror above but also into the edge of its window.

To understand what follows it is necessary to know that a trout focuses the eye by moving its lens by means of a large muscle known as the retractor lentis.

With the lens at rest in the retina the lens is so positioned that anything in front and overhead is in close focus. When retracted, the lentis muscle moves the lens both inwards and towards the back of the retina in a straight line away from the nose, thereby providing focus to infinity directly in front and also to some degree above.

John Goddard then sought to determine the width of the cones of binocular vision benefiting from this focusing ability. I quote:

First of all we must take the two arcs discussed;

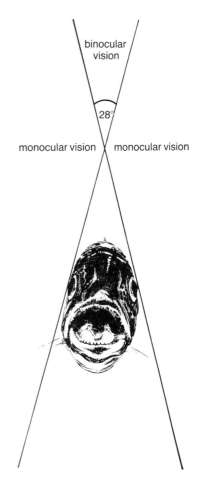

Fig 5   Zones of binocular and monocular vision. Because of the inward tilt of the eyes there is a zone of binocular vision overhead of approximately 28°.

the one in front at 35° and the one overhead at 28°, a rough average would be 32°. This means if his eyes were focused at less than infinity he would only be aware of approaching food within a narrow arc no more than thirteen inches wide at its maximum. Even with his eyes focused to infinity and concentrating on approaching food within its area of binocular vision, the band of water above and in front covered less than thirty inches wide at his probable maximum distance of vision in relatively clear water.

John Goddard found himself in the fortunate position of being able to test out some of the findings with a co-operative trout. He

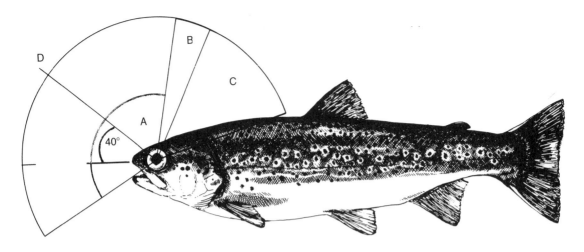

Fig 6   Zones of binocular and monocular vision. (a) Angle of binocular vision, approx. 130°. (b) A zone where probably the eye focus changes. (c) Eye permanently focused at infinity over this area. (d) Approximate optimum angle of binocular vision (40°) when trout is lying horizontally. John Goddard suggests that the 130° angle of binocular vision may well be increased at infinity. If so, the optimum angle would also decrease to less than 35°.

found a position that offered cover behind and partly above him and was able to lower a dry fly with extreme accuracy over the lie from a position directly above. I quote:

To start with I was drifting the fly down to him at predetermined distances to each side, and by this method I quickly established that my theory seemed reasonably accurate, as the trout lying only about twelve inches below the surface completely ignored my fly if it was more than eighteen inches to either side of his lie. I was about to retire and leave the trout in peace when to my astonishment he broke through the surface in the most perfect arc and took my fly in the air as it was hanging about fifteen inches above the surface and about twenty inches upstream of his lie.

Now the only way he could have seen this fly in the air was over the edge and in front of his window, and as I was reasonably sure that he had not tilted upwards before jumping I realised if I could persuade him to jump and accept the fly a few more times I might also be able to prove, or disprove, my first theory as well that they may indeed have cones of binocular vision to some extent overhead as well as in front. Never have I met such a co-operative trout as during the next fifteen minutes or so I persuaded him to launch himself into the air seventeen times. His reactions were absolutely fascinating as each time I lowered

the fly and swung it down towards him I was in no doubt at all as to whether he had seen it, as when he did all his fins, particularly the tail, would start vibrating. These vibrations would increase in intensity as I swung the fly closer until it was in range of his lie, when he would jump and take it in mid-air. I quickly established that he would first see the fly in the air when I swung it to within three or four feet directly upstream of his lie. Now of course what I wished to establish was whether or not the trout was observing this fly over the edge of his window through his ordinary vision or binocular vision.

If my theory was to be confirmed he would be unaware of the fly if I positioned it in the air between three and four feet upstream and more than eighteen inches off-centre, and so it proved to be. If I swung the fly down to him anywhere near that centre line he would see it every time but I could swing it down right past him repeatedly if it was more than about two feet off-centre and not once did he seem to be aware of it.

Certain conclusions can be drawn from the experiment:

(1) A trout lying and feeding within, say, 18 inches or so of the surface will probably be concentrating through its binocular vision and therefore the approaching fly-fisher would probably not register

unless he made any sudden movements. (2) A trout lying very close to the surface will probably be focused below infinity so any approaching objects, including the fly-fisher, will be even less likely to be seen. In both cases, however, accurate casting will be necessary, as the fish is unlikely to be aware of any fly drifting down to it either on or below the surface either side of its narrow arc of binocular vision.

Focusing

The construction of the trout's eye allows very close focusing. It doesn't need a scientist to confirm the all-too-common experience of a trout's close scrutiny of an artificial fly on the surface. If some got any closer they would scratch the cornea on the hook point. Trout lying just a few inches below the surface focusing on items on the surface have a very small depth of focus. In simple terms, the closer an object is to a lens of either a camera or an eye the smaller will be the area in front and behind the object that is also in focus. When a lens is focused at infinity the depth of focus is huge.

Trout lying immediately below the surface focusing on surface food have only a small depth of focus. They are reluctant – or, more likely, unable – to move to surface food beyond a short distance from their feeding lane. Admittedly, they have only a small window, but, more significantly, their attention is not drawn to items further away if their focus is centred on the surface above them. Deeper-lying trout are more willing to move further sideways or forwards to take food. This is in part due to their increased window but also due to their much increased depth of focus at a greater distance.

Trout focusing on an object just a few inches away cannot at the same time focus on the fly fisher some yards away, but this is not to say that the angler is not in the field of vision or won't be detected regardless of movement or outrageous clothing – he simply will not be in sharp focus. That close focus can be altered in a split second to home in on something that has caught the trout's attention. Moreover, when a trout is focused on something at or beyond just less than two

feet it probably has everything in focus from a distance of rather less than two feet through to infinity – a salutary thought indeed.

John Goddard's recent research has revealed a new and highly important facet of trout vision. As it expands or contracts to focus the lens, the lentis muscle moves in such a way that the front of the lens is always equidistant from the front of the retina. 'This means that even when a trout is focusing at very short range on food immediately in front of it, an arc of about 45 degrees on each side and to the rear of the fish is still focused to infinity. This would indicate that a trout feeding very close to the surface and focused at short range would be less likely to see you if you were either opposite it or even upstream, rather than well downstream, where you would come within the range of its 45° arc at its rear' (*see* Fig 6). This should not be confused with the blind zone immediately to the rear of the fish, in which it may be possible to approach quite close without detection. The consequences of an approach from within the 45° zone could be catastrophic, and yet it is often from this angle that the traditional across and upstream presentation is made.

The Effects of Light

The combined effects of refraction, reflection off the surface and the absorption of light by water means that the amount of light a trout receives is generally less than that in the air above the surface. The amount of light decreases with increasing depth. There is also considerable variation in the amount of light penetrating the surface at various points. Because the light rays at the edge of the window are the most compressed, so too will be the light intensity, which on a bright, sunny day could be considerable. Around the immediate window edge there is about 4½ times the amount of light because of the compression of light rays.

The trout's eye has a fixed aperture, which means that it cannot vary the amount of light it allows in. This is in contrast to man, whose pupils dilate and contract to accommodate different light intensities. Bright sunlight when the sun is directly overhead can be very uncomfortable for trout, which explains their frequent resort to shade or deep water.

With a little thought the fly fisher can use bright sunlight to aid his approach to trout, but it can also work to his disadvantage.

HEARING

From Alfred Ronalds onwards, interested parties have sought to discover the effects of airborne sound on subsurface fish. Twelve-bore shotguns have been discharged four or five feet from trout with no visible effect upon them. Very little sound that is airborne above the surface penetrates below; as much as 99·9 per cent of sound energy in air is reflected off the water. Virtually nothing penetrates the surface and certainly not the normal conversation of two anglers. Take a dip in a swimming pool and try to hear any of the sounds from above the water. Subsurface noises or vibration are much easier to detect. Sound transmission is about four times more powerful in water than in air. The hearing of trout is very well developed and they can detect sound waves in water through the lateral line along each side of the body. They also have a detection system deep under the skin with no direct access from outside. Trout are extremely sensitive to low-frequency vibration, even to the extent of being aware of other fish moving. It is also possible that they can detect obstacles by the reflection of water waves back to them.

Because the riverbed is no more than a continuance of the riverbank, vibrations on the bank will be transmitted to the riverbed and from there through the water to fish. Heavy-footed bankside disturbance can easily scare trout, as can careless wading in a small stream. I prefer to use non-studded waders on rocky streams because I suspect on stone metal studs can be detected more easily than rubber soles. If you have any doubts about sound carrying under water,

next time you take a bath try sticking your head under the water and gently knocking on the bath side. Even the slightest sound is picked up and trout hearing is much more attuned than the human ear to underwater vibration.

TASTE

There is every indication that trout possess some sense of taste. Some flies are almost invariably ignored by trout despite their abundance and ease of capture. The obvious explanation is that they are unpalatable. At the other end of the menu some other food sources are rarely passed by. Perhaps when trout are being selective during a multiple fly hatch part of their selectivity is based on taste, but I confess I know of no studies to support the idea. Taste and texture are experienced by the trout's tongue and inner mouth and not by the tough jaw, which seems to be quite insensitive. The sensitivity of the inner mouth and tongue is sometimes demonstrated by the instant rejection of an artificial fly if the trout is given the time to do so.

All the trout's senses are keenly attuned to its survival from predators, including man, and to maximising its feeding capability on and below the surface. It is the air–water interface that is the great concern for the dry-fly fisher, and here we can utilise the few deficiencies of trout vision where flies on the surface are viewed through less than favourable conditions. Next to a hatch of fly, the best sight on arrival at the waterside is a rippled surface, which serves to mask a critical view of the fly. Still the odds against any one cast being successful are heavily stacked in the trout's favour. Too often trout seem to have all the answers. Charles Brooks was right – 'In the field of fly fishing for trout, the only expert is the trout.'

2 The Trout's Environment

A river is water in its loveliest form; rivers have life and sound and movement and infinity of variation, rivers are veins of the earth through which the life blood returns to the heart.

Roderick Haig-Brown, *A River Never Sleeps*, 1948

One of the fascinating aspects of trout fishing is that you can choose between a small moorland beck or spring creek that you can leap across or the La Chine Rapids of the St Lawrence Quebec, a stretch of water a half-mile wide, and still be fishing dry flies for trout. In between these extremes there is a wide variety of water all containing different species of trout. There is probably nothing quite like the English chalk stream, though some of the French streams come close. The nearest American equivalents are the spring creeks that are scattered across the country. The water is filtered through limestone and is clear and high in alkalinity. These creeks vary greatly in size from the meandering trickle through a meadow to the large Henry's Fork, which is much more than twice the width of any British river. The world abounds with freestone rain-fed rivers. Probably some of the best of them from the trout fisher's point of view are the North American tailwaters below dams. Water accumulates in the reservoirs, where its temperature stabilises, and it is released at a constant pace to provide a clear, even flow enhanced with food from the lake to create a stable trout environment. The regulated flow does a great deal to minimise the harmful effects of drought and flood.

Classic dry-fly water on the River Test.

The South Fork of the Snake river, Idaho, where some of the best dry-fly fishing is often from a boat drifted downstream. The margins right under the tree branches are very productive lies.

It is a popular notion that if you want to improve a fishery you should build a dam on it and educate the dam managers into the needs of a trout fishery.

The fact that the dry-fly fisher tries to represent surface flies and terrestrials should not mean that he lives in ignorance of the world below the surface. The type, frequency and size of hatches of aquatic flies are determined entirely by factors and influences affecting the world below the surface. Similarly, trout propagation, growth rates and lifespan are intricately linked with the subsurface environment. For a fly fisher to fish a stream with a list of patterns simply because he knows they are successful or has had them recommended is to fish in considerable ignorance. An unawareness of the trout's world makes a very incomplete angler. So far as the dry-fly fisher is concerned, much of what happens on the surface is determined by the environment below. The factors that influence both trout and aquatic flies are source and temperature of the water, the type of riverbed, the gradient, the rate of flow and volume of water, and weed cover. All these determine the type of fly life, the places where the flies hatch, and, consequently, where trout lie in anticipation of food.

The quality of the water is of extreme importance. Water quality in this context means temperature, alkalinity and oxygen content. The degree to which these three factors influence a stream will dictate the trouts' food chain.

WATER TEMPERATURE

Trout are cold-blooded creatures, which means that their body temperature matches that of their immediate surroundings. As the water temperature fluctuates so does the trout's body temperature. Brown trout are cold-water fish and therefore extremes of heat can be fatal. They can withstand very low temperatures so long as the water immediately surrounding them does not freeze, and they survive in water covered with ice. An increase in body temperature brings about a similar increase in energy expenditure. The temperature tolerance of trout is greater if the heat is matched with increased oxygen levels, but this rarely occurs in the wild, where the amount of oxygen which can be dissolved in water falls with increased temperature. At 54°F the amount of dissolved oxygen that can be retained by water is one-sixth more than at 70° – a significant variation. The effect of increased water temperatures is to increase energy expenditure. Trout need to consume more food as their metabolic rate rises. Summer feeding levels are generally higher because at higher temperatures food is digested more quickly and consequently the trout is hungry earlier; because more food is required to maintain the metabolic rate of the fish; and because a greater quantity or variety of food is available. This is why growth rates are higher in the summer months.

There is probably no other influence on trout behaviour so important as water temperature. The more stable a stream's temperature is over the fishing season the more predictable will be trout activity levels. Extremes of temperature reduce trout activity. In very cold water the metabolic rate drops, less energy is expended and the need to feed diminishes. It is quite possible that an early-season hatch of fly will stimulate little interest because the water may still be very cold. At high temperatures the need to feed is greater but the ability to do so is restricted by the falling oxygen levels. In contrast to these extremes, in water at a temperature comfortable and conducive to trout activity they may rise to even the smallest, scattered hatches of fly. Temperature plays an important part in the hatching times of all aquatic flies and consequently on the surface feeding times of trout.

The temperature of water is primarily determined by its source. Freestone rain-fed rivers and streams generally experience a wider temperature range than a spring-fed or chalk stream. Spring water may take some months from falling as rain before being discharged from its subterranean reservoirs. Its temperature is much more settled than that of rainwater pouring rapidly into the rivers off the land. Even when the air is relatively cold a spring-fed stream can produce a constant flow of significantly warmer water at a temperature which suits both the fly and trout growth rates.

Water temperature also has an important influence on the activity of fly life. In general, the aquatic fly life is much less tolerant of fluctuations in temperature and oxygen levels than trout. Some fly species are able to tolerate relatively high or low temperatures or oxygen levels but it is the wide variations that are unendurable. The more stable the environment in terms of water flow, temperature and oxygen content the greater total population of insect life it will support. The narrow temperature range of the relatively warm water of a spring-fed river is particularly suited to the requirements of aquatic flies. These warmer waters will often produce two generations a year of some upwinged fly species, whereas in colder streams only a single generation is likely. Periods of temperature extremes, of either cold or heat, will also prevent or postpone fly hatches.

Some interesting research has been published in the United Kingdom by Dr J. V. Woolland. He examined the stomach contents of brown trout in the Welsh River Dee and made some discoveries relevant to the dry-fly fisher from which I shall quote later in the chapter. In relation to water temperature he had this to say: 'In this study there appears to be a definite correlation between feeding activity and water temperature – trout fed throughout the year but less intensively at times of low and high water temperatures.' Table A illustrates the correlation between the fullness of trouts' stomachs and water temperature.

ALKALINITY

Having considered temperature, which to some extent determines oxygen content, we turn to the alkalinity, or 'hardness' of the

Table A   Seasonal variation in the fullness index of trout stomachs in the River Dee

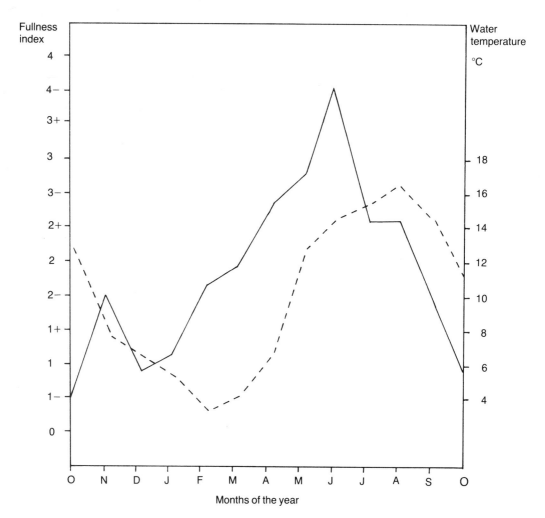

water. Alkaline water engenders life, from the simplest, microscopic aquatic creatures and vegetation to fish life. As well as the plentiful food chain ensuring an abundance of fly life for good trout growth, other attributes of alkaline water are also of great benefit. The spring-fed chalk streams of southern England (and a few other isolated chalk streams elsewhere in England), the limestone waters of northern France and America are all able to support much greater fly life and faster trout growth rates than most rain-fed streams. The alkalinity or acidity of water is measured as a pH (parts hydrogen) value. A pH of 7 is a neutral water. Figures below 7 have an increasing degree of acidity or 'softness' and above 7 an increasing degree of alkalinity or 'hardness'. Generally speaking, alkaline water contains a greater percentage of carbonates, the mineral essential for a rich plant and fly life. There are two further largely underestimated side effects of high

22

The author netting a brown trout from the West Beck, Driffield.

carbonate levels. The first is that they have a favourable effect on fish respiration rates, which aids their survival at critical periods. During periods of low oxygen levels in the water carbonates cause the respiratory system to slow down, enabling fish to survive on a reduced oxygen intake. The reverse effect is true in times of high oxygen levels, when the respiratory rate is quickened. The second benefit of carbonates is that they speed up the process of decay of dead organic materials, preventing an excess accumulation of decaying debris on the bed of a river or a lake.

The chalk through which the rainfall seeps before collecting underground acts as a fine filter, ensuring that chalk-based and spring-fed streams are generally of a clarity unsurpassed by freestone streams.

Because there are differences between spring-fed chalk and limestone streams and freestone rivers trout within them are affected in different ways. The two types of river are compared below so that the dry-fly fisher can understand the differences that affect both the fly life to be represented and the trout lies and feeding patterns. What follows are generalisations which can be applied to a typical chalk stream or freestone river. Each aspect will apply to a greater or lesser extent to individual rivers.

Important Characteristics of Chalk and Spring-fed Streams

Because they are spring-fed from water rising from underground reservoirs rather then controlled by the immediate recent rainfall there is a relatively narrow fluctuation in

23

The River Test.

water temperature. This provides a much more stable environment for all aquatic life and for fish. Eggs of flies, immature nymphs and fish fry are much more likely to survive without suffering the extremes of flood and drought. There is generally a greater quantity of fauna on which to feed.

For similar reasons there is also a relatively constant flow of water, resulting in much less rapid variation in water levels and current strength. Most of the water is moderately paced. This is important for trout growth as fish which live in faster water grow more slowly, since a larger proportion of their energy intake is spent simply in holding their position in the current.

The water is frequently exceptionally clear. In practice this means that individual trout can be spotted, stalked and cast to by the fly fisher, and that trout behaviour and reactions can be monitored. The drawback is that trout can also have an equally clear view of the angler. It is more likely that light leaders and a delicate presentation will be required.

There are often long stretches of river of a constant depth and width, which would suggest a fairly even surface flow and relatively little turbulence. A closer examination of the surface reveals often difficult currents caused by the extensive summer weed growth. Additionally, there may be mill-pools, weirs and artificial obstructions constructed by the fishery management to provide more interesting fishing.

Substantial weed growth will host a wide variety of fauna upon which trout feed. Ephemeropteran nymphs, shrimp and snails are probably the most important. The weedbeds also offer cover from predators. In high summer, when the flow might be expected to drop, profuse vegetation grows, enabling a water flow to be maintained in channels between weedbeds.

Because of the stable environment the aquatic fly life and other food sources are found in abundance. The wide variety of flies provides more interest for the fly fisher.

There are regular and often prolific hatches of upwinged duns. Complex or multiple hatches, when two or more species hatch in

A freestone river in Western America. This fly fisher is searching for trout in the lee of the rocks and in the protection of the fallen branches.

quantity at the same time, can also be experienced. As a result of regular hatches trout are often selective towards one species.

Frequently the river banks are open, surrounded by meadows. This may make for easier casting but the angler is more visible against an open skyline. All species of fish have growth rates well above average.

Characteristics of a Typical Freestone Rain-fed River

The key distinction is that flow and temperature can be irregular, following recent rainfall levels very closely. When winter snows melt, the rivers immediately fill up with very cold water, which may retard the growth of most aquatic fly life. Periods of low rainfall in summer may mean a very low water level with a low oxygen content. Wide fluctuations in temperature also make the water less tolerable for trout. The extremes of flood and drought are more frequently experienced than on chalk streams, reducing the survival rate of immature aquatic fly life and fish.

As a result of the irregular flow and relatively wide temperature fluctuation and sometimes varying water quality, the quantity of available food may be markedly less than in a spring-fed stream. It may mean that the numbers of upwinged duns are not as great as on a chalk stream, but this is debatable since different species prefer different types of river. Many species of aquatic flies may be supported because of the wide range of substratum but their numbers will not be so great. Stoneflies will play a more important role.

The speed of change in water level may be very rapid. A rise in level may be very apparent even over half an hour's fishing as rain further up the valley fills or discolours the stream.

Because the water is drained straight off the land most rain-fed streams are not as clear as spring-fed rivers.

On more turbulent rocky streams, the water tumbling and cascading over rocks gains more oxygen, to some extent compensating for any possible deficiency in summer.

The River Wharfe, one of the best fly-fishing rivers in the north of England. A highly productive river for fly life and one of the most scenic.

The river may be of mixed substratum offering a rapid change from solid rock to gravel, boulders, sand or mud over a short distance. This results in a very irregular depth and width, offering a wide range of deep pools, riffles, glides, pockets, eddies and backwaters, all of which provide a wide range of holding lies and interesting places to fish with different tactics.

The main thrust of current is likely to be in one place. Often on a chalk stream the current is widely spread over the width of the stream. Because the current is channelled into a single force this often results in under-cut banks.

Often it is only at low summer levels that individual non-rising fish can be spotted and stalked.

Because there are less frequent and smaller fly hatches trout may be less selective in their surface feeding. This is very much dependent upon fishing pressure, which will influence trout behaviour on any stream.

During periods of low water the aquatic fly activity is reduced and then terrestrials probably figure more prominently in the trouts' diet.

Tailwater Rivers

Where do tailwater rivers, those splendid North American trout fisheries below dams, fit into this scheme? It depends on whether the water is released from the dam at a steady rate all day or in a huge flush for a few hours each day. The latter, known as peak power dams, create great trout fisheries but not great dry-fly waters; the daily rise and fall of the water proves too unstable for most insect species and the main food of trout is the freshwater shrimp (known as scuds).

The steady flow rivers are incredible insect factories, producing great hatches not just in the summer but throughout the year. A comparison of the insect species in a tailwater river and a spring creek shows striking similarities – and that's the wonder of these flows. They are actually like giant artificial spring creeks, with stable water temperatures and rich food chains. The trout rise over weed beds in the slow, smooth currents to heavy hatches of upwingeds, caddisflies and midges.

TWO BASIC REQUIREMENTS: FOOD AND COVER

'Innocence is a wild trout.'

Datus C. Proper, *What the Trout Said*, 1982

'Stupidity is a recently-stocked trout. Sophistication is an educated trout.'

J. R.'s corollary to the Proper Principle

Whether stocked or wild brown trout or rainbow trout are under consideration, their basic requirements are the same. Their behaviour may be dissimilar but their survival requirements do not differ. They need to have an adequate food supply that will not cause them to expend too much energy in satisfying their hunger, and also the security of cover to protect them from enemies. If the trout angler bears these two aspects in mind he will go a long way towards discovering where fish are lying.

There are some behavioural differences between stocked and wild trout and between browns and rainbows. A stocked fish is in some part conditioned to man. It has been accustomed to associate him with feeding, and until its release in a stream the stocked fish has had its survival instincts suppressed. Food has been provided and man has protected it from predators. Suddenly releasing hatchery fish into the wild does not immediately make them behave differently. Their feeding and survival instincts, which have so far been subdued, slowly begin to take effect. Some hatchery influences diminish within quite a short time, others are retained for longer. Art Lee put it this way in *Fishing Dry Flies for Trout*: 'You can take the trout out of the hatchery, but you can't take the hatchery out of the trout.' Wild trout are much less predictable than hatchery fish. The indigenous fish has survived because it has avoided predators, feasted when food was plentiful and scavenged during times of insufficiency. Hatchery fish are used to feeding simultaneously and even after some time in the wild they may continue to do so. A hatch of fly for some reason ignored by wild fish may initially trigger a feeding response from some stocked fish. Soon all the recently stocked fish will be joining in. Hatchery trout are conditioned to expect food to arrive overhead in the form of pellets thrown into the stewponds. Initially, until those recently stocked trout become more stream-wise, they will be looking to the surface for food and for some while after release into a river they may react with much less suspicion towards the surface fly. If I may be permitted to add my own principle: trout rise to the level of their own gullibility.

The differences between mature brown and rainbow trout can be quite marked but much depends upon how wild, if at all, the fish are. As a generalisation, browns are much more territorial than rainbows, which are apt to be cruisers. These characteristics can be quite visible in a clear stream. A brown trout will hold its feeding position and is prepared to defend it from an intruder but rainbows cruise both up and down stream and across the current searching for food to a far greater extent. Of course there are exceptions to every rule and I have seen both chalkstream and freestone rainbows adopt territorial attitudes, guarding their lies jealously. In a stream where the aquatic fly life and other food sources are substantial, brown trout have a tendency to be more discriminating in their diet. Rainbows are more adventurous and their intake more diverse than the sometimes ritualistically feeding browns. I emphasise that these differences are marked only on rivers where there is an abundant variety of food and dependable hatches of fly. Browns may be more selective and much more wary of unusual natural foods and their artificial counterparts.

Just as 'tame' hatchery fish grow to become wild after release in the river, so it is possible for the reverse to happen. Tony Waites, the head keeper of the Driffield Anglers' Club, pointed out to me a wild 6½ pound hen brown trout that had appeared in their beautiful chalk stream a couple of seasons earlier. Tony had watched the fish almost every day for those two years and had thrown her pellets and became quite fond of her. He made very sure that on the half dozen occasions of her capture she was carefully returned to the stream. Whenever he approached the water to look down from a parapet about ten feet above the surface she would come to the margins expecting something to eat. Every other trout bolted for cover at our appearance on the skyline while she made for a shallow bay at our feet. Tony named her Monica after a lady of ill repute who had been involved in a much-publicised political scandal. In answer to my puzzled look, he explained: 'She's given so much pleasure to so many!' For all that Monica was so tame she was extremely stream-wise, as befitting one of her years, and very aggressive in defending her territory. Other brown trout between two and four pounds often encroached on her territory, approaching within two or three feet, and she immediately drove them away.

TROUT LIES

The dry-fly fisher can survive being a bigger ignoramus about trout lies than the nymph or wet-fly fisher because a rising trout betrays its presence. Unfortunately, there is a considerable length of fishing time when trout may not be showing themselves by feeding on the surface, or the river is such that non-rising individual fish cannot be spotted. The better the understanding of the trout's behaviour and its environment the fly fisher possesses, the more likely his success in finding trout and persuading them to rise. An experienced trout fisher should be able to fish an unfamiliar stream and have a good idea where the principal lies will be.

Trout have three requirements when selecting a lie: easy access to or a permanent position in the food lane; relief from strong currents; and cover from predators. These lies may not accommodate trout twenty-four hours a day. The position of some lies will mean that trout have to move into the main stream to feed on a hatch of fly; others offer little protection, though suitable cover will be close at hand; and some trout will be found in

Monica (see text), a wild 6½lb brown trout. Captor Roy Shaw.

very strong currents for short feeding periods. All fish practice economy of movement in running water. They must do so. Just to maintain their position in the stream they must swim against the current, expending energy. Therefore trout taking up temporary positions in fast water are generally on the look-out for food. All fish need the maximum intake of food for the minimum of effort. The most suitable lies are those that offer the most in terms of food supply but demand little energy expended in return.

Trout in different rivers have different feeding habits. In moderately paced alkaline streams, rich in food, fat, faster-growing trout have a wide variety of food to choose from. In rocky, faster, less alkaline rivers there are more likely to be leaner, hungrier fish.

River trout rarely search for food; they let it come to them. They live in the midst of a food factory where a conveyor belt brings almost all their requirements. For the most part they position themselves in or with easy access to the number one production line, the main

path of the current, the food lane. On a chalk stream or spring creek there may be no single major food lane but a series of different lanes between weedbeds across the breadth of the stream. On a typical freestone river there is much more likely to be a single principal food lane around which trout will take up station. Some larger freestone rivers may have a number of food lanes where the currents divide and take their own course, but even then there is often a single major lane. The food lane is usually the route of the strongest current, although this is not always the situation. Even on a freestone river the food lane can be dispersed across the width of the river. Trout expect to find most of their surface and subsurface food in the food lanes and most adult trout will feed there at some time during the 24-hour period. Sometimes the food lane is just too fast for trout to stay in other than during a period of ample food provision. They would spend more energy than they could replace. Moderately paced currents are more comfortable for trout to stay in, especially if a pocket of quieter water

29

Searching a food lane for a rising fish. Here the principal lane has been divided in two by the large rock and fallen tree-trunk midstream.

can be found in the lane – a hollow in the riverbed, in a cushion of water in front or behind an obstruction, or in a bank-eddy pocket on the edge of the lane. Trout also move into and patrol eddies and backwaters, expecting to find food that has been washed out of the main current. Such occasions present one of the rare examples of trout going searching for food. Experience will have taught them that midges prefer calmer water and that spent spinners and adult flies which have died trapped in the surface film will have accumulated there. Not only will the current pick up most of the subsurface food and adult flies on the surface, it will also be the main source of terrestrial flies which fall on to the river. They may not fall directly into the food lane but they usually end up there as minor currents feed them in.

It is possible in some circumstances to create an artificial or man-made food lane. I was fascinated to find on a visit to the Yellow-stone river in the Yellowstone National Park, Wyoming, that while I was wading the river a small shoal of between six and a dozen cut-throat trout of between fourteen and twenty inches would come to feed at my feet. They fed on nymphs and other dislodged fauna as I shuffled my feet in the stones and gravel on the bottom. The nearest would be four or five inches away with the furthest varying from six to ten feet away. The Yellowstone is a strictly catch-and-release fishery and it has become a trout fisher's paradise because of that far-sighted policy. Trout grow bigger and wiser and little or no stocking is required. This artificial food lane of nymphs, caddis and other tiny fauna provides a food supply wherever one wades and almost invariably trout assemble directly downstream. Unfortunately, they are too preoccupied to rise to the surface.

The fly fisher needs to be aware of where trout lie. In clear spring-fed streams and less frequently in other streams individual fish will be spotted, but if there are no trout rising on a river where the stalking of individual non-risers is not possible the answer is to cast the fly over the likely lies. Studying the surface of the food lane may give some indication of trout lies. Clues will be given by surface currents but one needs to know the topography of the riverbed to discover those places that offer breaks in the current in which a trout can rest, expending much less energy but still able to react quickly to food. In learning the physical features of a riverbed there is no substitute for being able to examine and memorise a river under very low water conditions. I doubt whether any other information is more valuable than knowing before a fish shows where the likely lies will be. Walking the banks and wading the stream under low water conditions, without worrying about the fishing but merely to

study the contours of the river bed and observe disturbed trout bolting from their lies, is invaluable. You are a spy in the enemy's camp. The reconnaissance should be a revealing and worthwhile exercise with long-term benefits.

Describing the different types of water in a river has become quite a science in itself. Art Lee has a nomenclature for no less than thirty-five different sites or types of water. For example, a *riffle* is 'water tumbling over relatively few rocks or stones', a *riff* is 'a series of riffles', and *rapids* are 'big riffs through which great volumes of water speed over large rocks and boulders'. He also carefully distinguishes between water surfaces – for example, 'run, slick, side eddy, dead water, stickle, jabble, shoot, riffle, rush, surge, pocket, boil, backwash' and others. Such a narrow classification of water is the result only of careful observation of a river. Water

A brown trout fighting for its freedom on the West Beck, Driffield.

that is summed up by others as either 'slow, fast or medium-paced' is much more critically assessed by Lee. I am amused at his method of classification of a river or stream. 'If I can't comfortably cast across it, it's a *river*. If I can, it's a *stream*.' Using such a yardstick we would have many fewer trout rivers in the United Kingdom than we currently claim. North American fly fishers in general can teach the average British trout fisher a great deal about reading the water. In New York State alone there are 17,000 miles of rivers and stream, most of which offer a very wide range of trout water. No wonder the American angler has evolved a comprehensive terminology.

To describe a river in scientific terms by examining its physical properties and the nature of its water does no justice at all to its magical beauty. A technical appraisal of a beautiful woman would do little to quicken the pulse, but a glimpse across a room or a hint of her perfume or time in her presence might leave you wanting to know her better. Only by being on the riverbank or wading its bed over a period of time can one appreciate the intimate beauty of a stream. I could never fall in love with a stillwater, much less the fruits of the trend towards ponds over-stocked with gullible trout. When I find my pearl of so great a price that I sell all but my soul it could only be a river.

All water is different. Certainly no two rivers are the same, no two pools or runs alike. Even from day to day the river changes as levels and flow fluctuate. The surface is ever changing with each boil, whirl and bubble. Even from cast to cast the current moves at its own whim. Subtle and almost imperceptible variations are forever being made as the gradient alters and the current is shaped by the invisible contours, obstructions and depressions that make up the riverbed. There is an almost infinite variation in a stream's flow and in its surface and subsurface movement. The speed of the water below is slower than that at the surface. As a general rule the current speed slows the nearer to the riverbed. The fact that surface water appears uncomfortably fast to hold a trout does not

rule out trout lying deeper in calmer water, watching for surface food. Fish in such lies must make a split-second decision about rising to take surface food; thinking twice will mean that the food is missed. Charles Fothergill, a guide on Colorado's swift Roaring Fork, put it like this: 'Any fish in currents like that makes his mind up fast – or goes hungry!' On most water a rising trout is easy to detect; the sight and sound of the splash as the nose breaks the surface and returns below is obvious. On calmer water the expanding rings of ripple betray the rise for some seconds afterwards. But many rises, particularly in fast water, are much harder to see. The fly fisher should make himself aware of where trout should be expected to rise because if he doesn't know where to look the tiny sips, the barely discernible rises will never be seen.

Usually, trout take up protective lies except when feeding. There are exceptions to this. Much depends upon how recently the trout were stocked. Wild trout adopt exposed positions near the surface of the principal food lane only when they are feeding. If they are seen near the surface the chances are they will respond to the stimulus of food. At other times they will be under cover and they must be looked and fished for in likely lies. When trout are not feeding, some streams, particularly those holding a high percentage of wild trout, seem almost void of trout because they are under the protective cover of weedbeds or undercut banks. Rainbow trout and recently stocked fish are much less cautious.

Another general but flexible rule is that the largest trout hold the best feeding positions. I have watched smaller fish which have taken up the prime position during a time of relatively little fly activity being ousted by bigger trout when a hatch of fly has started or been anticipated. The rule is less true of slower streams than faster ones, where the chance to take fast-moving food is much more critical. In faster water trout are much more aggressive in the defence of the prime feeding position. This is also true of good cover from predators. The best shelters are usually occupied by bigger trout. But sometimes the

A huge back-eddy where trout patrol in a leisurely manner picking off spent flies and stillborns.

size of a trout is not necessarily the determining factor as to who wins the prime lies. It has been known – although, I confess, not in my own experience – for wild ½lb brown trout to drive out much bigger rainbow trout from good lies. This is probably something to do with the survival instincts of the truly wild fish being more active than those of the stocked rainbow.

The prime feeding position is not necessarily at the very head of a pool. Much depends on whether subsurface nymphs or adult flies are being taken. A nymph is more likely to be taken at the head of a pool and the adults further downstream. The reason is simple. If the nymph swims to the surface at the head of the pool, it takes some time for it to emerge on the surface, by which time it could be many yards further downstream, depending upon the speed of the current and where the nymph activity starts. Trout rising to duns are therefore often found at the cen-

tre or tail of a pool because that is where the fully emerged duns will be found. It is sometimes the case that the initial nymphal activity stimulates trout into feeding towards the head of the pool and as the duns emerge trout drop downstream to adopt a lie to pick off the adults.

SPECIFIC LIES

The authors of *Stalking Trout*, Les Hill and Graeme Marshall, conducted a survey of lies on some of their New Zealand rivers over a period of two years. The object was to note the position of every feeding trout. Although the specific details of their findings cannot be applied to every trout river thousands of miles away, their general conclusions have some significance for most streams. It should be noted that the survey was conducted only from 9 a.m. to 3 p.m. each day and a diffe-

This angler is casting a fly on to the zone of water where the calm backwater borders the main current.

rent pattern could emerge for evening findings. The sample involved 1,476 trout. The main conclusions were that the most popular lie for feeding trout (26 per cent of observed trout) was in the eye of the pool; that a large percentage adopted lies in front of and in the lee of rocks and in the lee of extended banks; and that the number of surface-feeding trout in the centre of pools increased as summer heightened.

One lie not specifically mentioned below simply because it can occur anywhere in the stream is in an area where two current speeds meet. Trout adopt positions in calm water where they have easy access to and a clear sight of food in faster water. Therefore in almost any area where a faster current borders calm water trout can be expected to lie in the edge of the slower water.

The Eye of a Pool

The eye of a pool (Fig 7) is an angular area of quiet water at the head of a pool, between the fast current and the bank. As the fast current comes into the run it produces a zone of quiet water on one side or on both. Whatever the type or size of the river, this is one of the most popular lies for a good fish to adopt. It is relatively quiet water where the trout can remain with the minimum of effort; they have easy access to the food lane and can find cover close at hand under the bank or in deep water. If a pool is on a bend then the eye is on the inside of the bend. On a pool on a straight section there could well be an eye at either side. On a straight section, or if the angle of the bend is slight, the flow of the eye is in the same direction as the main current. If the

34

Fig 7   The eye of a pool is a comfortable lie with easy access to the food lane. If the pool is on a bend or behind an obstruction a back-current may develop in the eddy. Here trout may lie facing the opposite way but still facing upstream.

angle of the bend is sharp a back-current is created in the eye, where the flow of water turns back on the main current. Therefore it will be likely that trout in the back-current will be facing the opposite direction from trout in the main current. Where this is the situation trout may patrol the back-current looking for food. Where there is no back-current trout can either wait for food items on the very edge of the current or make a temporary excursion into the main food lane for

sighted food. The fly fisher will do best to cast his fly on to the very edge of the fast water or actually on the slower-moving zone between the main current and the eye. Presentation on the backwater is straightforward if the problems of drag can be overcome to allow the fly a reasonable time on the surface. The presentation is best made from anywhere except directly opposite the lie, across the intervening fast water, where the effects of drag will be immediate.

The Centre of a Pool

A trout usually takes up station near the surface in the centre of a pool only if flies are hatching or if it is on the look-out for surface food. Little cover is offered unless it is resting over a weedbed or has some other bolt-hole near by. It is usually not until evening or dusk that trout will venture here and stay in anticipation of a hatch or a fall of spinners.

The Tail of a Pool

I am sometimes surprised by the number of trout I scare if I start to wade the tail of a pool instead of first casting a fly over it. Trout drop back to these shallows and forage in surprisingly shallow water – often no deeper than enough to cover their backs. Watch the V-shaped wakes dart upstream as you carelessly approach the pool from below. Many trout in front of the run-off shelf at the tail prefer to stay close to the bank because of the cover it offers. I've often cursed my own eagerness to get into the water as good-sized fish bolt from the shallows.

Rocks

There are varying opinions about whether trout take up positions immediately below rocks in mid-current (Fig 8). In fact, much depends upon the current strength. Water immediately behind a rock or a similar obstruction where the current is very strong may be too turbulent to be attractive. There are basically four lies around a rock: immediately in front, where the current has created a quiet cushion of water through back pressure; on either side of the rock, if the current is not too strong; and, in a moderate current, the space immediately behind a rock may be occupied by a trout. One important fact should not be overlooked: water velocity at the surface is much greater than that lower down. I was very surprised when fishing some of the freestone rivers of the western United States how many trout could be caught immediately behind big rocks in quite turbulent water; indeed, some of these were the most productive lies. Although the water surface appeared turbulent the current moved at quite a slow pace (the subsurface water velocity would be even slower) and gave trout plenty of time to react to the fly.

In the Lee of an Obstruction or Bank Extension

Boulders, logs, fallen trees, outcrops of the bank – all form zones of calmer water in their lee. The calmer zones offer benefits similar to those in the eye of a pool. The quiet area offers sight of food on the edge of the food lane and also receives surface food washed into the lee. Where the obstruction drastically

Fig 8   Lies around boulders or subsurface obstructions.

cuts into the current a back-current is created, obliging trout to face into it, the opposite way to trout in the main current. Here trout are more likely to patrol the lee rather than waiting for food to come to them. The effect of any bank extension or barrier is to slow down the current velocity for a short distance upstream with a cushion created by back pressure and for a longer distance downstream. The area of the downstream zone will be influenced by the speed of the current, the size and shape of the barrier, and whether or not it is wholly submerged. The size of the lee – or of any lie, for that matter – is practically immaterial: trout will take up lies little bigger than themselves. Sometimes even the tiniest of bankside lees attracts a trout. I have caught many trout in freestone rivers from lees and pockets that have been barely big enough to accommodate a fish. Professor H. B. N. Hynes of the University of Waterloo, Ontario, suggested that the larger the obstacle behind which a trout is sheltering, the larger the trout. Alas, it isn't quite so straightforward.

Under Overhanging Trees

Bushes or tree branches that hang down just above the water provide attractive lies (Fig 9). Even if they are not over a food lane they provide terrestrial food as it is blown or falls on the water below. Good cover is also provided. On a well fished stream they also provide cover from fly fishers. Often good trout that have proved too difficult for less persevering anglers are taken from such lies. Too many lost flies amongst the foliage are a great deterrent. Lies that are difficult to fish frequently produce bigger-than-average trout.

Pockets

Pockets are cushions in the current created by the presence of rocks or obstructions, either completely or partially submerged. In between will be pockets of calm water attractively out of the velocity of the main current. Pocket water is rarer on chalk streams than

Fig 9   Shade and protective cover are offered beneath overhanging branches. Additional food in the form of terrestrials will also be anticipated.

on faster rocky waters. Fishing the pockets is often productive in warm weather because the tumbling, churning effect mixes more oxygen into the water, keeping the trout active. Trout may move into these lies seeking well oxygenated water. Fishing the pockets with a dry fly is highly productive but often difficult as the intervening currents play havoc with any attempt to minimise drag on the fly. The answer is to approach as near as possible and fish with a very short line. Pick-pocketing with a good search pattern can be a highly successful tactic.

Along the Banks

Trout will take up positions by the water's edge along most streams (Fig 10). They offer calmer pockets of water within reach of the

This fly fisher is casting into the shaded area under the trees where trout are rising. The rest of the river was in bright sunlight, with hardly a fish to be found under the open sky.

Fishing the pockets between rocks on the River Ure.

Fig 10   A lie in an undercut bank.

food lane, particularly if the bank is along the outside edge of a bend where the current runs close. Most terrestrial food first enters the water at the bankside. On one of my favourite Yorkshire streams I offer the same advice to all guests fishing the water for the first time: if you want grayling fish the middle of the stream; if you want brown trout fish close to the banks.

The current on the outside of a bend may erode the bank to the extent that it is considerably undercut. I know this only too well as many banks seem to collapse under me. Under the overhanging bank is an ideal trout lie. The fish is still in the food lane and the bank affords excellent cover. The only drawback is that such lies are often difficult, sometimes impossible, to fish with a dry fly. Much depends upon the height of the water.

The Confluence of Incoming Water

Whether the new water source is a tributary stream or a drainage ditch, it is the additional water (unless polluted) that proves attractive. New food may be brought in and in midsummer when water and oxygen levels may be low the fresh water could well be cooler and have a higher oxygen content.

Depressions in the Riverbed

Even the smallest hollow in the riverbed offers relief from the current. Trout in these lies are often difficult to detect if they are well camouflaged or in deep water. In all but shallow water trout may be reluctant to feed on the surface from such a lie.

Weedbeds

Weedbeds offer relief from the current and cover from predators and, although they may not be actually in the main food lane, the weeds hold plenty of nymphs, snails and shrimps on which to feed. Trout wait in the calmer water just inside the cover offered by vegetation so that they can quickly move into the food lane to feed and return again to the calmer waters. Often on spring-fed rivers where weedbeds abound there will be many food lanes between the weedbeds and trout will be watching the surface for food from the relative tranquillity of their cover. Frequently

The confluence of the main river and a feeder stream. The incoming water from the side stream may be cooler, contain more oxygen and provide an attractive lie for trout to adopt when the main river is low.

In midsummer many spring-fed and chalk streams suffer excessive weed growth. Most fish take refuge under the beds of ranunculus on the tiny River Allen in Hampshire.

water above a weedbed is slower-paced than that at either side. Trout in such a position are watching the surface for food and have the benefit of being able to melt into the weeds very quickly.

The Deeps

On most rivers there are areas of slower, deeper water where trout lurk near the bottom. These inviting pools are not difficult to fish with the dry fly but trout are very reluctant to rise from such depths. As summer progresses their reluctance wanes. The leviathans of local legend invariably haunt such deeps. I dare say some fish are more apocryphal than factual, but behind most stories there is probably more than an element of truth. One pool on my local stream yielded such a fish. The bridge pool is the deepest part of the river, the flow is very slow and any surface-feeding fish takes a fly only if it has passed careful scrutiny. An avenue of overhanging tree branches makes the pool

very difficult to fish except by horizontal casting whilst standing in water up to one's wader tops and making a longish, difficult upstream cast. In the Mayfly (green drake) season anglers have been broken on big fish. A 1lb trout is a good one in this unstocked stream, which holds only wild brown trout and grayling. Whilst attempting to remove from the pool a few unwanted pike by spinning one member took a wild brown trout of over 3lb. Those broken 6X or 7X leaders of summer took on a new significance. The best chance of tempting fish to the surface begins with the Mayfly, and thereafter in the twilight of a summer evening.

Problem Lies

The easy-to-approach, easy-to-fish lies may have been cast over hundreds of times by other anglers; consequently, such lies will be inhabited by rather wary fish. If there is the chance to fish lies that are out of the way, difficult to approach or in near-impossible

The cover provided by a bridge offers an attractive lie. This bridge is very low and a horizontal cast is needed.

Fig 11   A problem lie which presents the fly fisher with a difficult cast.

places to cast to, my advice is to make the most of them. The probability is high that other anglers will have passed these by in favour of easier lies or they may have left the evidence of their failure with flies and leader tippets in overhanging trees and bushes. The cost of a lost leader tippet and a fly is a few pence, almost negligible when compared with the true cost of most people's fishing.

Persevere in these places and often a good trout that thought itself safe can be caught. Successfully winkling out a trout from a difficult and taxing lie is worth a dozen easy fish from open water.

I have detailed above the principal lies but I never cease to be amazed at the places where trout seem to be caught. There are rules as to

Fig 12   A plan of some of the trout lies.
1   Around rocks and boulders.
2   Under overhanging branches.
3   In the eye of a pool.
4   In a back-eddy.
5   At the confluence of a tributary stream.
6   In the centre of a pool.
7   Along the margins, especially in areas of shade at times of bright sunlight.

where trout should be lying and there are exceptions to every rule. The Madison is one of the West's best trout rivers and yet in parts it has been described as a 'fifty-mile riffle'. All water will hold trout; if they don't appear where you would expect them, try the less obvious. The American fly fisher Joe Brooks put it this way: 'Cover it all. Sometimes you'll find a real dinosaur in the riffles, lying in water hardly deep enough to cover its dorsal fin!'

Part Two
Surface Food

An intrinsic part of the dry-fly fisher's skill lies in his knowledge of the entomology of the streams he fishes and in his ability to relate that knowledge to the choice of fly he presents to trout and the manner, time and place in which he offers it. The greater the fly fisher's interest in entomology, the more likely he is to catch fish.

A natural interest in entomology is of great benefit to the fly fisher and I know of many men who have first been drawn to fly fishing and then branched out into amateur entomology. Their knowledge of the fly life on local streams, accumulated over many years, is invaluable to their fishing. Excessive entomological interest often interrupts fly-fishing time, as I know all too well. Too often the means have become more important than the end, and I have left my landing net in the car in favour of a fly-catching net and spent more time catching flies than rising trout. The entomologist's interest stops short of looking beyond the insect world and the role of the angler is to catch fish. The fly fisher should be interested at the point where the two worlds overlap, when insects become the centre of a trout's attention. Being aware of which flies might be expected at a particular time of day, during a specified month of the season, on a given river, or being able to recognise the important natural flies on the water, is an integral part of persuading a trout to rise.

The life-cycle of a number of flies and other insects has a considerable bearing on surface-feeding trout. No book purporting to offer advice on dry-fly fishing should fail to examine to a reasonable and necessary depth the very food source being represented. For the fly fisher to be entomologically ignorant is akin to running for political office without being aware of the issues that influence the voters.

I apologise for what to some might appear an excessive use of the Latin scientific names for species. The fly fisher's names for flies vary from country to country and even regionally within countries. It is therefore necessary when discussing a species to avoid any confusion by using the scientific name. One man's blue-winged olive (*Ephemerella ignita*) is another man's blue-winged olive (*Baetis vagans, B. Parvus* or *B. bicaudatus*).

3 The Trout's Menu

You are to know, that there are so many sort of flies as there be fruits: I will name you but some of them; as the dun-fly, the stone-fly, the red-fly . . . and indeed too many either for me to name, or for you to remember.

Izaak Walton, *The Compleat Angler*

Many studies have been conducted into the diet of trout by a wide range of interested parties, from the inquisitive angler with his marrow scoop to detailed research by worthy scientific bodies in different countries. The broad geographical base of the research reveals widely differing findings. Not surprisingly, feeding habits differ from one river to the next, between lake and river, between differing parts of individual rivers, between seasons of the year and between times of the day. It ought not to have taken a wise man long to realise that such a diversity should have been anticipated.

If we restrict our interest to those parameters that affect the trout fisherman and consider (a) rivers and streams and (b) the spring, summer and early autumn months, the fields of research are narrowed down. The only research of value to the fly fisherman at the waterside is the examination of the stomach contents of a freshly caught trout. Scientific research into what trout should be feeding on, or fed on last year on

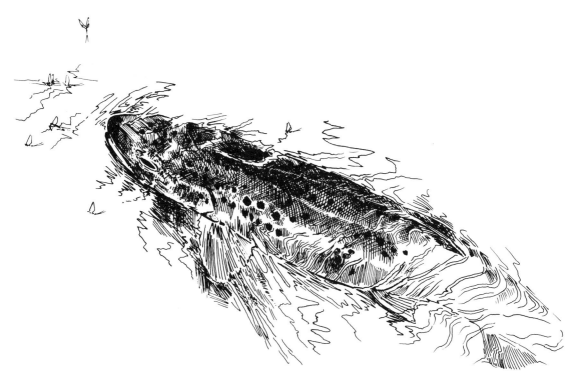

Fig 13   A feeding trout.

such and such a stream, is of minimal value to the fly fisher at the water's edge wanting to know what fly to cast over a likely lie. The great benefit of knowing what a trout has been feeding on in the last half hour is immense. The major snag is that you must catch the first trout of the day to get the answer. Even then you will know only what it has been feeding on, not what other trout might be taking in half an hour's time. Unfortunately I find myself spooning trouts' stomachs less and less over the years as I kill far fewer than I once did. One alternative is to use a stomach pump, a simple hand-held suction device, which pulls out a small amount of food without injuring the fish.

The reasons for choosing to fish with the floating fly at a particular time are entirely personal and sometimes illogical. Usually it is because trout are surface-feeding, or we think they ought to be and we search for a co-operative fish or simply because it is the pleasure of fishing in such a fashion despite knowing that at that precise moment a deep-sunk nymph is really what is needed; or, worst of all, because the fishery rules dictate the method. Whatever the reasons are, what we really want to know is what surface food source a trout would be willing to rise to. The answer will be one or more of many items of food that find their way by accident or design on the river surface. The menu is formidable. It consists of the emerging upwinged duns, stillborns, floating nymphs, winged duns, spinners, spent spinners, emerging and adult caddis, adult stoneflies, emerging and adult midges, adult alders, gnats, smuts, hawthorn flies, any one of scores of species of beetles, caterpillars, craneflies, ants and grasshoppers. Although the menu is extensive only a relative handful might interest the trout you are casting to. It may even be interested only in one species, at one precise stage in its life-cycle. Discovering which is part of the fascinating challenge of dry-fly fishing.

When the great angling writer Sparse Grey Hackle wrote 'Angling is Tradition' he could easily have been referring to dry-fly fishing. Most of what has been written about the subject has been almost solely concerned with representing the adults of the upwinged species of the Ephemeroptera, and many of our flies reflect the traditions established by men long dead. I personally have no doubt that the challenge of fishing an imitation of an upwinged species is the most interesting for the fly fisher, but I am equally sure that many of those revered figures of time past failed to appreciate, or failed to accept, the validity of representing the wide range of the balance of the trout's menu.

In Charles E. Brooks's excellent book *The Trout and the Stream* (1974) he quotes from two surveys of items of food on the surface of two American rivers, one in the east and the other in the west, and the stomach contents of trout from those rivers. I do not propose that the findings should be applied to every trout stream on every continent but they should stimulate some thought about trout streams everywhere.

Over the duration of an entire season nets were set to capture all floating creatures. So that surface food from all along the stretch was surveyed the nets were set every three feet. They were examined and emptied every few minutes so that very few creatures had time to escape. At the same time as the netting was in progress the stomach contents of trout were also analysed. The two sets of results were compared and summarised:

1. During the early season aquatic insects represented over 80 per cent of the surface food and the stomach contents.
2. During the midsummer aquatic insects represented 70 per cent of netted insects but 40 per cent of the stomach contents.
3. Towards the autumn the balance between surface insects and the stomach contents was in agreement again but the dominating food source (70 per cent), both on the surface and in the stomachs, was terrestrials.

The study groups drew four conclusions about trout feeding behaviour on the surface of the streams examined.

1. Over the season, terrestrials outnumbered aquatic insects on the surface.

This scoop of a trout's stomach is full of black gnats with barely another species represented.

2. In the spring, when aquatic insects were at their peak numerically, trout took them in almost exact proportion to their availability.
3. In the late summer and early autumn, when terrestrials were at their peak, trout took them in almost exact proportion to their availability.
4. Over the course of a season more terrestrials were taken by trout because they were available for more hours of the day than the sporadically hatched aquatic flies.

Charles Brooks uses these findings to back up his belief that 'availability is the prime factor in the selection of insects by trout'. He further concludes that fishing terrestrial imitations will bring more success over the hours of daylight because they are the major available food source. He does not say that trout feed upon terrestrials with the intensity and voracity of trout rising in the midst of a hatch of duns. His approach is summed up as 'Match the hatch when there's one on, but if there is not, look to terrestrials.' I confess that I have no personal studies to support my own belief that Brooks is not far wrong, just a gut feeling resulting from hundreds of hours scrutinising river surfaces for the first signs of a hatch. For some months on the majority of trout rivers hatches of aquatic flies occupy only a small part of the day. Other than during a hatch of aquatic flies or the return of mated females trout will feed either on sub-surface food, or other surface food (terrest-

Table B   Seasonal variation in the diet of River Dee trout by number.

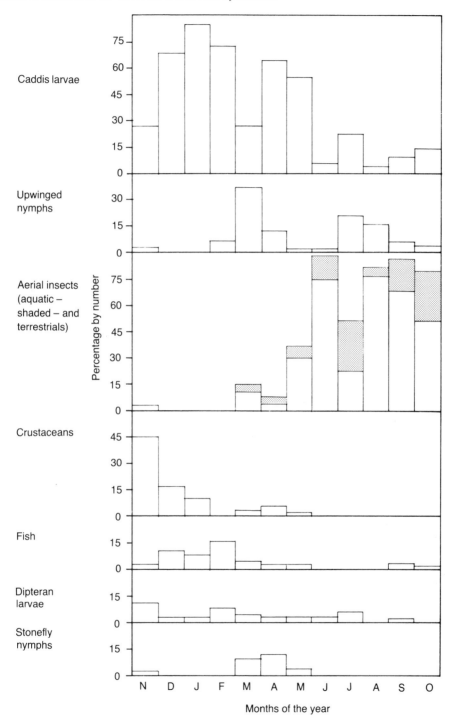

Table C The percentage composition of the diet of River Dee trout by number and volume

	Number	Volume
Upwinged nymphs	6.8	3.5
Stonefly nymphs	1.1	0.5
Sedge larvae	18.5	41.7
Dipteran larvae	1.3	2.9
Dipteran pupae	0.8	0.2
Crustacea	1.2	0.8
Coleoptera	1.5	0.1
Aerial insects	67.1	34.2
Aquatic	*13.1*	*11.0*
Upwingeds	*6.6*	*3.9*
Stoneflies	*3.1*	*2.5*
Sedges	*1.8*	*4.2*
Diptera	*1.6*	*0.4*
Terrestrial	*54.0*	*23.2*
Diptera	*36.8*	*17.0*
Hymenoptera	*0.5*	*0.5*
Hemiptera (bugs)	*16.7*	*5.7*
Fish	0.6	12.2
Miscellaneous	1.1	3.9

rials), or not at all. If you are on the river to catch fish and you want to cast a fly on the surface you can choose from any fly in your box and you might be successful, but the best bet is a terrestrial.

Dr J. V. Woolland's survey into the feeding behaviour of Welsh River Dee trout provides some very similar findings to the American study. The stomach contents of 105 brown trout were examined over the course of twelve months. These are presented in Tables B and C. The findings of interest to the dry-fly fisher are twofold:

1. Aerial insects (particularly of terrestrial origin) formed the major part of the summer intake of trout.
2. Aerial insects became more common in the diet of trout with increasing age.

189 hawthorn flies from the stomach of a twelve-inch chalkstream rainbow trout. All were recently taken.

This slow-moving corner of a chalk stream affords the trout a leisurely inspection of the surface fly. This fish fell for an imitation of the black gnats which were being blown off the nearby trees.

Other earlier surveys all recorded an increased consumption of terrestrial food in older trout. Dr Woolland's survey also commented that in some specimens the summer diet consisted of up to 90 per cent by number of aerial insects. Both the surveys quoted by Brooks and Dr Woolland's results provide food for thought for all fly fishers – particularly the latter survey, which discovered that from June onwards aerial insects were not only the single major food source but that they were the majority food, being greater than the total of all other food sources. As trout grew older they consumed more surface food, and from May to October, in all but one month, terrestrial insects were taken in much larger numbers than aquatic flies.

The problems of selectivity are examined more closely in a later chapter but while we are discussing the menu the fact should be recorded that even though a wide range of food sources may be on the surface at a particular time trout sometimes choose to feed on only one species of insect. The problem can be infuriating but finding the answer should be a stimulating and exciting prospect for the fly fisher. The problem is not simply one of matching the species being preferred, but also adequately representing the insect

on the surface. Extreme exclusivity in feeding is commoner on chalk streams, where there may possibly be a wider range of food to choose from at any one time.

Trout are extremely catholic in their feeding habits. If you want to fish on the surface you must also adopt the same degree of flexibility. To continue to cast an imitation of an upwinged dun in the absence of a hatch is not a logical nor a very satisfactory approach. In the following chapters you will find some alternative solutions. Most trout are opportunists, often needing to feed on whatever food comes their way and taking advantage of any tasty additions to their aquatic food sources. Commenting on a trout's response to the sight of surface food, Art Lee wrote: 'Each action, therefore, represents a quick and automatic response without resort to any consideration whatsoever.' This might be true of a trout in fast water which develops a Pavlovian response to the light pattern but it certainly is not so of a leisurely feeding trout at the centre or tail of a pool or in the sluggish current of a backwater. Some trout can be all too selective about which flies they take. Careful inspection at very close range is very commonplace, and therein lies the problem for the dry-fly fisher.

4 The Natural Fly

Angling is an art, either by practice or by long observation.

Izaak Walton, *The Compleat Angler*

THE UPWINGED SPECIES
(Ephemeroptera)

I prefer to describe the species within the Ephemeroptera order as 'upwinged' flies rather than calling them Mayflies, since many anglers reserve the latter name particularly for the three species *Ephemera danica*, *E. lineata* and *E. vulgata*. There are four distinct stages in the life cycle of the upwinged flies: egg; nymph; dun, or subimago, the first adult stage; and the spinner, or imago, the second and final adult stage. As adults their lives are extremely short, varying from just two hours for the caenis to about two weeks. Most live about twenty-four hours; it seems that their sole function as adults is reproduction.

Most ephemeropterans emerge during the warmer months of the year. The development of eggs and nymphs of some species is significantly regulated by temperature. Temperature may also be the trigger which starts emergence and brings it to an end. Although temperature is important, very sparse hatches of upwinged duns have been recorded during every month of the year.

Different species of fly prefer different habitats. Some indication is given of their chosen habitat by the shape of the nymphs. The flat nymphs are the stone-clinging type commonest in the fast water usually associated with stony riverbeds. Agile-darting nymphs live in weedbeds and burrowing Mayfly nymphs prefer streams with a sandy or muddy bed. It follows that the type of riverbed and the source of the water – whether from underground reservoirs, from springs, or recently drained off the land – are major factors in the presence of different species. The angler should be aware that different species emerge in different types of water and even over a short length of river individual species will restrict themselves to areas that fulfil their specific requirements. A summary of the characteristics of the commoner British and North American species is given in Tables D and E.

The nymphs grow by a series of moults of the outer skin until the final larval stage is reached. As the water temperature approaches its critical point the nymphs begin to leave their protective environment between stones, in weedbeds and moss and in the muddy bed and prepare to make the most hazardous journey of their lives. Just before emerging the stone-clinging nymphs venture on to the upper surfaces of stones; according to some sources, these nymphs make the journey to the surface once or twice during the day before emergence. Why these preliminary ascents are made is not known but at least one authority suggests that it is to take in air to aid the splitting of the nymphal skin. The actual place of emergence varies between species. Most emerge on the water surface; a few do so entirely or partly out of water, on a stone or stick; and at least one British species, the dusky yellowstreak (*Heptagenia lateralis*), emerges as an adult below the surface. Emergence below the surface is commoner amongst North American species and the Quill Gordon (*Epeorus pleuralis*) is a famous hatch on eastern and midwestern rivers. In all species the skin of the upper surface of the thorax splits and then the skin over the nymph head splits for the dun to emerge and erect its wings by pumping blood into the wing veins. The shed skins or shucks (exuviae) usually float away on the water surface. Those species which emerge wholly on the surface must first break the film as surface tension works both ways.

An easy target: a crippled dun. This fly has failed to erect one of its wings and has it folded and trapped, unable to take flight.

This emerging dun was watched by the author. It had difficulty breaking through the surface tension from its nymphal shuck and its wings were so wet they would not erect. It struggled briefly, then remained motionless, trapped for ever.

The cataclysmic breakthrough from the environment in which it has spent all its life to a totally new one is no easy transition. They don't all make it. Not only is the emerging dun struggling to leave its nymphal shuck and penetrate the film a prime target for feeding trout, it also has to adapt itself from functioning as an aquatic nymph to being an airborne fly. The trauma of battling through the film and shedding their old skins takes its toll on the emergers. Many die in the process. It may also be true that some species are prone to a higher mortality rate at this stage. It has been observed that the blue-winged olive (*Ephemerella ignita*) suffers more than most species when trying to break free of its nymphal shuck. The inch of water below the surface provides the most dangerous moment of the nymph's journey from the riverbed, even the most critical and vulnerable seconds of its life so far. This vulnerability does not go unnoticed by trout, and particularly in the early stages of a hatch trout feed upon the emerging duns.

In addition to consuming the emergers as a prelude to a concentrated onslaught on the floating duns, trout are also aware of the stillborn duns that fail to make it. The dead and dying half-nymph, half-dun, and duns which are trapped in the film with their wings so sodden and creased that there is no hope, are easy and attractive targets. Trout know that they have no chance of escape and rise confidently and leisurely to the stillborns and trapped adults. In a sparse hatch of duns the likelihood of trout concentrating on the stillborns or emergers is slimmer than in a large hatch. The bigger the hatch, the greater the probability of trout regularly taking the trapped emergers and stillborns in preference to the floating winged adults.

The characteristics common to all duns are upright wings, six legs, a segmented body and two or three tails. Most species have two quite large forewings and two much smaller hindwings. These smaller wings are easily visible in some species, much harder to detect in others, and totally absent in a minority

Table D   A key to the features of the commoner British river species of upwinged duns and spinners

Common and scientific name	Distribution	Habitat	Appearance and time of emergence
Autumn or August dun *Ecdyonurus dispar*	North and west of England, South Wales	Stony rivers	June–Oct.; daylight
Blue-winged olive *Ephemerella ignita*	Widespread	All types of river	May–Nov.; daylight and dusk
Caenis *Caenis spp*	Widespread	Slow-moving rivers	May–Sept.; dawn and dusk
Claret dun *Leptophlebia vespertina*	Widespread but localised	Slow-moving rivers; preference for slightly acidic water	May–July; daylight
Dark olive *Baetis atrebatinus*	South, south-west and localised in north of England	Alkaline water	May–Oct.; daylight
Dusky Yellowstreak *Heptagenia lateralis*	Scotland, south-west and North of England	Smaller rivers and streams	May–Sept.; evening and dusk
Iron blue *Baetis niger, B. muticus*	Widespread except south-east England	All types of river	April–Nov.; daylight
Large brook dun *Ecdyonurus torrentis*	Widespread but localised	Small stony streams	March–Sept.; daylight
Large dark olive *Baetis rhodani*	Widespread	Faster-flowing water	Feb.–May, Sept.–Nov.; daylight and dusk
Large green dun *Ecdyonurus insignis*	North and West England, South Wales	All types of river	May–Oct.; daylight and dusk
Large spurwing *Centroptilum pennulatum*	Localised in South Wales, south and north England	Alkaline rivers	May–Oct.; daylight
Late March brown *Ecdyonurus venosus*	Widespread, except south and east England	Faster-flowing water	April–Oct.; daylight and dusk
March brown *Rithrogena germanica*	Localised in Wales, Scotland, north of England	Faster-flowing water	March–May; daylight
Mayfly *Ephemera danica, E. vulgata*	Widespread	All types of rivers	April–Nov.; daylight, dawn and dusk
Medium olive *Baetis tenax, B. venosus, B. buceratus*	Widespread	Prefers alkaline water	April–Nov.; daylight and dusk
Olive upright *Rithrogena semicolorata*	Mainly in the west of the UK	Faster-flowing rivers	April–Sept.; dawn and evening
Pale evening dun *Procloëon bifidum*	Widespread	Prefers alkaline water	April–Nov.; evening
Pale watery dun *Baetis fuscatus*	South and north of England, parts of Wales	Prefers alkaline rivers	May–Oct.; daylight

Characteristics of the dun	Characteristics of the female spinner	Egg-laying behaviour of the female spinner*	Angler's names
Large; 2 tails; grey or light fawn wings; olive-brown body	Reddish-brown body with darker underside; dark brown tails	2	Great red spinner
Medium-large; 3 tails; bluish wings; various olive-brown body shades	Olive-brown to sherry-red body with green egg-sac; tails olive-grey	3	Sherry spinner
Very small; 3 tails; creamy-white overall appearance	White body and tails	4	Broadwing or Angler's curse
Medium; 3 tails; very dark grey wings; dark-brown body, paler underside	Brown body, tails pale brown	4	–
Medium; 2 tails; grey wings; olive-brown body	Dark-olive body, light olive underside; grey-olive tails	1 (probably)	–
Medium; 2 tails; very dark grey wings; grey-brown body	Olive-brown body, last 3 segments orange-brown; brown tails	3 or 4	Dark dun
Small; 2 tails; blue-black wings; grey-brown or dark brown-olive body	Dark claret body, paler underside; tails pale grey	1, 4	Jenny spinner or Little claret spinner
Large; 2 tails; mottled wings; dark brown body	Dark olive-brown body, purple-brown underside; purple-brown tails	4	Great red spinner
Large; 2 tails; pale grey wings; olive-brown or olive-green body	Dark olive body, paler underside; dark olive-grey tails	1	Early olive, large spring olive
Large; 2 tails; light fawn mottled wings; dark olive-green body	Olive-green body; dark olive-grey tails	4	–
Medium-large; 2 tails; blue-grey wings; olive-grey body	Olive body, paler underside; pale grey tails	uncertain	Large amber spinner
Large; 2 tails; fawn wings; brown body	Reddish-brown body; dark brown tails	2 and possibly 4	Great red spinner
Large; 2 tails; fawn wings; dark brown body	Dark red-brown body; brown tails	4	Great red spinner
Large; 3 tails; grey wings; yellow-cream or grey-white body	Pale cream body, last 3 segments brown streaks; tails dark brown	3, 4	Green drake, Grey drake or Spent gnat
Medium; 2 tails; grey wings; brown to yellow-olive body	Brown body, paler underside; off-white tails	1	Olive dun, Red spinner or Blue dun
Large; 2 tails; dark blue-grey wings; grey-olive body	Yellow-olive body, cream-olive underside; tails pale buff	2 possibly	Yellow upright
Small; 2 tails; pale grey wings; straw-coloured body	Olive-brown body, translucent grey-white underside; tails grey-white	uncertain	Little pale blue dun
Small; 2 tails; pale grey wings; grey-olive body	Pale watery body, last 2 segments yellow-olive; grey tails	1, 4	Golden spinner

Purple dun *Paraleptophlebia cincta*	North and west of England	Small fast or larger medium-paced rivers	May–Aug.; daylight
Sepia dun *Leptophlebia marginata*	Scotland, south and north of England	Slow-moving rivers	April–May; daylight
Small dark olive *Baetis scambus*	Widespread	Prefers alkaline rivers	Feb.–Nov.; afternoon and evening
Small spurwing *Centroptilum luteolum*	Widespread except Wales	Prefers alkaline rivers	May–Oct.; daylight
Yellow evening dun *Ephemerella notata*	North-west and South- west England, Wales	Moderately paced water	May–June; late evening
Yellow May dun *Heptagenia sulphurea*	Widespread	All types of river	May–Oct.; daylight and dusk

*Key to the egg-laying behaviour of the female spinners
1 Female spinner goes underwater and eggs laid on substratum.
2 Female spinner rests on stones above the surface and eggs are laid on substratum below the surface.
3 Female spinner flies down to the water and releases the eggs in one mass.
4 Female spinner flies down to the surface a number of times and eggs are laid in batches.

The large brook dun (*Ecdyonurus torrentis*).

Medium; 2 tails; blackish-grey wings; dark brown body	Brownish body with purple tinge, paler underside; yellowish tails	uncertain	–
Medium; 3 tails; brownish-grey wings; dark brown body, paler under	Dark red-brown body, lighter underside; long dark brown tails	uncertain	–
Small; 2 tails; medium dark grey wings; grey-olive body, paler underside	Dark or deep red-brown body, last 2 segments yellowish; grey-white tails	1	July dun, Small red spinner or Olive dun
Small; 2 tails; grey wings; pale watery olive-green to olive-brown body, paler underside	Yellow-brown to amber body, underside cream-yellow; olive-white tails	3	Little amber spinner
Medium-large; 3 tails; pale grey wings; pale yellow body, last 3 segments pale amber	Yellow-olive body, last 3 segments brown-olive; yellow tails	3	–
Medium-large; 2 tails; pale yellow wings; yellow body	Pale olive-yellow body; dark grey tails	4	Yellow hawk

of species. The colour of the subimago is, as their common name suggests, a rather dun, sombre shade. The colour of a species may vary in its shades from river to river and from month to month on the same stream. Spring or autumn hatches are frequently darker than the midsummer hatches of the same species. The air temperature at the same time of emergence is also believed to affect coloration; the cooler the air, the darker the colour of fly.

Upon emergence the dun rests on the surface with only its six legs in contact with the surface. Neither the tails nor any part of the body touch the surface. To do so would make it much harder to shed the water before flight and probably lead to the dun drowning. The dun rests on the surface with its wings fully upright drying itself. As a rule, in warm weather this period is much shorter than on cool, dull days. Sometimes the period seems to be infinitesimal as duns appear on the surface and fly off with barely two or three seconds elapsing. In the very early season when large dark olives (*Baetis rhodani*) are prolific I have timed duns on the surface of rivers in the north of England for over four minutes before flight. They are certainly living dangerously, risking capture by fish or birds. I do not think that air temperature

alone determines the time spent by the dun on the surface. On quite warm days I have noticed some species on the surface some little while and on other days of similar temperature duns seem to burst through the surface like submarine-launched missiles. (In fact they will have struggled through the film but they certainly did not so much as pause for a second on the surface.) My own experience suggests there is a link between the type of water and the speed of take-off. For whatever reason, the chalk stream hatches seem to linger longer and give trout the opportunity for feeding while the freestone-stream hatches leave the water more quickly. This is, of course, a sweeping generalisation, but one that has been observed many times. There are other factors influencing the time on the surface, including humidity and wind in addition to temperature.

Whilst on the surface the duns seem to have very little control over their drift. The current takes them where it will and the effects of wind on their high wings is to turn them into the wind much as a weathercock behaves.

The duns head towards the shelter of vegetation, where, usually within the next forty-eight hours, the transformation to spin-

Table E   A key to the commoner North American species of upwinged duns and spinners

Common name Scientific name	Distribution Habitat (type of river)	Seasonal emergence Hatch time	Tails	Dun body colour (length in mm)	Dun wing colour	Spinner body colour	Spinner fall
Tiny white-wing black *Tricotythodes minutus*	E, W slow	July–September morning	3	greyish to blackish-brown (3–6)	white	blackish-brown	morning
Slate-wing mahogany dun *Paralepto-phlebia adoptiva*	E, M medium	April–June afternoon	3	reddish-brown (7–9)	brownish-grey	reddish-brown	afternoon and evening
Dark blue quill *Paralepto-phlebia heteronea*	W fast	June–August morning	3	reddish-brown (7–9)	slate	light brown	evening
Dark blue quill *Paralepto-phlebia debilis*	M, W slow-medium	August–October afternoon	3	reddish-brown (7–9)	slate	light brown	evening
Hendrickson *Ephemerella subvaria*	E, M medium-fast	May–June afternoon	3	reddish-brown or olive-brown (11)	slate	reddish-brown	afternoon or evening
Hendrickson *Ephemerella rotunda*	E, M medium-fast	May afternoon	3	browny-olive (7–9)	slate	reddish-brown	afternoon or evening
Sulphur dun *Ephemerella dorothea*	E, M medium-fast	May–July afternoon/ evening	3	beige to yellow (7–9)	yellow-grey	yellowy brown	afternoon or evening
Slate-wing olive *Ephemerella lata*	E, M medium-fast	July–August morning	3	olive (7)	dark grey	dark olive	evening
Pale morning dun *Ephemerella infrequens*	W medium	July–August midday	3	creamy-yellow olive cast (7–9)	light grey	brown	morning or evening
Western green drake *Ephemerella grandis*	W slow-medium	June–July midday	3	dark olive (14–16)	bluish-grey	dark brown	night
Slate-wing olive *Ephemerella flavinea*	W medium	June–August evening	3	dark olive (8–10)	bluish-grey	reddish brown	morning or evening
— *Ephemerella doddsi*	W medium-fast	July–August midday	3	dark olive (13–14)	grey	dark brown	evening
Green drake *Ephemera guttulata*	E medium-fast	May–June mainly dusk	3	olive (17–20)	grey-olive, black markings	creamy-white	dusk

Yellow drake *Ephemera varia*	E, M medium-fast	June–July dusk	3	yellow (13–16)	yellow-grey, brown markings	yellow-cream	dusk
Brown drake *Ephemera simulans*	E, M, W medium-fast	May–July dusk	3	yellowy-brown (10–20)	brown or grey, blackish markings	brown or grey	dusk
Quill Gordon *Epeorus pleuralis*	E fast	April–May afternoon	2	greyish-brown (9–11)	slate	yellow-brown	midday
Pale evening dun *Epeorus vitrea*	E, M fast	May–July evening	2	pale olive (9–11)	light grey	creamy-yellow	evening
Slate-brown dun *Epeorus longimanus*	W fast	June–July morning	2	grey	slate	reddish-brown	evening
Great red quill *Epeorus grandis*	W fast	July–August sporadic	2	dark brown (9–12)	slate	reddish-brown	evening
March brown *Stenonema vicarium*	E, M slow-medium	May–June sporadic/ evening	2	olive-brown (10–16)	olive, brown markings	olive-brown	evening
Grey fox *Stenonema fuscum*	E, M medium-fast	May–July sporadic	2	olive-brown (9–12)	olive, brown markings	olive-brown	sporadic
Light cahill *Stenonema canadense*	E, M medium-fast	June–July sporadic	2	creamy yellowish-olive (10–12)	cream, brown markings	cream to orangey	evening
Olive dun *Rithogena hageni*	W fast	July–August morning	2	brownish-olive (8–9)	slate	brown	morning and evening
— *Heptagenia simpliciodes*	W slow-medium	June–September sporadic	2	pale cream (10–11)	light grey	yellowy-cream	morning and evening
Large mahogany dun *Isonychia sadleri*	E, M fast	May–August afternoon/ evening	2	dark reddish-brown (16)	dark slate	reddish-brown	evening
Drake *Siphlonurus occidentalis*	W slow	June–October midday	2	grey (15)	slate	grey-brown	morning and evening
Blue-wing olive *Baetis vagans*	E, M medium	April–August midday/ evening	2	brown-olive (6–7)	slate	olive-brown	morning
Blue-wing olive *Baetis bicaudatus*	W medium-fast	April–October sporadic	2	light reddish-brown (4–5)	light grey	reddish-brown	early morning and evening
Blue-wing olive *Baetis parvus*	W medium	May–September sporadic	2	olive-brown (6)	slate	dark brown, 2 segments white	early morning and evening

Tiny blue-winged olive *Pseudocloëon anoka*	W slow-medium	June–September sporadic	2	olive-brown (4–5)	light grey	brown olive	evening
Tiny blue-winged olive *Pseudocloëon edmundsi*	W slow-medium	July–September sporadic	2	olive (4–5)	light grey	light reddish-brown	evening
Speckled dun *Callibaetis nigritus*	W slow	May–November dusk	2	olive tan (9–12)	grey, white veins	speckled grey brown	morning and dusk

ner, or imago, the final adult state, takes place. The length of the delay probably decreases with increased air temperature. The wings are spread apart and a split appears on top of the thorax and head. Then the head, thorax and legs emerge, and the spinner uses his legs to pull itself free from the skin. The skins are the shape of the original fly, except for the wing skins, which are too fragile. There are a number of distinctions between the two adult states. The legs and tails of the spinner are longer, the body is brighter and the wings shiny and transparent and more heavily veined in most species. In the case of males the legs are generally longer than the female's and the eyes larger. Most spinners darken with age, particularly the females after copulation.

Shortly after the final moult the reproduction process occurs. The male spinners collect in swarms sometimes comprising thousands of individuals. Many species have their own preference for swarming areas and have characteristic flight patterns. In wet or windy weather they are usually found in the shelter of trees. Swarming usually takes place in the late afternoon and evening but this could be delayed until the following day if the weather

Fig 14   A trapped-wing stillborn.

The recently emerged spinner with its dun exoskeleton on the left.

The spinner. Note the longer front legs and tails, and transparent wings.

turns suddenly colder. Copulation takes place in the air although at such times flight is almost impossible and the mating pair often sink slowly to the ground. Copulation does not take long and upon parting the females head towards water to lay their eggs. Most male spinners die over land and are of no interest to the fly fisher, though a few species may end up on the surface.

After copulation the females immediately return to the water to deposit their eggs, which with a few species are plainly seen in the egg ball at the rear of the abdomen. They do this in one of a number of ways. Some species fly down to the surface and release the eggs in a single batch either by dipping the abdomen tip in the water whilst flying or by briefly resting on the surface for a short period. Some visit the surface on several occasions, depositing the eggs either by alighting on the water or by dipping the abdomen whilst in flight. A number of *Baetis* spinners climb down stones and stakes at the

waterside and deposit the eggs on stones and moss below the surface. After oviposition these females are sometimes able to break through the film and fly away; others die under the surface and are a target for trout. In rarer instances a few species rest on partially submerged stones in shallow water. The tip of the abdomen is lowered below the surface and the eggs deposited between stones and gravel. The manner of oviposition of each of the common British species is detailed in Table D.

It is worth noting that when a spinner lands on the surface the wings are in the upright position. They do not droop into the spent, horizontal position until the eggs have been extruded. Therefore, if accurate imitation is sought, artificials that incorporate egg-sacs should not be tied in the spent position. After oviposition the spinner on the surface may struggle, trying to erect its wings in an effort to lift itself free. This disturbance and the ripple it creates is impossible to repro-

A female spinner with its wings in the spent position.

duce with an artificial. After oviposition the abdomen of some species dramatically lightens in colour in the absence of the eggs. Much of the colour is drained away and it becomes semi-transparent. This results in the differences between some species being negligible. Often the spent spinners are difficult for the fly fisher to see. Many have virtually no profile as they lie in the surface film. Trout feeding upon them may appear to be taking something almost invisible and often take them in a quiet and methodical manner. They are aware that there is no escape for the spinners and feed accordingly with the minimum of effort.

CADDIS OR SEDGES (Trichoptera)

Most fly fishers pride themselves in being able to identify and name as many of the upwinged flies as they come across. This is certainly not so for the sedges, which with a few exceptions, are simply referred to by their general appearance – for example, 'black sedge', or 'small dark sedge', and so on. Few fly fishers are able to identify accurately more than a handful of species. This is not surprising in view of the similarity of the species and the trout's lack of fastidiousness over the selection of an artificial when the naturals are about. It is usually sufficient for the fly fisher to have an imitation of approximate size and colouring, but not always.

Some species are distinctive enough to create very selective feeding situations to the adults. There is a sedge, the Zebra Caddis (*Macronema zebratum*), on the Housatonic River in Connecticut that has a bright green body and striped wings. Throughout the summer months, during early mornings, the large brown trout of this river lie tight to the banks and sip spent egg-laying adults. Woe to the angler who doesn't have an imitation of proper shape, size and coloration. One group of New Zealand fly fishers, after a series of frustrating mornings, apparently began to believe locals' stories about '. . . a unique strain of brown trout in the river with no mouths'.

The grub-like larvae of many species build protective cases. Many have their own highly distinctive cases always constructed in the same shape with the same materials. The cases are usually made from the small stones, sand or vegetation on the riverbed and may vary in size from a few millimetres to well over two inches in length. Other important species are net-makers, the larvae not building cases but a silken web that snares food from the current. Some larvae are highly carnivorous and consume enough ephemeroptera nymphs to seriously reduce the population of a stream. As it nears maturity the larva seals up its case and spins around itself a silken cocoon in which the legs and wings are formed. Some weeks or months later the pupa chews through the case wall and swims to the surface.

The metamorphosis from pupa to adult winged fly takes place either at the water surface or on stones or vegetation at the water's edge after the pupa has climbed ashore. The problems of breaking through the surface film are insurmountable for some individuals and they die trapped in or below the film. The emerging adult as it hangs below the surface breaking free of its pupal case and the stillborn and trapped adults are easy targets for trout. The biggest mistake many anglers make when they see trout rolling and jumping during a sedge emergence is to fish a high floating dry fly. Those cavorting fish are taking emerging pupae, insects half in and half out of the surface film, and they ignore most adult imitations.

The biggest trait on the pupa is the brightness of the air bubbles trapped in the transparent sheath draped around the body. The correct imitation not only rests in the film like the natural but also carries that aura of reflective brightness. The popular pattern in North America for this situation is the Emergent Sparkle Pupa, a fly tied with Antron yarn.

Some adults do not delay on the surface and take flight quickly; others skitter across the surface before take-off. The dry-fly fisher may successfully employ a floating pattern for species that stay on the water any length of time; however, it is when the females return

Table F   Common British species of river sedge and their characteristics

Common and scientific name	Period of emergence	Size of adult	General characteristics
Black sedge *Anthripsodes nigronervosus*	Daytime; June–Sept.	11–13mm	Prefers large rivers; long slim black wings and antennae
Brown sedge *Anabolia nervosa*	Evenings; Aug.–Oct.	11–16mm	Medium brown appearance; emerges via vegetation
Black silverhorn *Mystacides azurea, M. nigra*	Daytime; June–Aug.	8–9mm	Prefers slow rivers; black; antennae curve over body in flight
Brown silverhorn *Arthripsodes cinerus*	Daytime; June–Aug.	8–10mm	Prefers slow rivers; brownish with black markings; antennae curve over body in flight
Caperer *Halesus radiatus, H. digitatus*	Evenings; Aug.–Nov.	20–23mm	Common; mottled yellow-brown wings, orange-brown body
Cinnamon sedge *Linnephilus lunatus*	Daylight; June–Oct.	14–15mm	Slim; cinnamon-brown wings with black markings
Grannom *Brachycentrus subnubilus*	Daytime; April–June	9–11mm	Common; fawn-grey wings; mated female has green egg-sac at rear
Great red sedge *Phryganea striata, P. grandis*	Evenings; May–July	20–27mm	Fairly common on slow-moving rivers; mottled reddish-brown wings with black bar
Grey flag *Hydropsyche instablis,* *H. pellucidula*	Daytime; June–July	10–12mm	Common on faster water; grey wings with black markings
Grey or silver sedge *Odontocerum albicorne*	Daytime; June–Sept.	13–18mm	Prefers faster water; silver-grey wings
Large cinnamon sedge *Potamophylax latipennis*	Evenings; June–Sept.	18–19mm	Common; mottled yellow-brown wings
Marbled sedge *Hydropsyche contubernalis*	Evenings; June–July	11–12mm	Marbled brown patches on a greenish wing; orangey body
Medium sedge *Goëra pilosa*	Daytime; May–June	10–12mm	Widespread; very hairy, greyish to darker yellow wings
Mottled sedge *Glyphotaelius pellucidus*	Daytime; May–Sept.	17mm	Widespread; cream to yellow-brown wings with brown patches
Sand fly *Rhyacophila dorsalis*	Daytime; April–Oct.	variable	Widespread; wings various shades of brown
Small red sedge *Tinodes waeneri*	Evenings; May–Oct.	8mm	Widespread; reddish or yellowish-brown wings
Small silver sedge *Lepidosstoma hirtum*	Evenings; May–June	9mm	Widespread but localised; grey or grey-brown; mated female has green egg-sac
Small yellow sedge *Psychomyia pusilla*	Evenings	5–6mm	Very common; brown-yellow wings
Welshman's button *Sericostoma personatum*	Daytime; May–June	12–15mm	Widespread; dark brown wings with golden hairs; grey-black body; mated female has dark brown egg-sac

to lay their eggs that most surface-feeding activity starts. The females of a few species crawl below the surface to deposit their eggs, some drop the eggs in flight over water but the majority land on the surface. The manner of alighting on the surface varies widely from the gentle ripple-free landing to a ten-foot drop and the ensuing splash created by the diving sedges. Even when hitting the water from such a height they may fail to break through the surface tension and quite a commotion results. Other species specialise in the Olympic event of the hop, skip and jump, or running across the surface.

Many sedges are quite pale on emerging, before darkening to their true colour. The commonest colours are various shades of brown, although some are silvery-grey or black. There is a wide variation in size from the micro-caddis a few millimetres long to others of an inch or more. All have four wings which extend roof-like over the body. The wings are covered with tiny hairs. Most sedges have prominent antennae, which on some species may be three times the body length. They live longer as adults than up-winged flies, some species for as much as a fortnight.

STONEFLIES (Plecoptera)

It is as nymphs that stoneflies are mainly of interest to trout and they are really only of interest to the dry-fly fisher when the females return to the water to lay their eggs. There are thirty British species of which only a handful can command the attention of the fly fisher. The characteristics of each of the principal species can be found in Chapter 9 under their individual common names: February red and yellow sally. All have a similar life-cycle and share some common features.

The majority of the order prefer rivers with a stony or gravel bed and consequently they are common on many upland and some low-

An adult stonefly.

land streams with these requirements. In general, the diversity of stonefly species increases with a steeper river gradient and decreasing alkalinity. Other factors have been considered in relation to stonefly distribution – for example, temperature, altitude, substratum and current speed – but no one factor has proved to be of greatest importance.

In western America the appearance of some of the large stoneflies on the faster rivers provides some spectacular fishing. Lee Wulff comments that on certain western rivers the large stonefly 'is *the* most dramatic aquatic trout food'. I have seen the huge species called the salmon fly, as big as a man's thumb, and I've experienced first-hand the trouts' reaction to these giants on the surface. It was a strange feeling for me as an English fly fisher to cast to one trout with a size 16 caddis and to the next with a size 4 longshank floating Salmon Fly. The return to the water of the mated female salmon fly rightly attracts trout fishers from far and wide for the amazing phenomenon of trout rising to such large flies.

There are fly fishermen in the United States who plan their entire season around the salmon fly. They start in May on a low altitude river, like the Deschutes (Oregon), and follow the hatch to waters like Henry's Fork (Idaho) in late May, the Big Hole (Montana) in early June, and the Yellowstone (in Yellowstone National Park) as late as July. They slap large dry flies for trophy-sized trout for almost three months.

The nymphs are easy to distinguish from ephemeropteran nymphs as they all have two tails, whereas the latter have three. When the mature nymph is nearing its time for its transformation to adult the wingpads on the back of thorax blacken noticeably. The nymphs crawl ashore and on the stones and vegetation on the riverside they shed their nymphal skin and emerge as winged adults. The dry-fly fisher has no opportunity to imitate them at this time. Soon after the females have emerged, which takes place a few days after the first males appear, they mate on the ground. They are poor flyers and spend most of the time at rest in the shade in trees and

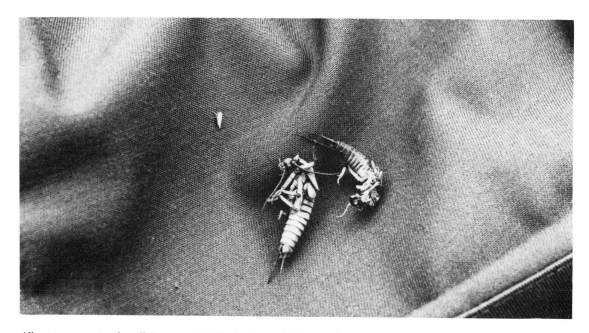

All creatures great and small. Two nymphal shucks of one of the largest American stoneflies, the salmon fly, and a tiny leafhopper to their upper left. Both species are trout favourites.

bushes, taking flight only in calm, warm weather. All the adults have four hard, shiny wings, which are long and narrow and when at rest lie flat over the body. The wings of the female are much longer than the body, but those of the male are usually much shorter.

The females return to the water surface to deposit their eggs, which are held on the underside of the abdomen. The females of the larger species do this by swimming or running on the water, usually in a diagonally upstream direction. Imitations fished in this way when the naturals are seen on the water can be effective. The smaller species dip the egg-mass into the water, where it disperses. A few species fly over the surface and suddenly drop from two or three feet.

DIPTERA (Aquatic Species: Midges and Reed Smuts)

Midges (Chironimids)

There are many hundred species of midges, almost all of them aquatic. They are a substantial food source for stillwater trout and a lesser one for river trout, although there is a general belief that midges have become more prolific on slow-to-medium-paced trout streams over the last twenty years. I hope that this is not an indication of the midges' tolerance of even quite polluted water.

They are members of the Diptera order of flat-winged flies which have two flat wings folded across the back. The adults vary in size and colour but most of the species found on running water are very small indeed. They are certainly too small for the angler to see on the surface at any distance and trout quietly feeding on what were hitherto thought to be smuts might in actual fact be taking midges. American fly fishers have developed the skill to a fine art, and its exponents are able to tie imitations and fish with them on hooks even as small as size 32. On both rivers and stillwaters I do not doubt that it is the midge pupae that are most attractive to trout, but there are times, which seem to be becoming more frequent, when trout concentrate on the adults.

Hatches occur almost daily throughout the trout season. Griffith's Gnat is an excellent imitation of the emerging midge.

Reed Smuts (Simulium)

Not without good reason are these tiny flat-winged flies sometimes known as the black curse. The adult fly, emerging from its pupal case, rises to the surface in a gas bubble. Because they arrive at the surface relatively dry from their protective bubbles, the adults do not have to dry themselves, and fly off almost immediately. The winged adult is between 3 and 4 millimetres in length and has a dark-brown to black body and broad transparent wings. One man whose imitations are fished the world over is a Dane, Preben Torp Jacobsen. He commented to me that 'the hatching smuts penetrate the surface very fast – you will never see them 'standing' on the surface. Only those that can't penetrate the surface film will be hanging in it and caught by trout.' He devised an excellent parachute-hackled fly for just this occasion. It is described in Chapter 9. In the same way as midges are becoming more important on rivers where upwinged species are declining, so too are the smuts. If you think that fishing with tiny surface flies is a recent innovation J. C. Mottram's *Fly-Fishing, Some New Arts and Mysteries* (1915) carried this observation. 'The season of 1913 was remarkable for the dearth of Ephemeroptera and abundance of smuts, and on referring to my log I find that almost as many chalk-stream fish were killed on smuts as on duns.'

TERRESTRIALS (Beetles, Caterpillars, Hawthorn flies, Gnats, Grasshoppers, Leafhoppers, Ants)

Some British fly fishers never fish with terrestrial patterns – 'It just isn't *fly* fishing.' I concede that a few patterns look more like extra-terrestrials than anything else but if you are on the river to catch trout with a floating fly and trout are rising like there's no tomorrow for some juicy, succulent but land-based morsel I'm not going to refuse them. If it floats and they want it, I'll fish it.

Charles E. Brooks quotes aquatic biologists as saying that hatches of upwinged duns on most streams account for less than 10 per cent of the fishing day, and that analysis of stomach contents of trout indicates that winged aquatic flies represent no more than 20 per cent of the food present. Although Brooks's and Woolland's survey differ in the proportion of aerial insects taken by summer trout, both confirm the importance of terrestrials. Woolland found that they are the biggest single item of all summer food sources and Brooks suggests that over the season they are taken in greater numbers than aquatic surface flies. Unless the dry-fly fisher can find some alternative food source to represent or is prepared to fish the water, he could be spending as much as 80 or 90 per cent of his time waiting for trout to rise to a hatching fly.

Of the twelve flies in the *Treatyse of Fysshynge Wyth an Angle* (1496) there are two patterns which are the first examples of the use of terrestrials. Even Alfred Ronalds's *The Fly-Fisher's Entomology* (1836) was able to refer to the imitation of beetles, caterpillars, ants, and even the leafhopper a century before Vincent Marinaro offered his solution to the problems of its imitation in his *A Modern Dry-Fly Code* (1950). Following Marinaro's pioneering work in the United States, his fellow countrymen have developed terrestrial fishing to a degree unknown in the United Kingdom.

The American obsession with terrestrials began with Marinaro and his fishing companion, Charles Fox, who for many seasons fished the Letort Spring Run together. The new era began one day when both men were fishing to trout steadily rising with bulge rises. Not a fish was hooked and frustration and failure resulted. Marinaro lay on the riverbank peering at the water surface. There he discovered thousands of tiny, almost minuscule duns, ants, beetles and other assorted tiny terrestrials. The two men assembled a makeshift fine-mesh net and col-

Midsummer and low water on this freestone river. At this time of year during the afternoon period when few aquatic flies are hatching a terrestrial pattern is often an excellent search pattern. The tree-lined bank will provide plenty of terrestrial food.

1,800 black gnats, all freshly taken by a 2lb chalkstream rainbow trout, laid out in a photographic tray.

lected from the surface upwinged duns with wings less than ⅛ inch high, ants between ⅛ and ⅝ inch long, beetles less than 3/32 inch in diameter, and an extraordinary number of leafhoppers of barely measurable proportions. This was the start of Marinaro's realisation of the potential and actual food source provided by terrestrials. The impression these findings had upon Marinaro inspired him to experiment. His subsequent imitations proved very successful, particularly his Jassid to imitate the leafhopper. This one pattern assured Marinaro of fly-fishing immortality. His patterns are based upon the premise that trout have difficulty sensing the thickness of small insects floating on the surface and that it is the silhouette, opacity and light pattern that are the critical factors when imitating terrestrials.

The British trout fisher has not fished ter-restrials with the same enthusiasm as his American counterpart. This is in some ways surprising. Thirty-five years before Marinaro and Schweibert, the English fly fisher J. C. Mottram knew full well the value of this alternative food source:

On the other hand, there is a kind of smutting fish that is not truly a smutting fish. Very often one hears the angler say, 'The fish were smutting the whole day long.' This occurs especially in still, thundery weather, and in September; examination of the water shows it to be covered with all manner of small insects, green fly, tiny ichneumons, hoppers, minute beetles, gnats, midges, smuts, and a host of other unnamed, unknown minute insects which have fallen or flown upon the water.

All terrestrials on the surface find their way there by accident rather than by design as they fall, fly, leap kamikaze-style or are wind-borne. During the warmer weather of mid-summer most terrestrials become more active. Their increased activity raises the likelihood of their ending up on the water. At specific times on a warm, windy summer's day, when the abscence of aquatic fly due to water flow and temperature makes trout look elsewhere, terrestrials will play a very major role in their diet. As summer progresses some aquatic fly life decreases and the tasty bonus of a juicy terrestrial is something trout are on the look-out for. It is amazing how far some fish will move to take some of the larger terrestrials. It is also a sad but true fact that on many rivers and streams aquatic fly life, in particular the upwinged species, has declined in recent years. Pollution, run-off of agricultural chemicals, abstraction are the likely causes. Inevitably, terrestrials become far more important to fish and to the dry-fly fisherman.

If there is still any doubt in your mind about the significance of terrestrials I can offer a poignant illustration of one trout's selectivity over its choice of terrestrial. I have been fortunate to fish an east Yorkshire chalk stream as a guest of Roy Shaw, an excellent fly fisher and wildlife photographer. Roy caught the trout in question and examined its stomach contents, of which a single species made up 99·9 per cent. More than 1,800 black gnats had recently been taken by the fish. Other autopsies have revealed hawthorn flies in their hundreds and all these in trout from a chalk stream where traditionally the aquatic fly life is most abundant.

5 The Trout's View of the Fly

The first qualification for judging any piece of workmanship from a corkscrew to a cathedral is to know *what* it is – what it was intended to do and how it is meant to be used.

C. S. Lewis

It has been reasonably established that a trout can see only those items on the surface which are in its window. The water may of course be so rippled by the effects of current or wind that very little is seen through the window. Given clear relatively calm water, trout can be expected to see flies on the surface and objects in the air and on the bankside if they fall within the field of view. Nothing that is on the surface in the zone beyond the window can be seen unless it is tall enough for its tallest parts to be caught by the effects of refraction. With this exception, trout are unable to see flies on the surface beyond the window. But the *effects* of the surface flies may be seen on the undersurface, the mirror.

A TROUT'S VIEW OF EMERGERS

There is little doubt that trout often concentrate on the emerging nymphs and hatching duns in preference to the fully winged adults. Full consideration of trout preference for the nymph just below the surface is given in my book, *Trout On A Nymph*. There is a stage where the emerging fly is neither fully above nor below the surface. If at least part of the artificial to be used remains dry, consideration of the natural and its fishing imitation fall within the scope of this book.

The key feature of the emerger is the body of the nymph, which in due course becomes the empty nymphal shuck, hanging in the film. The thorax, legs and eventually the adult's abdomen are all pulled through the surface film. According to Gary LaFontaine, who studied mayfly emergence in great depth for his book *The Dry Fly*, there is a very important secondary trigger characteristic during emergence. This trait exists for only ten to twenty seconds of emergence but on a relatively calm surface is very obvious, and occurs at the critical time when trout are keying into the emergers. The characteristic is an aura, a soft glow around the thorax area of the fly. The upper side of the thoracic skin splits and is pushed to either side of the thorax as the adult emerges. To quote La-Fontaine: 'The aura is this stretched, thin flange of skin, infused by light from the open sky and the reflection of air bubbles along the inside rim. From below it looks like the insect is wearing a halo.' His Halo Emerger was devised with just this occasion in mind.

A TROUT'S VIEW OF DUNS

The emerging and adult duns probably constitute the majority of flies the dry-fly fisher represents, so there is nothing more important than an understanding of the trout's comprehension of a floating dun. Upon emerging the dun rests on the surface to dry its wings before flying off. It supports itself on the surface only by its six legs. No other part of the body or tail touches the water. The entomologist J. R. Harris suggested that if the tails did touch the water it might be difficult to lift them clear again, which would probably lead to the dun drowning. For the majority of fly fisherman and fly tyers it has been of paramount importance that the artificial fly should match the natural in its attitude on the surface of the water. Logically, then, the floating imitation should have its body and tail supported clear of the surface. The natural dun really is a *dry* fly. Latterly there has been a school of thought that maintains the view that allowing the body on the surface does not matter one jot and to this end hackles have been abandoned completely. The theories of both schools will be considered later.

The first indication of any fly on the surface is often not its appearance in the window but the light pattern created by the effects of its resting on the reverse side of the mirror, in the surface beyond the window. In the case of an upwinged dun each of its six legs makes a tiny indentation on the mirror through which light penetrates, forming a pattern of bright dots or streaks of light. There is no doubt that this can be the first indication that surface food is on its way and alerts a fish to the presence of a fly in the mirror. It has been suggested that many species of dun have their own light pattern and that trout can decide even at this stage whether it is the food they are looking for. It seems to me improbable that trout can distinguish be-

tween species whilst they are in the mirror. An overall impression of size might be indicated, but the possibility of discriminating on any other basis must be discounted.

Once alerted to the presence of a dun in the mirror, a selectively feeding trout will wait to make a closer inspection of the fly in the window before deciding to take it. In very rippled water where a clear inspection of the fly is not possible, it may be that the effects of the light pattern alone, or in combination with a general impression of size, a blurred outline and colour, will prompt a fish to rise. This explains why the exact pattern of artificial fly is less critical in rippled water. Trout seeing the light pattern well ahead or to one side sometimes move forwards or to one side to bring the fly into the window for a more critical examination. It is often possible to observe trout and grayling move to a natural fly that is out of the window and then, after approaching less than halfway, turn back. They had positioned themselves so that the fly came into the window and for one reason or another they didn't fancy what was on the menu.

While the dun is on the mirror, only the light pattern is visible. As it approaches the edge of the mirror the effects of refraction allow a fish a sight of the tops of the wings before it sees anything else of the fly. There is a short period when just the light pattern and an increasing portion of the wings is visible (see Fig 2). As the fly nears the window the wings get nearer the light pattern until the two merge as it passes into the window and can be seen as it really is. There is some debate about what, at this stage, a trout can understand of the dun (and our artificial). This has resulted in the different styles of artificial fly – some emphasising wings, others eliminating wings, some emphasising body colour, some fly tyers insisting upon achieving a natural light pattern from the hackle and others rejecting hackles as useless. The surprising thing is that these seemingly contradictory theories are all soundly based on observation.

Vincent Marinaro describes a remarkable experiment in the context of discovering

As the dun on the mirror nears the edge of the window the wing tips appear in the window detached from the body or light pattern. As the fly enters the window the wings and body merge.

more about the relative importance of the mirror and window; it also reveals a great deal about the imitation of the natural's wings. Trout were feeding regularly during a hatch of Henricksons on the Yellow Breeches. One trout was feeding in a narrow lane that enabled it to pick off any dun it chose. Marinaro's colleague positioned himself upstream of the feeding fish and collected naturals from the water. He then removed the wings from thirty-seven duns and placed them, alive and able to adopt a natural position, on the water at intervals along with the winged naturals. The rising trout continued to take the winged flies but *not one wingless natural was taken*. That is indeed a powerful argument for the inclusion of wing representation in an artificial fly. Marinaro called the experiment 'earth-shaking'. It also proves that the trout didn't rise on the basis of light pattern alone. In the above experiment the light pattern stimulated some initial response in the trout, which evaporated when trout were able to inspect the wingless fly in the window only a foot or so away.

In the last paragraph I suggested that 'wing representation' might be needed. Note that I did not say that wings were essential. Fly-fishing experience proves that wings on an artificial are not a prerequisite for success. On a standard wingless fly the upper fibres of the hackle will be seen in the window whilst the fly is on the edge of the mirror, and when in the window no doubt the upper hackle fibres give some impression of wings. In *A Modern Dry-Fly Code* Marinaro writes: 'the wing, its height and breadth and flatness, is the most important part of a floating dun!' The last two attributes are certainly not found in a wingless artificial although the height factor is fulfilled by the hackle. The breadth and flatness can be copied only by a specific wing imitation or very many turns of hackle over half the shank. If Marinaro's theories are right they would make the wingless artificial next to useless. Perhaps he fished to extremely selective trout which were fully able to assess wing width and flatness. I've met a few like that, but more than half my trout are taken on wingless patterns.

In contrast to Marinaro's emphasis on the wings I conducted a small experiment last season to try to confirm that sometimes it is the light pattern alone that produces a positive trout reaction. I tied up a few flies that consisted of no more than a wound olive parachute hackle on the top of the hook shank in the style of the USD series of John Goddard and Brian Clarke. There were no wings, tails or bodies save the tying thread holding down the hackle and the bare hook shank. These flies are impossible to fish with; they refuse to land in the upside down position such is the weight of the hook. However, by placing them on the water they drifted down on quite a calm surface over rising trout and grayling. The only visible feature to a fish is the light pattern and the spread hackle imitating the six legs of the natural. These flies were avidly taken by rising fish so indicating that sometimes the light pattern alone is sufficient stimulus for a trout to rise.

An even earlier trigger to the rise is the activity of nymphs as they swim to the surface. This may well stimulate a rise period as trout move progressively on to the duns. The nymphal activity is definitely a significant trigger that will warn trout to the likelihood of surface food becoming available. As the nymphs begin to move out of the weeds or from under stones trout feed on them and follow their progress to the surface. At the head of a pool or in other areas where nymphs rise this may well be an important trigger, but elsewhere where there is no nymphal activity it can only be the light pattern and the appearance in the window that are the necessary stimuli. Some trout feed in areas too far away to be aware of the ascending nymphs. I suspect that most trout rise to duns for the same reason they rise to spinners and other surface food – because they see them on the surface.

Often trout will be found in a taking mood and are in a frame of mind where almost any fly will do. Similarly, they may be rising in rippled or rough water, or are stocked fish not yet fully wild and will rise to almost any reasonably dressed and adequately presented fly cast their way. It is tempting dur-

Fig 15 A close scrutiny of the surface fly. The moment of truth – of the choice of artificial, of the accuracy of the dressing, and of the presentation.

ing periods of such obliging co-operation to try out one's own experimental patterns and claim success for them. It is great fun to fish at such times but the success of our patterns teaches us little about how to overcome the problems of selective trout.

Selectivity is not the monopoly of chalk-stream or spring-creek trout. If it were, dry-fly fishing elsewhere would soon pale into boredom. Angling pressure on any river makes for more selective fish if a catch-and-return policy is in operation. On a freestone river in the summer months when river levels are at their lowest and water clarity is at its highest trout are able to have a very clear view of surface flies on calm water and can be extremely selective about the imitation offered. When this is a problem I am convinced that a combination of a number of factors will satisfactorily answer a trout's inspection of a fly.

First, there is little doubt that the first trigger to stimulate a rise may be the earlier nymphal activity, but the first trigger to a particular individual fly is the light pattern in the mirror confirmed by the sight of the wing tips on the edge of the window. Either one or both of these may prompt the trout's interest. Its fins work a little quicker and as the fly comes into the window the trout begins to

move closer. The speed of these reactions depends entirely upon the speed of the current and the depth from which the trout must rise. It should be borne in mind that the deeper trout lie, the greater the diameter of their window. The beginning of the rise has been triggered. If the water is rippled or trout are not being very fastidious, the trout may continue to rise on the basis of the light pattern alone. If the view of the fly is a clear one, the movement to the surface will continue unless something about the fly warns the fish that it is not what it wants. This might be a failure in presentation, or it could well be that the presentation is fine but the trout says, 'It's a dun OK, but it isn't the one I'm after.' Far too often for my own liking a trout has seen my fly on the mirror, risen to inspect it in the window, and, being unconvinced, has followed it downstream for a foot or two, scrutinising it from a distance of less than three or four inches. Its suspicions have been aroused by some aspect of the presentation or dressing. Half of these fish remain unconvinced and melt back into the stream, but the other half find their inquisitiveness satisfied and a minute later they are returned to the river a grade higher in their education.

Viewing a fly from such a close distance for a few seconds allows a wise trout to study its characteristics. Features such as size, overall shape and silhouette, relative proportions and colour are easily observed if current speed and water clarity allow. It is Marinaro's contention that trout rise in a way 'that places the fly always at the edge of the window for all purposes: viewing, inspecting, and taking. He does not use the clear central area of the window.' I cannot fully support Marinaro's theory that the central window area is not used for inspecting a fly. My own experience is that time and time again trout use the central zone for viewing surface food, and often do not decide to rise until the fly is directly overhead or even beyond the trout. Of course there are many times when a trout makes its mind up on the basis of what it sees of the fly on the edge of the window, where its view of the colour of surface flies is clearer than at the centre of the window, and reacts accordingly. But some selective or fastidious trout make a judgement only when the fly is in the centre of the window, where they have a more accurate view of the critical features of size, shape and silhouette.

Size is very important. Few fish feeding even with only a modicum of selectivity are willing to take an imitation of the same aquatic fly of an unnatural size. It is the easiest characteristic to represent, for which there is no excuse for failure. Even a few millimetres difference in size appears as a huge disparity to a trout.

Shape, silhouette and the relative proportions of the fly are extremely important. The shape and silhouette of the dun on the surface differ from that of the 'standard' floating imitation. On a wingless pattern the side view offers no attempt to represent the natural's wings unless the turns of hackle are wound over the front third of the body to provide a semblance of the wing width. Any 'standard' dry fly viewed from the front has a circle of hackle fibres. Nothing like this exists on the natural, which, when similarly viewed, displays only the front legs, thorax and the narrow head-on view of the upright wings.

The body too may be closely examined by selective trout. The light, delicate, and at times translucent body of the natural is difficult to represent. Many artificials have thick, heavy and opaque bodies which simply will not adequately represent the body of a dun or spinner. I am convinced of the need for at least an approximation of the abdomen and thorax colours of the natural fly when fishing to selective fish. Some rising fish are less discriminating, others demand a closer imitation. There are times when I feel I could support Marinaro's theory, but for some trout Marinaro's observation holds very little water. In his introduction to the 1970 edition of his book *A Modern Dry-Fly Code* he wrote: 'If you believe as I do that the bodies of duns are meaningless and superfluous, then with one mighty stroke you have eliminated a great deal of confusion and uncertainty. You need only imitate the wing, which is of paramount importance.' I have no wish to cross swords with such a fly-fishing heavyweight as Vincent Marinaro or Doug Swisher and Carl Richards, who took an opposite view when they wrote in *Selective Trout*: 'In considering the dry fly, however, we must be equally concerned with the shape of *both* body and wings . . . The wings of our artificial must provide a close representation of the wings of the natural so the trout will respond and begin to rise. The body, however, is just as important.' Between these two extremes are the majority of trout which will rise to something looking vaguely like what they are after, with or without wings or bodies, so long as it is presented naturally, and artificials tied to both Marinaro's and Swisher and Richards's prescriptions will work. In my own experience different selective trout, when they are being truly selective about a pattern and not the presentation, are making their choice over different aspects of the surface fly. Some are selective because of an inadequate light pattern – which explains the times of failure for the no-hackles, which emphasise the body; others are selective about the abdomen, thorax or wings.

The overall colour presented by the dun will be recognisable by trout, as will the colour of specific parts of both the natural and the artificial fly, particularly the wings and the undersides of the thorax and abdomen. Fortunately, the differences between some species of fly are so minimal that they would be undetected. The body and wing colours of many species are very similar and this is used to the fly fisher's advantage when he uses a single fly to represent a number of naturals. A trout's assessment of colour in the surface fly depends very much on the light, whether reflected or transmitted, in which the fly is viewed. The view of a dun in the window is very much governed by the strength of the light behind the fly. The brighter the light, the more difficult it is to detect colour in the fly, and silhouette and size are more important features. There is an argument to be made out for the exaggeration of certain key colours in the natural fly. This is considered in the section on fishing for selective trout in Chapter 6.

A TROUT'S VIEW OF SPINNERS

The mated female spinner must return to

A hen spinner viewed from below the surface through the window.

water to deposit her eggs. Those of interest to the dry-fly fisherman are the species which deposit their eggs by dipping the rear of the abdomen in the water in a single or a series of drops on the surface. When the spinner alights on the surface to deposit the eggs her wings will be in the upright or slightly parted position. As the fly rides the water depositing her eggs the wings begin to droop. After ovipositing, the majority of spent females die on the surface with their wings splayed horizontally so that the body, tails, legs and wings are on or in the film. It is in this spent position that trout find them easy prey.

It follows that because the spent spinners are not supported by their legs, as were the duns, the image in the mirror is very different. It is not a question of a light pattern from the legs since the whole fly – wings, tails, abdomen and thorax – is visible in the mirror. The two key features are the body and the outstretched wings. Because the fly is in the film, and not above the surface, the trout's view, both in the mirror and in the window, is much clearer and the body colour of the fly is much more apparent. The thorax colour is more pronounced than the abdomen colour, which may be almost drained of deep colour after ovipositing. Why we insist on representing a spinner with a fully hackled fly that holds the body above the surface is a mystery. The fly is certainly not being presented as trout expect to see it – flush with the surface. The fly fisher needs not so much a dry fly but a damp one. Despite the fact that spinners are most vulnerable when flush in the film and at this stage attract most trout attention, the hackled patterns with bodies part out of the water still catch a great many fish. They are taken for newly alighted spinners in the process of ovipositing and not the fully spent stage.

Probably the majority of trout feeding on spent spinners feed very confidently and position themselves very close to the surface in the feeding lane. Because of the trout's closeness to the surface it will have a very small window. It doesn't need a large window because the bodies of spent spinners will be visible on the underside of the mirror.

It is in the late evening and dusk that many species of spinners return to the water and the falling darkness means that the angler finds these spent flies very hard to see. The failing light also influences the trout's view of surface flies. It should be remembered that trout eyesight is more efficient than human eyesight in low light conditions. Therefore, if we care to view spent spinners through the bottom of an aquarium against a dusk sky, our view will be poorer than a trout's. In John Goddard and Brian Clarke's book *The Trout and the Fly* there is an interesting, and at that time probably unique, photograph of the trout's view of spent spinners at dusk under the influence of a red sunset. The spinners' bodies in the photograph are virtually invisible but I suspect that the more efficient eye of the trout may comprehend more than the camera lens or the human eye. The significant aspect of the photograph is that the last rays of light are refracted around the fly body and through the transparent wings, making the latter very clear against a dark sky. On the occasion of the photograph when there was a red sunset the light refracted was also red. Goddard and Clarke suggest that since trout eyesight is more sensitive to red than other colours flies at such times are easier to see. This would explain why some spinner imitations with orange hackles, such as the Orange Quill, are so effective (*see also* the Sunset Spinner in Chapter 9). Another aspect of the trout's view of the spent spinners against the dull grey sky of late evening is that the wings become practically invisible. This resulted in Doug Swisher and Carl Richards tying their No-Wing Spinner considered in Chapter 8.

A trout's view of the natural upwinged fly on the surface in ideal, unrippled, clear-water conditions can be summarised as follows:

1. In the mirror, a light pattern is created by the feet of the duns; the bodies of spent spinners are visible because they lie in the surface film.
2. In the window, the legs, bodies, wings and possibly the tails of duns can in all probability be seen, as can similar features of spent spinners lying in or on the surface. In the duns the tails are probably the least likely to be seen, and in the spent spinner the legs are of the least significance.

Caddis, stoneflies, midges and smuts have their own light patterns, which in general terms can probably be distinguished from each other by their size. Terrestrials too will create a light pattern but many of these are more likely to rest in the film and be visible to fish in both the mirror and the window.

The trout's view of surface flies is one that is impossible to define clearly simply because it is exceedingly variable as wind and wave, ripple and current have marked or more subtle effects on the mirror and the window. In broken water the effects of refraction on a fish's view of a fly are varied as the fly rises and falls over ripple and wavelet. The size, shape and colouring of the fly will appear to be continuously altering as it traverses a highly disrupted window. In calm water, a much clearer and more critical view is possible.

A TROUT'S VIEW OF THE CADDIS

The light pattern created by the returning female caddis is the principal trigger to the trouts' rise. I am grateful for Gary LaFontaine's permission to quote from his classic work *Caddisflies*:

In the case of the active caddisfly adult, in fact, the light pattern is sometimes the only problem the adult imitation must solve to be realistic. This is typically true, for example, when ovipositing females hop and skitter over the surface. If an insect or a fly is outside visual range (the trout's window) spreading a flash of light with every bounce and kick, the fish rushes toward the light pattern and never examines the finer details of the adult caddisfly. The major point emphasized by all the hours observing trout feed on the surface is clear and simple: the light effect of the insect whenever it is a prominent trigger for a strike, is so overwhelming that it is usually the only important characteristic.

A hot day on the Yellowstone river, Wyoming, and nothing rising. Gary
LaFontaine, Jack Dennis and Mike Lawson discuss tactics.

The decision to fish a caddis pattern as a search fly has paid off.

Mike Lawson releases a fine cutthroat trout.

There is no single way in which the female sedge rests on the surface; that is to say, there is no clearly defined or easy to describe light pattern. Some may rest sedately and statically on their six legs, some have their abdomen submerged, some are running or skating with or without abdomens below the surface, others are struggling to break through the surface tension so that they can swim to the riverbed and another group are landing in kamikaze style, hoping to crash through the surface film. As a result, the natural fly might sit high above the surface or flush in the film or with just its rear in the film, and all with varying degrees of movement, activity and surface commotion. The resulting light patterns vary accordingly from six dimples of light created by the feet through to a confused blur and streaks of light as an agitated fly dances on or dives through the film. Trout feeding on the relatively inactive sedges being carried along in a natural drift will wait for their food to be brought along on the current. When fluttering sedges are landing trout will cruise an area expecting to see the agitated light pattern.

The view of the caddis through the window varies too, with some species having some or part of their bodies in the film or submerged and others floating high supported by their legs. Different traits are displayed by the various behaviour patterns. Flies flush in the film produce a very obvious break or bulge in the surface, with splayed wings either side of the body being an important feature. The active caddis produces dots and streaks of light, the latter particularly from the wing edges of a skating sedge. Needless to say, the trout's view of the near-motionless insect is much clearer than its view of the fluttering fly. The physical characteristics in terms of size, shape, silhouette and colour are more important in the static fly; in the active insect the light pattern and movement are the crucial imitators.

It isn't hard to understand why the most popular sedges have been ones that obligingly drift with the currents. In a genus like the North American Black Caddis (*Chimarra*) the females collapse after depositing their eggs.

They can be imitated with the standard dead drift presentation, the one 90 per cent of the fly fishermen are going to be using anyway, and a simple downwing dry fly.

On the Au Sable in Michigan the fishermen come every May for the Little Black Caddis flights. What a difference there is, though, between the beginner and the advanced fly fisherman. The ones new to the hatch flog indiscriminately, covering every riser and catching mostly small fish. The experienced angler does more studying than casting, watching the sipping rises for the slight differences that point out a larger fish.

The main difference is the rise rhythm. Small fish work quicker, moving a bit to take every insect that drifts down. The large trout is more patient, tipping up steadily to the spent females but never hurrying.

THE EFFECTS OF LIGHT ON SURFACE FLIES

Bright sunlight is often a deterrent to surface feeding. The sun may be directly overhead and be simply too bright to allow trout to see clearly any surface objects. Although duns might be plentiful it may be very difficult for trout to see them. Conversely, in very low light trout cannot perceive colour very well and they are much more likely to make an assessment of surface flies by their size and silhouette or light pattern.

Two types of light may come into play when surface objects are seen from below. The first is reflected light. Light reflected off objects shows them as opaque and in solid colour. Trout are able to see flies in reflected light even though surface flies appear to be almost permanently back-lit. A trout can inspect a fly closely when it views it from the same side as a strong light source illuminating the fly. The colour of any object is most difficult to assess when it is strongly lit from behind, and I suggest that sometimes trout take flies because the shape and size are the critical factors, not the reflected colour.

The second type of light is transmitted light. Many natural duns and spinners have at least part-translucent bodies which allow some light to pass through. When a fish is positioned below a back-lit natural fly (in all but excessively bright light) the effects of translucency will be visible if surface conditions permit. The difference in appearance between a fly in reflected light and in transmitted light is sometimes considerable. Light passing through the wings and bodies will appear different under a range of light and surface conditions. Not all naturals have the same degree of translucency and each sex and species is slightly different. The thorax of a dun or spinner is completely opaque but the abdomen is not. The abdomen of a spinner is much more translucent than a dun's especially after ovipositing, when it is most attractive to trout.

The first serious attempt to consider translucency in artificial flies has generally been attributed to J. W. Dunne's book, *Sunshine and the Dry Fly* (1924). Most fly fishers appear to have overlooked a remarkable volume some ten years earlier by John Cecil Mottram, *Fly-Fishing, Some New Arts and Mysteries* (1915). Mottram, whom Arnold Gingrich refers to as 'angling's Invisible Man' and praises as 'the completely unsung genius of English angling literature', anticipated many later American angling writers in his awareness of the importance of terrestrials on the water and of the value of fishing tiny smut imitations. Writing of transparency in the natural fly he had this to say:

People do not as a rule examine objects against a bright sky, yet this is how a fish must view a floating fly. It follows, therefore, that the fly-tier must by no means neglect this quality; he must examine the natural flies against the sky, take note of those parts that are opaque and those that are transparent, and further, of the transparent parts he must note the colour, for whilst traversing the fly's body the sun's white light becomes coloured. If, then, the fly-tier thinks colour of importance,

here is a type of colour which is of far greater value than any that is reflected.

Translucency was referred to by implication as long ago as Charles Cotton's supplement to *The Compleat Angler*. Referring to the body dubbing, Cotton wrote: '. . . step to the door and hold it up betwixt your eye and the Sun, and it will appear a shining red; Let me tell you, never a man in *England* can discern the true colour of a dubbing any way but that'. By considering his artificial flies in this way, Cotton alluded to the translucency of the natural fly, but few fly tyers between him and Mottram gave it much consideration. F. M. Halford's patterns show no sign of resolving the problems; they are mostly opaque quill bodies offering no translucency. Dunne understood the problem well enough and exhorted the fly fisherman to examine the natural fly 'against the light' and to dress an imitation bearing the results in mind. He thought he had solved the problem with his 'Sunshine Fly'. I believe his patterns, which were very complicated to dress, worked well enough on sunny days but on dull or cloudy days the patterns were no better than any others.

The colour of the natural fly is constantly changing as it is viewed in varying degrees of transmitted and reflected light. I have little doubt that when assessing a natural fly with the intention of making a suitable imitation the considerations of translucency should be almost as high a priority as its reflected colours. Fly bodies appear both opaque and translucent; much depends upon the angle of the light on the fly and the position from which a trout views the fly. Finding the answer to the problem of dressing an imitation that appears translucent in direct light and yet still natural under reflected light is not easy. Some of the answers are considered in Chapter 8.

Part Three
Fishing the Dry Fly

The following two chapters 6, and 7, are the ones on which success or failure hangs. If you tie your own flies, chapters 8 and 9 may cause a few headaches, but if all fails at least high-quality flies can be purchased. The strategy adopted at the waterside and how the fly on the end of the line and leader is presented are the sixty-four thousand dollar issues. Flunk these and you'll return home fishless.

Anyone can be successful, but consistency comes only with practice. Watercraft, presentation techniques, reading the river, discerning the rise forms, identifying the hatches and generally pitting your wits against the trout's all come to him who perseveres. That is not to say that success is guaranteed; if this book were to make any promises the fine print would reveal that all too often a large portion of humble pie is on my supper dish. Every fly fisher experiences days when he goes home water-licked. Much of the answer lies in becoming single-minded and adopting a predatory instinct which allows nothing to come between the fly fisher and persuading a trout to rise to the fly. It has been said that a good fisherman thinks like a fish. By being on the water long enough and being willing to learn about trout and natural flies and about bringing the artificial into contact with the former, the observant fly fisher soon becomes the efficient predator.

There are more times than I care to admit when I am convinced that I have had the correct pattern of fly, representing the exact stage of the life-cycle that the trout has been concentrating on, delicately presented, alighting on the surface like a melting snowflake, and conforming perfectly in drift to the naturals – all to nil effect. For some indiscernible reason – perhaps it is imperceptible drag, or perhaps the trout counts seven dimples in the light pattern, not six, or perhaps the Almighty exercises divine intervention, or perhaps the trout simply don't take all the naturals – I just can't rise a fish. Such frustration is no better summed up than in the German proverb 'Alle Kunst ist umsunst wenn ein Engel auf das Zundloch brunzt', which translated goes: 'All skill is in vain when an angel pees in the touch-hole of your musket.' There's not a lot you can do about it.

6 Dry Fly Strategy

It is here that the intellectual exercise begins. For especially on our more prolific streams, each day brings its own problems, its different insects; indeed, each hour may bring its changes, now the fish taking one insect, now another; sometimes the nymph, sometimes the dun, and sometimes the spinner. No two fish rise in the same way, and each one presents its own individual enigma, in which the uncertainties of the terrain, the wind, the current and the fly are intricately intertwined. For dry-fly fishing is a continual challenge to our faculties if it is taken seriously. The fly which is infallible today may be an abject failure tomorrow, and the solved mysteries of one season may become the unsolved mysteries of the next season.

David Jacques, *Fisherman's Fly*, 1965

CHOOSING THE RIGHT FLY

The 'right' fly is the one that rises the trout. It is rarely the only pattern that will rise a particular trout, no matter how selective. It is more than likely that a brown trout locked into the rhythm of taking the duns of a particular species will be duped by an imitation of that species. It may of course take other patterns, but the odds are lengthening. Fishing an imitation of the natural fly on the water, if there is any, is the key to successful dry-fly fishing. No one advocates fishing an alternative pattern to the species being consumed. And yet . . .

I have met a few skilled fly fishers who have used a mere handful of flies all season, no matter what the fly on the water. Two have been 'one fly only' men. The first used, and probably still uses, the Pheasant Tail as tied originally by Payne Collier, with the only concession being a couple of different hackle alternatives. I watched and fished with this angler for two seasons and his results were consistently better than most of the other rods in the club. 'I've a fly for every occasion' he'd say, 'and this is it!' The second angler is my colleague Arthur Oglesby, author of a couple of excellent books on Atlantic salmon and European Editor of *Field and Stream*. Some twenty-odd years ago, as secretary to a small club controlling some chalk stream fishing, Arthur experimented with using a single pattern of dry fly for a whole season. He opted for the John Storey and his efforts

produced a slightly better catch than his previous seasons' averages. Ed Van Put, an expert Catskill angler, uses only three dry flies all season, year in year out: an Adams, a Royal Wulff and a Pheasant Tail Midge. I am not sure what these examples prove except that all three men are experts in presenting a dry fly. I am sure that many trout which fail to rise to an artificial and are deemed 'too selective' are being selective not so much about the imitation as about the presentation.

Fortunately there isn't a narrow law which says that you must imitate exactly the insect on the surface. That would be an inflexible restriction and would discourage experiment and variation. There's no fun in what would become no more than a science. The best pattern is the one that gives the impression of being a wide range of flies, sufficiently vague as to imitate none in particular exactly but suggestive of a great many. Even then there is no 'right' fly unless it is presented properly and fished correctly.

The hope is that the dry-fly fisher will be able to cast a fly to a trout which is already rising. The benefits are obvious. The trout's position has been revealed, it is already in a feeding mood, actually on the look-out for surface food, and the manner in which it has taken the food from the surface – the rise form – may give a clue as to what it is taking. The most ardent dry-fly purist will cast a fly only to a trout already rising or at least visible just below the surface. This is fine if there are plenty of fish rising; I too adopt a similar

The author giving 100 per cent concentration.

policy, and if trout are regularly betraying their presence surface-feeding who wouldn't? There can be few more enjoyable experiences for the dedicated trout fisher than to wander a stream casting here and there, covering rising fish every few yards. Some are risen, some hooked, some landed, some are put down and a few turn their noses up at the flies offered. The angler moves on to the next riser, a cast further upstream, six feet further into paradise. A memorable day is completed when the trout have co-operated with an unexpected degree of altruism.

Alas, it is not always so simple. Hatches of fly sufficient to induce a steady rise period or a fall of egg-laying spinners, sedges or stoneflies never lasts the length of the fishing day. If we are fortunate a few spinners may be around in the early morning, a few duns and caddis may emerge intermittently during the day, and in the evening we might witness better hatches and egg-layers returning. I am unwilling to wait around for trout to show themselves before casting a dry fly. It boils down to approaching the subject in three ways: fishing only to rising trout; fishing the likely lies; fishing all the stream. The ideal is the first. It's dry-fly fishing to dream about. (Except that dreams sometimes turn into nightmares. Remember Skues's fictional Mr Castwell, who upon departing this life had his wish of fishing the gin-clear waters of a celestial River Test fulfilled by St Peter. The keeper pointed out a rising trout and Mr Castwell rose and hooked it and another from the same place, and another, and another, continuing until dusk . . . 'Hell!' said Mr Castwell. 'Yes,' said the watching keeper.) The second is a consequence of no fish rising, and the third is only for the angler who knows no better. Most dry-fly fishing is a combination of fishing to co-operative trout, using the skills of reading the water and knowing where trout might be expected to lie and offering suitable patterns.

FISHING TO RISING TROUT

Luck, fate, fortune, the stars or your god is on your side. Trout are rising. This is what it's all about. This is why we go fly fishing. It's the real thing. None of that hit-and-miss business of casting a fly where there *might* be a trout, with a pattern that *might* bring up a fish. Most of the problems have been solved. You know where trout are and that they are feeding. These are reasons for joy and optimism. You're going to be busier than a one-legged man in a forest fire. A dry-fly fisher who doesn't approach this stream with a smile on his face is pursuing the wrong sport. My biggest problem is restraining myself from crashing through the undergrowth and wading the stream as though storming a D-Day beach. Then there are those rarer days that are so few and far between, when trout are rising and it is almost as though I've been inextricably linked by some primeval bond to the flowing water and its surroundings. These days occur for me only when I wade some quiet stream alone and shut off the outside world, lost in wonder, as the hymm puts it. Somehow, a sixth sense anticipates every rise, and by some primitive intuition one knows where the trout are lying and when they will rise. The river and I are one.

Under normal fishing conditions when trout are surface-feeding, only one problem remains – discovering what the trout are rising to. Again, observational skill is crucial. Study the water surface.

Are there any flies visible? If so, are they

Fig 16   Surface-feeding trout.

duns, female spinners, newly emerged sedges or returning sedges, or some other aquatic fly? There may of course be a number of different species on the surface; hatches overlap or multiple hatches might be experienced, with two or more species emerging at the same time. Newly emerged duns might be on the surface at the same time as spinners or egg-laying sedges. During the mid-to-late evening, when large, seemingly mouthwatering duns are emerging, trout often prefer the small spent spinners which constitute a better bet, a mouthful that isn't going to disappear at the last moment. Also, during the complex hatches of a number of species, the Swisher and Richards law of pounds of meat comes into effect. This maintains that trout feed on the species which offers the greatest total volume of food. That is why during multiple hatches trout often prefer the smaller species which frequently emerge in greater numbers than some of the larger duns. Despite being a larger mouthful which appears to offer the biggest return for the least effort, the less dense hatches of larger duns are passed by.

The fly fisher should be aware of which species might be expected to hatch at the time of the season and day, and with this information one may be able to deduce what is being taken. Catching specimens in a net is the best solution. Tying a simple fine-mesh net to the end of the fishing rod is as good a method as any for scooping flies off the surface. Establish whether they are sedges, upwingeds, stoneflies, or terrestrials. If upwinged, are they duns or spinners? Which species? Examine the key characteristics: size, number of tails, colour of wings and body colour. Even if the exact species cannot be identified, as is sometimes the case, an overall impression of size and wing and body colour will enable you to select a suitable artificial. If sedges, are they active or motionless, emergers, or returning ovipositors?

There might be no visible fly. Are they taking emergers in the film, trapped terrestrials, spent spinners or tiny aquatic species – or is it that you need spectacles? When all possibilities are eliminated, only the impossible remains plausible. That, apparently, is exactly what happens on the Beaverkill (New York). In his River Rap audio tape (one of a series of 90-minute tapes by a local expert on many North American trout rivers – they are an invaluable guide, the like of which we have yet to see in the United Kingdom) Eric Peper describes his frustration of seining the water, both surface and subsurface, and finding absolutely nothing on which the rising trout could be feeding. He concludes, puckishly, that '. . . those trout are rising for style points'. Unfortunately I have days when for all my fishing effort style points for presentation are my only reward. If it is not possible to determine categorically what fly is being taken – either because the distance is too great, the flies are too small, or there are too many species to be specific – another method of identification must be used. The rise form is the biggest clue.

RISE FORMS

When trout take a fly from the surface or move just under the surface, water is displaced. Because natural flies and terrestrial insects adopt different positions on the surface or in the film, trout take them in different ways. Similarly, trout become aware of the length of time different species or different stages of life-cycle stay on the water and they rise with appropriate speed in a leisurely or frenzied fashion. Much can be learned from the rise form. It will never be possible to differentiate between a blue-winged olive or a medium olive in this way but other broader generalisations can be claimed. The size of the rise form may vary from looking like the results of a half-brick being thrown into the pool to the tiniest sip, a mere pinprick of a whirl. Part of the excitement is that you don't know whether the trout is a ten-incher or a three-pounder.

It is a general but flexible rule that the bigger the natural fly or the quicker it is to escape the surface the greater the probability of a noisy, splashy rise. The smaller the insect, or if it is trapped or struggling in the

A 2lb brown trout takes a dun in a tiny chalk stream.

film, or dead, then the quieter the rise. Sedges, moths and large duns usually prompt a rise with some commotion. Midges, spent spinners and stillborns evoke quiet feeding, sometimes resulting in barely discernible water displacement; the natural or artificial fly merely disappears without a sound and with only the slightest water movement. If there are multiple hatches of flies, or in the evenings when duns, spinners and sedges can be side by side on the surface, the rise form is an important indicator of food being chosen.

Big splashy rises do not indicate big fish, nor do quiet rises suggest small trout either. In fact it is surprising just how the opposite is true. It is often the smaller fish that create the most disturbance.

Watch for rhythmically feeding fish. Some may rise to every other fly or at some time interval during a steady hatch. They may not rise to the artificial if it falls drastically out of sequence. I am not suggesting that trout can count the flies overhead, merely that their

body clock allows them to rise at regular intervals in a rhythmic pattern. Trout feeding in such a manner are probably aware that food is in plentiful supply, such as spent spinners, smuts, midges, stillborns or early-season duns taking a long time drying before flight.

Be aware that trout do not surface-feed only on duns, spinners, sedges and terrestrials but often – and some would say more often than not – trout feed on emerging flies, stillborns and floating nymphs. This is particularly evident in complex hatches, according to Doug Swisher and Carl Richards, who wrote in *Fly Fishing Strategy* that 'During most hatches, two to eight floating nymphs will be taken for every winged mayfly' (up-winged flies, not *the* Mayfly). This sort of ratio might be true for some American streams but I have never found any quantity of floating nymphs in an examination of stomach contents of a British trout that amounted to more than a small minority of the total intake. One reason for this apparent absence in an autopsy is that the insect often completes the hatching process whilst in the throat of the trout. This also happens to emerging caddis flies. This startling statistic at least makes me more aware of what trout might be feeding on.

The Major Rise Forms

The degree to which each rise will be seen and heard depends upon two factors: the angler's own experience and powers of observation and the speed and turbulence of the current. On a flat calm surface all the rises are observable and most are audible. In fast water only the slashing rise might be seen or heard, or, with a bit of luck, and by studying the water if it is not too distant, it may be possible to pick out the plain rise. All surface rises are betrayed by a tiny bubble of air. As the fly is taken in so is a small amount of air, which is expelled immediately through the gills. Only on a calm smooth surface is the

bubble seen clearly, and it usually bursts almost immediately.

The Simple or Plain Rise

The simple or plain (Fig 17) is the commonest of rise forms and the one which results from most rises to duns. It is the standard rise, the manner in which trout would ordinarily rise to take surface food. In fact most surface food is taken in this way at some stage. The earliest spent spinners, some motionless sedges and terrestrials are taken with the simple rise before they appear on the surface in greater numbers, and an alternative rise form develops directly relating to that particular food. The characteristics of the rise are the breaking of the surface by the trout's mouth (which may be too fast to be visible) followed by concentric rings ebbing across the surface, which in rippled water will soon disappear. In rough, fast water the evidence is dispersed before the first ring gets a foot away. If trout

Fig 17 The simple or plain rise.

appear to be rising with simple rises but the dun patterns fail to rise a fish, it may be that trout are actually taking nymphs on the point of emergence. The water displacement is almost identical to that when they are taking duns. An emerging or floating nymph pattern could well be the answer.

The Slashing Rise

As its name suggests this rise is as though a trout slashes at the fly (Fig 18). A considerable disturbance is caused, a lot of water is displaced, the trout has moved at speed to take the fly and broken the surface with a splash. Sometimes the head and shoulders or more of the fish breaks the surface; at other times it surges towards the fly with its mouth protruding out of the water. Occasionally a slashing rise is produced from a deep-lying fish bolting to intercept some surface food

and returning to the riverbed. These are often recently stocked fish still learning to be stream-wise and not yet attuned to established feeding patterns. The slashing rise is more likely to be a trout moving quickly to take a fly that it expects not to stay in a straight drift. Why else must it move so rapidly to make sure of the kill? The one fly that regularly has surface movement is the sedge, either as a newly emerged adult fluttering its wings in a blur before take-off or as a returning egg-laying female alighting. Some of the larger terrestrials such as craneflies, moths, grasshoppers and larger beetles are snapped with considerable disturbance. The only other species that I have experienced the slashing rises to is the true Mayfly, *Ephemera danica*. On the few streams I fish with good hatches trout frequently rise in such a fashion. I am not sure what produces these rises of reckless abandon. Perhaps they

Fig 18   The slashing rise; sometimes even the head and part of the body will break the surface.

The nose of this trout breaks the surface to snatch a newly emerged sedge.

are associated with the easy pickings of a large quantity of big flies or the fear of losing such a mouthful.

Trout rising in this way are prepared to move some distance to intercept a fly and will not stick rigidly to a narrow food lane. This is one time when casting accuracy is not at a premium.

The slashing rise is also experienced on faster water where the current ensures that trout must react with appropriate speed to intercept a surface fly. Inevitably, the speed of the rise and the faster movement of the water can create quite a disturbance. The slashing rise under these circumstances is more a result of the water speed than an indication of the fly being taken.

The Sip, or Kiss, Rise

Of all rises the sip (Fig 19) is the most difficult to detect on a rippled surface and is extremely rare in fast water. Trout producing these rises are usually stationed just below the sur-

face, or deeper if the current is very leisurely. The energy expended by a trout holding a position close to the surface is much more than in the lower zones; consequently, it is only the slower and medium-paced water that enables trout to feed in such a way. The faster the water, the more insects are needed to make holding a position just below the surface worth while. Being so close to the surface the trout's window is small and an accurate presentation is necessary. Because sip rises are associated with an abundance of surface food trout are relectant to move for a fly outside a narrow feeding lane and the fly must be presented exactly in line to drift over the fish.

The surface disturbance from the rise is minimal. On occasions I have watched trout less than three yards away take my fly with barely a ripple or bulge resulting. It has been as though the fly has been pulled through the film by some unseen force. I would go so far as to say that in some instances no part of the trout's body breaks the surface; the only

Fig 19   The sip or kiss rise.

ripple is produced by the fly being drawn through the film. I prefer to call these rises 'sips' as it seems to sum up the trout's behaviour accurately. Some are accompanied by an audible sip when air is sucked in as well as the fly. It must always be that some air is taken in but, because of the quiet nature of this rise form and the fact that they often occur on calm water, the intake of air can be heard.

The sip rise indicates that trout are feeding in a leisurely fashion. There is no urgency about the rise. It would suggest that the food is not going to escape very quickly or else a more urgent, noisier disturbance would be warranted. These rises invariably mean that the food items are either dead, dying, or trapped in the film. From this we deduce that the targets are either trapped emergers or stillborns (caddis or upwinged species), floating nymphs, trapped terrestrials, or spent

sedges or spinners. If no sedges or duns appear to be hatching it is likely that returning females or terrestrials are the food source. Other factors must be taken into account to narrow the field down. For example, take two extremes: if these rises occur during the heat of a midsummer afternoon, the odds are that some, probably small, terrestrial is trapped (ants on the water are invariably greeted with the sip rise). During late evening the sip rise is most likely to be to spinners or spent caddis, as this is the time when they are most prolific on the water.

Some streams at certain times have more scum on the surface than others. The wind and current accumulate the scum on the edge of the current and in backwaters. Here the trapped emergers, stillborns and spent insects are gathered and it is not unusual for fish to patrol these zones in a leisurely manner, picking off their food in sip rises.

The Head-and-Tail Rise

Harry Plunket-Green, in *Where the Bright Waters Meet* (1936), wrote: 'I do not know anything more beautiful in nature than the head-and-tailing trout.' They are more than simply beautiful; a big head-and-tailing trout is a heart-stopping sight for the fanatical trout fisher. I know of nothing I can mention here to make my adrenalin surge in this way. The fish feeds in such a way that often its entire back breaks through the surface. Invariably this leisurely rise is found on the slower-moving water and is an indication that trapped spinners, emerging midge pupae or nymphs, or stillborns are being taken.

The Nearly-Rise

The bulge or hump of water of the nearly-rise indicates a trout feeding on ascending nymphs or pupae just below the surface. Unfortunately, persuading them to rise to the dry fly is not too easy. A floating pattern *might* bring up a trout feeding in such a manner, but it is quite likely that if the emergence period has just started trout will feed on

A large eddy on the River Wharfe. Notice the scum lane where spent flies and stillborns accumulate.

the rising nymphs before moving on to the emerging and adult duns. It may only be a matter of minutes before their attitude towards a dun imitation changes. Because trout are taking ascending nymphs on the verge of emergence one answer is to fish a nymph as a floater on the surface. It is the silhouette of the nymph that the trout will be looking for. One of the nymph patterns with a dubbed body will work if it is well soaked with floatant. In all but very calm water the artificial is very difficult for the angler to see and you have to know exactly where the fly has landed and where the current is taking it. An alternative food source could be the ovipositing *Baetis* spinners which swim or crawl below the surface to deposit their eggs.

The most difficult scenario to envisage is a river surface with a number of species laid out on the menu. It is more than possible that simultaneously two or three species of duns are emerging, some spinners are returning to lay their eggs, sedges are hatching or returning, and a few unidentifiable micro-flies and the odd terrestrial are also found. What a selection! Trout may decide to take just one species, but how does the angler discover which? The combination of observation of the flies and inspection of the water surface and rise forms might narrow the field considerably. After as much information as possible has been gathered it becomes a matter of trial and error. Even if it is only possible to identify the wing colour of an upwinged species, try a suitable imitation. If there is still no joy it may be necessary to go to extreme lengths to collect flies from the surface, even if it means completely putting down a whole pool to get the necessary information.

Don't overlook the possibility of trout feeding on stillborns. The heavier the hatch the more likely that stillborns will be on the surface. It's Doug Swisher and Carl Richards's opinion that 'the wiser and larger the fish, the more apt he is to feed on stillborns'. They suggest that during a hatch when there might be relatively few natural stillborns on the surface their stillborn patterns are more effective than normal emergers. The stillborns are attractive because trout are aware that here is one item of food that is not going to escape. A dun could disappear in a second, the emerger is more of a certainty, the stillborn a 100 per cent non-escaper. Quiet, confident, steady rises often indicate rising to stillborns or emergers. Casting accuracy is essential with stillborns as trout enjoying a heavy hatch of fly have no need to move from a narrow feeding lane. Contrary to what might be expected, according to Swisher and Richards, the specialists in this field, the artificial must float high in the water.

SELECTIVE OR PREOCCUPIED TROUT

(The Agony and the Ecstasy)

If the dream is to arrive at the waterside to find trout surface-feeding, the nightmare must be subsequently to return home fishless in wretched desolation and frustration. To see trout gorging themselves on big hatches of fly is quite fantastic, often sufficient to send fly fishers into an equivalent frenzy. But as fly after fly fails and attractor follows imitation as surely as night succeeds the day, and muscles ache, all optimism is wiped away by mounting despair. If the truth was squeezed from me, I would rather leave a water unsuccessfully without a trout having shown itself than depart in total failure from a river in which every fish was rising. Fly fishing can be a humbling, even humiliating experience.

The probability is that some fish will rise quite readily to the artificial fly but others will take more persuasion. The greatest challenge is presented by the ultra-selective, educated trout which shuns 'standard' patterns or presentation. Three characteristics can be observed in such trout. Some fish are simply just cautious; they won't be duped by a second-rate imitation or a slightly suspicious presentation. Others are genuinely locked into feeding exclusively on only one fly, and because water conditions permit a close scrutiny of the surface fly, a close-imitation artificial is demanded. A further few are older, wiser and warier trout which have seen too many artificials and fly fishermen not to know an imitation when they see one. Only when these three factors combine do you get a truly ultra-selective trout, the one per cent of a stream. You can bet your last fly that any fish displaying all these characteristics will be a good-sized one and well worth persevering with. It is not often that the larger fish in a stream rise with regularity. They reserve their surface feeding for night-time or the Mayfly season. If one of these can be caught when it's being highly selective, it will be a fish to remember.

Trout intelligence is the fly fisher's greatest invention, behind which we hide a multitude of our own deficiencies. However, within a narrow margin there is scope for varying degrees of a low level of trout intelligence.

A trout that has been hooked and released is that bit cleverer next time – if there is a next time. The third capture will be even more difficult. Within a narrow margin there is scope for varying degrees of trout intelligence. Some learn more and learn quicker than others. Before its release in the stream a recently stocked fish may have never seen a natural dun. When it takes its first blue-winged olive it learns that they taste fine and are edible. If it is hooked on an artificial pattern it will become a degree more wary next time. All trout look for points of *recognition* in a fly, ensuring that it conforms to what they are looking for. The key points for stimulating the rise might be light pattern, wing height and colour, size and silhouette, or body colour. Selectively feeding trout will begin to check these more critically and might, through experience, begin to notice points of *difference*. If anything in the imitation or presentation is not like the natural fly it is allowed to pass by.

David Howden netting a brown trout on the River Wharfe.

There is a strong possibility during a multiple hatch upon which trout are feeding with little discrimination that at some time they will become selective over just one species. It is not possible to predict this or to say in advance on which species the favour will fall. But the angler should be aware if a number of flies are on the water and a variety of artificials are rising trout that at some stage they may feed selectively.

Here are eleven alternative courses of action for the problem of selective trout:

1. Fish on and hope. This is the line of least effort and minimum success. On the thirtieth cast the trout might rise, but the chances are it won't.

2. If all the rising trout are being selective and rising to just one species which you cannot adequately represent then you could wait for the hatch to die down. They may then look for other food sources.

3. In circumstances as No. 2, if you really want to admit defeat move elsewhere where trout might be more co-operative or the hatch is thinner.

4. Very selective individual trout might demand a closer imitation than the pattern we actually offer. If the water conditions are heavily in the trout's favour – clear, with a slow current and an unrippled surface – a close inspection of a fly is quite possible. Such a trout will have to be totally satisfied before rising. Some fly tyers have offered a number of dressings for just such fish. Each dressing is heralded by its creator as being that extra bit special, a degree closer to what a trout needs to see than the 'standard' dressings. The USD series of Goddard and Clarke or the No-Hackle flies of Swisher and Richards may be an answer. The latter are particularly useful when imitating very small surface flies.

5. When rising trout refuse my fly the following solution is the key to about half of those fish I subsequently rise. It's a good rule of thumb which works on any water when trout refuse a reasonable imitation of the natural fly: on fast water move up a size, on calm water drop down a couple of sizes. In fast or rippled water it may pay to move up a size or two and present a slightly larger fly that is more visible. This tactic won't work on the calm flats where the first alternative should be to reduce the size of the artificial. Size is much more crucial on calm water, and the smaller the natural fly, the greater the need for matching its size with the artificial.

6. Sometimes a pattern that contains some exaggerated aspect of the dressing does the trick. I have known fish rising to duns that have been uninterested in all I could offer until I tried a fly with a forward-slanting wing. It may be the early sight of the wing or the fact that the wing is emphasised that is the key. The wing style may be suggestive of a part-emerged fly struggling to erect its wings. This alone might make it an attractive target.

In some 'standard' dressings some features may be unintentionally exaggerated – for example, size, the number of legs through excessive hackling, or gaudy colouring. Planned exaggeration is different where a key feature is emphasised.

Richard Walker suggested that some species of flies have key colours, which may not be obvious to the human eye but are recognisable by trout. He cited the iron blues, blue-winged olive and pale wateries as examples, the key colours of which are crimson, orange and primrose-yellow respectively. These colours may not be obvious on examination of a dun but frequently the female spinners and sometimes the female duns display them in their body colours. Richard Walker suggested that if these colours are incorporated into the dun stage the artificial becomes significantly more attractive. He quotes G. E. M. Skues, who also seemed to have noticed the connection: '. . . it is well to study the underlying colour of the spinners of the natural insects of the same species, and to suggest that colour as the base colour of one's nymph by the use of the appropriate tying silk'.

Graham Marsh and Gary LaFontaine have been studying upwingeds through high-intensity photography, filming them from underneath with the light source above. The

Oliver Kite fishing the Foston Beck, East Yorkshire.

The Davidson River, North Carolina.

Robinson Creek, Idaho.

Roy Shaw dry-fly fishing on the West Beck, East Yorkshire.

Stephen Rhodes fishing the River Wylye.

Lars-Ake Olsson releasing a fine 3 lb brown trout on the River Kaitum, northern Sweden.

A No-Hackle dun resting on the surface.

(*Opposite*)
Female blue-winged olive spinner
with egg ball (*Ephemeralla ignita*).

A USD dun resting on the surface.

Playing a trout on the West Beck.

A beautifully marked 6 lb brown trout cruising and taking flies from the surface with sip rises.

Pocket water on the River Ure.

Oliver Edwards playing a trout on the West Beck. On this day nearly every fish caught was from under the far bank. A strong wind soon blew any duns into a narrow feeding lane.

Excellent water for the Klinkhamer Special – the Idsjostrommen in Sweden.

Rolf Pasteuning dry-fly fishing on the River Dove, North Yorkshire.

Pale Watery Thorax Dun

Olive No-Hackle Dun

Leckford Professor

Funneldun

Black Pensioner

Light Ollie

Misty Blue Dun

Adams

No. 3 Para

Itchen Olive

Iron Blue Dun (Russell)

Beacon Beige

Grizzle Mink

Sanctuary

Poly May Dun (Goddard)

Lively Mayfly No. 1

Lively Mayfly No. 2

Low-Wing Caddis

USD Paradun

Poly May Spinner (Goddard)

Deerstalker

No-Hackle Spinner (partridge wing)

Sunset Spinner

Jardine's Emerger

Jardine's Floating Nymph

Stillborn No-Hackle (reverse-hackle shuck)

Humpy or Goofus Bug

Royal Humpy

Grey Wulff

Royal Wulff

Emergent Sparkle Pupa

Klinkhamer Special

Spruce Moth

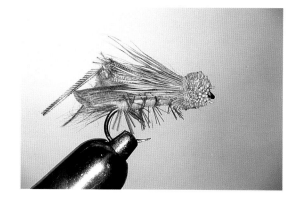

Hybrid Hopper

Hawthorn Fly (Jacobsen)

Walker's Red Sedge

Calf's Tail Emerger
Klinkhamer Special
Usual
Culard

Muddle May
Halo Emerger
F Fly
Sparkle Parachute

High-Riding Elk/Caddis
Silhouette Caddis
Dark Kyll
Floating Caddis Pupa

Squirrel Sedge
Wright's Royal
F Sedge
Voljc Sedge

translucency of the body is obvious, and just as obvious is what creates the undercolour, usually yellow, orange, light crimson or pale green, that the fly fisher cannot see. It is the sunlight passing through the eggs of the female duns or spinners. It seems feasible that an imitation which emphasises the key colours to what would appear to be an exaggerated degree could be more successful. To this end flourescent materials could be incorporated in a small way, as an underbody, rib or tip. Excessive use should be avoided as this is likely to deter rather than attract (*see* also page 177).

7.   If the fish are rising to duns they might be tempted to go for a stillborn pattern of the same species which promises a mouthful that won't escape. Swisher and Richards comment that their stillborns persuade many selective risers.

8.   Offer a food source that might be more attractive. Lee Wulff calls it offering them 'peaches and cream'. This might mean a large terrestrial, a sedge, or the largest bushiest mouthful you can find. On calm water a large attractor is likely to put down a fish but a small terrestrial could well be the answer, or a small version – say, a size 16 or 18 – of an attractor pattern like those in the Royal series.

9.   If the straight drift presentation doesn't work, try the unorthodox. A skittering dragged sedge or bivisible might tempt or annoy a trout enough to make it rise. Try any other presentation – with upstream drag, or landing the fly on the trout's nose, or just behind and to one side, on the edge of the window, with a good splash.

10.   Selectivity is much more of a problem on the calm flats where a good view of the fly and its presentation is available. Present the fly from a position upstream, or casting the fly so that there is slack line thrown upstream so that none of the leader precedes the fly, might help.

11.   Fish with a finer leader point. This is particularly true on calm, clear water, where the circumstances work in the trout's favour. A finer or softer point might be less visible or aid a more natural float.

NO FISH RISING

I have met too many trout fishers whose angling education was based upon the premiss that if a little knowledge is a dangerous thing a lot of it could be lethal. Many fly fishers are splendidly equipped with many expensive items of tackle and clothing. If they arrived at the water equally well equipped mentally they would do even better. Fishing the same stream for a number of seasons will invariably educate the angler about the natural flies to be anticipated. When fishing an unfamiliar water without the benefit of local advice or guidance one of the most valuable aids is to be aware of what fly life may be expected on the stream during that month and even at which times of the day. Similarly, on a strange water trout may be difficult to spot without the benefit of a hatch of fly to rise them. Familiarity with the types of water that provide the best lies in terms of food, cover and comfort is invaluable. This knowledge can be applied wherever one fishes. Successful dry-fly fishing when there are no trout rising (this might amount to quite a high proportion of the fishing day) is as attributable to observational skill as much as to wizardry with the rod and line.

If there are no fish rising take time to study the water before making the first cast. Learn where trout might be expected to lie and what flies you can anticipate hatching. I offer the following advice when confronted with an unfamiliar stream seemingly void of trout:

1.   Make sure that trout really are not rising. Trout in fast water or those feeding with tiny sipping rises might be missed.

2.   Assess where trout might be lying. This will enable you to concentrate on the areas of maximum probable success for the minimum of casting effort. The lies can be stalked. Avoid scaring fish. Be aware of the places that will invariably hold trout. Some lies, where it is easy to pick off food and cover is close by, always seem to attract fish.

3.   If one has the benefit of spending the whole day or longer on the water, make use of the parts of the day when the sun is

No trout rising – time to cover the likely lies with a search pattern. Gary
LaFontaine on Robinson Creek, Idaho.

highest and the fish activity is lowest. This
seemingly dull time can be spent studying
the stream to be fished later, when conditions
and trout cooperation are more favourable to
the angler. Make full use of the light to see
into the stream and study the likely lies or
feeding places when a hatch comes on. Even
if the fish are temporarily spooked by such a
reconnaissance, they will settle again later
and then the information gained will be well
worth while.

4.   Look for any obvious lies where terrestrials might be taken. Under low-hanging
trees and bushes and undercut banks are
particular places where, even though no
trout are showing, the occasional terrestrial
will induce a rise.

5.   Remember that in times of summer heat
trout seek shade and cooler, deep water, or
the cover of the riffles. Fish the lies that offer
shade. When you are trying to rise fish from
the bottom, the deep lies are not so reward-
ing. Faster water, barely deep enough to
cover a trout, is sometimes surprisingly
attractive if it lies in shade.

6.   Try searching the lies in the faster water
with an attractor type of fly, a Stimulator or a
Klinkhamer Special. Quite a large fly may be
the answer but even a size 14 Variant or
Bivisible, or a hairwing pattern like one of the
Wulff series might bring up a fish. Try them
first in a straight drift over the lies and then
with drag or even skittering in an arc across
the current from an up-stream position.
Trout in such water have to react quickly to
the sight of food and a skittering fly might

High summer and well bushed grassy banks – the ideal time and place for
fishing a terrestrial pattern.

provoke an automatic food response with
little time for thought. Sedges on the water
can be expected at almost any hour of the day
and trout are accustomed to their presence.
As a search fly, a good locally approved caddis pattern is often my first line of attack.

7.   Be aware of the water along the forward
edges of obstructions such as tree branches or
debris, where food and general flotsam are
collected. All sorts of surface food ends up
here and trout will take up an appropriate
position.

Reading the water when no fish are showing
is a very important factor in whether the fly
fisher will be successful. Apply the theories
underlying Chapter 2 to the river you are
fishing and mentally map out those places

where trout might lie. If you were a trout,
what positions would you adopt? Where
would you expect food, cover and comfort?

Fishing to Non-Risers

This is a different problem from the one considered above, which concerned the choices
open when no trout are visible. Now we are
concerned with those fish which can be spotted in their lies but won't rise to natural or
artificial flies. The short answer is of course to
give them something on their level below the
surface. That is usually the most successful
tactic but it is beyond the scope of this book.

The author netting a cutthroat trout. Although the main current is quite fast there is a narrow zone in the margins where trout rise to surface flies. When there is no surface feeding a good search pattern brings them up.

The fanatical dry-fly fisher might view such an action with the same contempt with which one might regard the soccer player who widens the goal-posts. Some of these fish are by no means wholly non-risers, despite appearing so, and the problem then becomes finding just what the necessary incentive is. The other side of the coin is that after trout have gorged themselves on a good hatch of fly they lie replete, often stuffed to the gills with flies, and until these have been digested neither nymph, lure nor dun will persuade them to feed. Of the trout that can be tempted to the surface only a few will do so to 'standard' patterns. One can try with imitations of the duns they might be anticipating but in my experience it is not the most successful ploy.

One type of presentation, no matter what the fly, is to land the fly right on the trout's nose, when the sudden appearance of the fly might trigger a split-second automatic response to food. Arthur Oglesby put it this way: 'Show a man a hand grenade and he may be reluctant to pick it up. Throw it to him accurately and without his knowing what it is and ten to one he will catch it. We have the instinct to take things presented to us suddenly, and trout survive by being quicker than their brethren!'

The oft-quoted and frequently dismissed theory of George La Branche, author of *The Dry Fly and Fast Water* (1914), is that an artificial hatch can be created by repeated presentation of a fly over a trout with the notion that the fish can be duped into believing that a hatch has started. Many pundits have dismissed this practice as implausible but I have found it a useful tactic on certain occasions. Each repeated presentation must be perfect. If some aspect is unacceptable the trout may be totally put down. The tactic is most successful on the faster water La Branche wrote about and it is much harder to convince a non-riser in a very slow-moving current.

If the 'standard' flies do not work, whether cast occasionally or *à la* George La Branche, other methods must be employed. One answer is to use shock tactics, to offer a larger than normal pattern like a sedge, a bivisible

or an attractor pattern. If it doesn't work in a dead drift it should be tried with imparted drag in the manner of a skittering natural sedge. If this fails, the same pattern should be presented from an upstream position, allowed to float down over the trout and then retrieved at speed. Don't be surprised if the fly is grabbed with some force. All this may, of course, make the trout bolt for the nearest cover, but if the only alternative is to leave it grinning at you I'd rather at least have a go at rising it. If repeated presentation doesn't work, do as the man said – 'Don't force it; get a bigger hammer!'

A juicy terrestrial also works wonders when fishing in the height of the terrestrial season. They can be anticipated on the water at any time and trout will rise to them even though there is no general fall of beetles or gnats. The additional bonus of a meaty beetle

Pocket water on a freestone stream. The type of water where attractor patterns and caddis are good search patterns.

or other largish terrestrial is often too much to be allowed to pass by. The vast majority of non-rising trout that I subsequently manage to persuade to rise do so to a terrestrial pattern.

We would like to think that most of our dry-fly fishing could be with aquatic imitations. In reality, for much of the fishing day we might do better fishing alternative food sources.

TERRESTRIAL STRATEGY

Beetles, black gnats, hawthorn flies, ants, grasshoppers and the rest are considered with their imitations in Chapter 9.

It is a matter of personal choice whether you adopt a *positive terrestrial strategy* or a *terrestrial strategy of last resort*. The former is when the fly fisher is aware that terrestrials could appear on the menu during most of the fishing season and is prepared to use an imitation at any time to try and bring trout to the surface. Positive discrimination towards terrestrials is a wise policy. During the often extensive blank periods of no surface aquatic flies it is likely that the most consistently successful patterns will represent the frequent but irregular land-based species that end up on the water.

The strategy of last resort is practised by dry-fly fishers who use the imitation only when trout are so preoccupied with a terrestrial species that they won't rise to anything else. Such a narrow attitude, which only reluctantly allows a non-aquatic imitation on the leader, seems to suggest that somehow the fly isn't quite kosher. The attitude is usually restricted to streams that experience fantastic hatches of aquatic fly. The suggestion is that the terrestrial should be confined to streams with minimal fly hatches, where land-based flies are supposed to figure more highly in the diet. I refute this. Streams that enjoy a good fly hatch are invariably well fished and the introduction of an artificial terrestrial is more likely to prove the downfall of wary trout accustomed to seeing imitations of aquatic flies. I agree with Charles Fox, who

wrote in *Rising Trout*: 'The land-born insect style of tie is of greatest significance where fishing pressure is heavy and killing light, the combination which makes for a sophisticated quarry.'

I have no hesitation in fishing a suitable terrestrial whenever trout are feeding on them or might be anticipating an occasional sample, or if I can't rise trout which are otherwise preoccupied with aquatic flies. Again, the key to successful terrestrial fishing is observation of the water surface and trout behaviour.

At the risk of stating the obvious, the places where terrestrials are most expected on the surface are where long grass lines the banks or in water under overhanging trees, bushes and bridges, where trout anticipate the fall of a sundry collection of land-based bugs and insects. If I find myself on a stream with no sign of aquatic fly emerging and trout are not rising I frequently tie on the leader a small black beetle pattern and slowly and steadily work my way upstream casting ahead over any likely-looking lies. On some days it has been the only way I have been able to take fish on a floating 'fly'. There are some lies on a few streams I fish that I know will almost always hold at least one trout and if the standard presentation of a terrestrial over these lies doesn't work it is sometimes a useful tactic to land the imitation with a plop. This might attract the trout's attention, which on a hot sunny day may well not be focused on the surface. With the absence of fly hatches combined with warm waters, trout may lazily maintain their position in the stream with total apathy towards the dry fly. The more aggressive presentation of a plopped beetle or a twitched cranefly or hopper might stimulate or annoy a trout into rising.

Different species appear during different months, but the most prolific time is during midsummer, when terrestrials are most abundant. They are most likely to be encountered on windy days, when even the slightest breeze can dislodge insects and beetles, or send some of the ungainly fliers like the craneflies unwittingly on to the water. Trout rising regularly under trees and bushes or close to the bank when there doesn't appear to be any hatching or returning fly are a sign that some other food is available. The odds are it will be a terrestrial. Sometimes the tiniest ants and other very small creatures become trapped in the film. They may not individually look like much of a meal but collectively they provide an easy and plentiful food source.

At specific times, when certain land-based species are most numerous, at the first sight of them trout move into new feeding positions simply to avail themselves of these new and possibly temporary additions to the menu. During the hawthorn season, when the flies might be being blown off a bush on to an unattractive backwater, trout will move into the area from their normal feeding lies until the item becomes unavailable. Even though terrestrials are inclined to arrive on the surface rather near the water's edge they also are found in midstream, a factor sometimes overlooked by the fly fisher trying to puzzle out the mysterious fly a fish is rising to. Anything on the surface will be carried along on the current, which may be continuously diverted and divided by rocks or weedbeds. A bankside current can soon end up midstream.

Only a bonehead would advocate fishing a terrestrial during a hatch of aquatic fly. What dry-fly fisher would want to? (The exception, as mentioned earlier, is when all else fails to rise a trout and a juicier alternative might break the feeding rhythm of fish locked onto a particular species.) For the majority of the time when there is no hatch in progress trout would expect to take advantage of an occasional terrestrial. In midsummer terrestrials become a major food source. When cast over known lies they can be deadly. By the end of summer, trout on many streams have become conditioned to feeding on terrestrials and a suitable imitation will offer the most hope of success. Too many lethargic trout remain unmoved by 'standard' dry flies; a terrestrial fished at the appropriate time might change apathy into avarice. Fishing them can be as finely judged and entomologically exacting as imitating the upwingeds.

SEDGE STRATEGY

A sedge is a sedge is a sedge. No argument there. But a trout would not agree. They know only too well that there is a range of sedge activity and there are different indications in terms of light pattern and behaviour from specific sedge types.

Too often sedge patterns are fished in a straight drift as one would fish an upwinged imitation. To be sure, they catch fish, for some newly emerged and returning female sedges are also carried along in the straight drift. But many others are highly active. They skitter across the surface, frantically beating their wings in a blur to escape to the air; they flutter about over the surface, dropping down to deposit eggs for only a second and then taking wing again; they frequently move in an upstream direction on the surface. No wonder trout are inclined to hit them with a bang. The imitation must not just simply look like a sedge, *it must also behave like one*. This may mean that the fly fisher keeps his fly on the water for varying lengths of time, or allows the fly to drag, or purposely twitches it by raising the rod tip. Leonard Wright, author of *Dry Fly Heresies*, goes so far as to write that a caddis pattern nudged or twitched *upstream* just before it passes over the lie will 'more than double your rises'. One of the leading authorities on caddis fishing, Gary LaFontaine, offers this advice in *Caddisflies*: 'Probably the most useful technique for imitating caddisflies, however, is the twitch-and-drift sequence, the fly moved on a short upstream skip and then allowed to float down to a fish that has been notified of its presence.' The most dramatic presentation of all is to cast the fly directly downstream over a fish and then rapidly retrieve it. The success rate with this final tactic is not outstandingly high but watch out for some real rod-bending and savage takes when it does work.

Trout can be just as selective about sedges as about upwingeds. Most fish will require certain features in a dry fly to match any natural species – size, silhouette, light pattern, colour, behaviour. Of these five aspects size and colour are straightforward and pre-

South Fork of the Snake, Idaho. Gary LaFontaine works along the margins with
a caddis pattern.

sent no problems, but silhouette, light pattern and behaviour might. A close representation of the species is not so important when imitating a moving insect; almost any fly of the right size, approximate colouring and light pattern will work. (In this connection, my comments on page 77 about the trout's view of the caddis are important.) The key to imitating the behaviour is observation, a word that seems to be cropping up a lot in this book. Check what the caddis on the water are actually doing.

Silhouette and light patterns are solved by the style and design of the artificial. If the standard high-floating patterns do not work it may be that a low-floating pattern will. Sometimes the standard patterns look as though they are about to take to the wing as they float high or rock in the breeze. A fish feeding on the spent, sprawled females completely exhausted from ovipositing is not likely to rise to a well hackled fly balancing on its hackle points. These trout need a fly flush in the film. Even if you do not have a low-floating pattern a short-term measure is to cut away the lower hackle fibres or even all the hackle and just have a body and wing. In the second instance soak the wing well in floatant and it should, at least for a while, support the body of the fly in the film. If sedges are emerging and trout rising to them but not to your fair imitation on the surface, it may be that they are taking emergers or stillborns. This will be particularly evident when the hatch dies down but trout are still rising, mopping up the wounded in the backwaters.

Sedge patterns are excellent search patterns on all types of water when there are no fish rising. Because the adults can appear on the water at any time of day trout do not appear to be deterred by the presence of an artificial when there is no hatch or fall in progress. Skues's Little Red Sedge is my own favourite and is often the first fly on my leader if no fish are showing. I took great pleasure in taking trout on it when on a boat drift down the South Fork of the Snake River, Idaho, when I dared to fish my English pattern under the nose of my boat partner, caddis specialist Gary LaFontaine. We had been

catching trout on hoppers and the activity had gone flat. Although we weren't aware of any caddis activity I gave my trustworthy standby a cast. Gary was as delighted as, and no less surprised than, me at its success. Sedges can score at any time.

THE MICRO-FLIES

Tiny dry flies – whether caenis or other up-wingeds, smuts, midges, or terrestrials – offer one of the greatest challenges to the dry-fly fisher. In my own experience I have never come across a trout truly feeding on tiny flies that has been duped by a larger fly. When these flies are alone on a flat surface the sipping rises to them are easy to see. When there are a number of flies on the surface the very small species might be difficult to detect and the rises to them masked by the larger species. The impression may be conveyed that trout are rising to the larger species whereas actually they are taking something very much smaller. Reading these 'invisible' hatches can be difficult but a broad hint might be taken if the imitations of the obvious naturals on the water fail to rise a fish.

Dropping down to a very small fly is not a simple or easy answer. The problems arise as the fly gets smaller. Actually spotting the artificial on the surface and keeping track of it can be no joke. I've often followed bits of flotsam or natural flies in mistake for my own. When trout are preoccupied with the small flies the need to assess the fly size accurately and fish an imitation of the same size is more critical than with normal-size flies. With flies less than ³⁄₁₆in long, an error of just one hook size represents a variance of 30 per cent. If fish are rising to tiny duns, the small sizes of the No-Hackle Sidewinders are excellent. Whatever species of surface fly is being taken, the smaller the fly, the bigger the problem of the size of the artificial. The size of the imitation must be exact.

If trout are proving impossible to rise with a tiny imitation of a natural, one answer is to offer a similarly proportioned attractor pattern – a Royal Wulff or similar.

Where the tiniest of hooks is necessary, the biggest problem is using the very fine leader point necessary to go through the hook eye and required to make a reasonable presentation. Using hooks of size 26 and smaller means using a leader point of .003 inches or 8X, which is less than 1lb breaking strain. If trout demand an ultra-small fly then an extremely fine leader of less than 1½ pounds strength is necessary; there is little choice open to the angler. Use the softest leader point available, particularly when fishing upstream. A stiff piece of nylon in conjunction with a very small hook will reduce the chances of achieving a hook-hold.

Hooking is a problem. The wider the gape of the hook the better for making the initial penetration into the mouth. Penetration may also be better achieved if the point is honed sharper and bent offset from the line of the shank. Striking is to be avoided as the fine leader may be broken; hooking is more a matter of tightening on the trout as it turns down to its lie. Playing out a trout is more of a problem with such a small hook-hold and a fine leader. The temptation is to play them for a long time until they are well tired and then net them. It is very much a compromise between getting them to the net quickly, with the risk of a breakage, so that they have less time to find snags and weed to hole up in and doing the whole thing very gently, during which time they might well escape. If trout are not going to be killed I am wary of playing them out completely, since such fish have a much poorer survival rate. Even if they are seen to swim off on release they may only make it to the nearest cover, where they turn belly up and die. Better to net or lose a trout still fighting for its life than to play it until it is completely spent.

FISHING FAST WATER

Frequently dry-fly fishers bypass the faster water at the entrance to a big pool or the pocket water between rocks on the higher stretches of freestone rivers and streams. The more usual lies in the pools and smooth runs offer much easier fishing and are probably more likely to carry emerged aquatic flies. The easier lies will attract far more fly fishers and the trout in them will be that much warier and the more moderate pace of the current gives them the vitally important closer look at the artificial. Fishing the rough-and tumble waters is harder work on the casting arm and on the concentration and also on the feet and legs. Wading this water calls for more than a little care; rocks, holes in the riverbed washed out by swirling currents and the current force itself make wading precarious. Often the water is less accessible than the more popular parts of the river. The rewards for extra all-round effort can be worth while.

When confronted with a huge riffle without a sign of a rise the temptation is to move elsewhere where the lies are easier to read. Nearly all of a riffle may hold fish but if you can read the water it is possible to find the trout with the minimum of effort. The best lies are along the edge of the slightly deeper channel created by the main current. Trout take up positions along this edge where the slightly deeper water means a less turbulent current near the riverbed.

Even on a river like the Madison (Montana), a vast fifty mile riffle, there are variations. The angler should squat or kneel to get low and look upstream. He'll see variations in the gradient, steep slopes mixed with plateaux. The hotspots on the Madison are right at the base of every slope, just as the gradient flattens out, because there is a line of deeper holding water stretching all the way across the river. None of this is obvious to the nonchalant, stand-up fly fisher.

Trout rise more readily. Surface food bounces by on the wavelets in a pretty quick manner. A trout seeing something vaguely edible must make up its mind instantaneously. A second thought is one too many and the food has disappeared. They react accordingly. One aspect of this fishing is that trout here are much more easily duped by repeated presentations over them. La Branche's tactic of convincing them a hatch is in progress does work on fast water where a close inspec-

Robinson Creek, Idaho. The best fish lay along the margins on the edge of this riffle. It need not always take four anglers to catch a trout – one to fish, two to shout advice and the fourth to take the photograph!

tion of the fly is impossible. However I am convinced that the first cast over a new lie is the important one. If a trout is going to come from the lie it's a five to one on bet that the first cast will be the killer. The trout is on the look-out for food, and if it's taken, it will be quick and confident.

There is no place here for the micro-patterns or sparsely dressed upwingeds. The fly has to float well and withstand the tumbling, swirling currents. Two types of fly work best – the heavily hackled high floaters like the Variants, Bivisibles, Hi-C's and Skaters or the buoyant flies tied with deer hair such as the Irresistible, the Rat-Faced MacDougal and the Humpy. Big sedges and attractors bring trout up. All should be soaked well in floatant. Trout here are much less selective; they are unable to be anything else with their only clues the blur of a light pattern and a vague outline and colour. Big flies, be they attractors or large well hackled or deer hair patterns, all have three key features: they

float well, are easily seen by both fly fisher and trout, and their light pattern triggers a hungry trout to rise.

I fish one fast water pattern that in my experience outfishes all others. The Klinkhamer Special is a large, attractive mouthful for fish, but significantly it is an emerger with its abdomen hanging below the surface. The body hanging tantalisingly below the film will be clear to trout viewing the fly both through the window and in the mirror. The Klinkhamer is the best pattern I know to persuade non-rising fish in fast water to come to the surface.

The straight drift works well – which is a shame, because getting the fly on the water to conform to the drift can be difficult with all the intervening currents of different speeds. It is just as well that at other times a dragged fly is required. Dragging, skittering or twitching works, particularly if sedges are returning to lay their eggs. Many caddis landing on faster water skitter upstream as though

Fast water of a fairly uniform depth. A close reading of the water will reveal boulders and calm pockets. If there is no surface activity it is observational skill that will spot the lies.

trying to maintain their position on the water. To aid twitching and generally better control of the fly and line a longer rod is preferred. This enables more of the fly line to be held clear of the water between the angler and the fly – a feature more important on faster water.

Because of the fish's poor view beyond its window in the rough water, it is possible to approach much closer to trout, particularly on pocket water between rocks which shield a view of the angler. Fishing upstream, one can often approach even to within a rod's length and dap a fly without casting.

FISHING THE TWILIGHT ZONES

The last moments of half-light when the sun has already dropped from view can provide some entertaining fishing. It is generally true that some of the larger and wiser trout rarely rise to surface-feed except in the first light of dawn or the twilight or darkness of late evening, or during peak hatches of large insects, like the Mayfly of the United Kingdom or the salmon fly of North America.

Dusk fishing has its own adherents, men who wander down to the river as most fly fishers are already conducting the post mortem in the public bar. They come out with the bats and the first stars and fish on into darkness, knowing that their efforts may not be rewarded with the numbers of trout caught by their daytime-fishing counterparts, but expecting that of those trout that rise a few will be the biggest in the river. The fading light of dusk gives a false confidence to the wary, shy trout that have viewed with suspicion each surface fly during the day and watched, unnoticed, each angler from the safety of their hidden lies. Now as the danger passes they leave their lies to look for surface food. Alternatively, during an exceptionally hot day there may have been no general rise period, either because there was no hatch of fly or, more likely, because the fish were simply too lethargic to rise. Now, as the sun sets, may be the only time the trout make any concentrated effort on surface feeding.

Three principal types of fly are encountered at dusk: egg-laying spinners and sedges, and moths. Although the latter are not aquatic, they are nocturnal and frequently end up on the water surface. I remember well the first occasion I saw the full benefit of a moth pattern at dusk. Many years ago I was fishing the River Greta, a small tributary of the Lune, in the company of an acquaintance. The locals had told us that the brown trout in this unstocked stream ran at about two or three to the pound. The river was extremely low, however, and we had not risen a fish between us all day. In near darkness we trudged along the bank in defeat. Just then a trout rose in the eye of the pool, on the very edge of the faster water. I cannot remember why my colleague tied on a grey moth; perhaps we had seen one on the water or maybe this was the only artificial we could see clearly. One cast later he was playing and netting a wild brown trout of 1lb 7oz. Not much of a trout by some folk's standards, but my guess is that no bigger trout had been taken from that stream for many a season. Since that day I have fished a buoyant white moth pattern many times at dusk and in darkness and have been delighted with the bigger-than-average trout I have caught.

The sedge is probably the best all-round dusk pattern and whether it is fished in a straight drift or with a twitch and drift or with other variations it brings fish up. The exact pattern is immaterial. It is the silhouette, light pattern and behaviour that are the stimuli. Movement of the fly is often the key to fishing in darkness. A fly conforming to the current's drift may go unnoticed but the twitching fly often attracts attention and excites trout into a savage take. Keeping track of the fly on the water is a problem for the angler and a white moth has the best visibility. Sometimes one can only 'guestimate' where the fly is on the surface and tighten on trout by the sound of the rise only.

Spent spinners, too, are successful, but these are better in dusk or dawn rather than darkness, when they are more difficult for trout and angler to see. As the dawn mists lift

Dusk and almost no light at all on a small freestone stream. This deep pool holds trout which rise only in the fading light. Surface food drifts round full circle on this difficult water. Surrounding trees make casting a very unorthodox affair with the method used not found in any textbook. Rolf Pasteuning, a Dutch angler approaches on hands and knees to present the fly at very short range.

off the river on a July or August morning trout will begin to rise to the returning female spinners and to those dead or spent caddis and spinners trapped in eddies and backwaters from the previous night. The daybreak rise is rarely to a hatching fly, except perhaps to the caenis, which can emerge in prolific numbers and produce a fantastic rise period. More often than not the dawn rise is to spinners. Trout rise steadily with slow, methodical sipping rises, knowing that their target will not escape. If these quiet rises are in evidence, the chances are that spinners are being taken.

7 The Art of Presentation

It is not the fly; it is the driver.

G. S. Marryat

Dry-fly fishing is as much about precision and accuracy as rifle shooting or archery. Additionally, it offers a much greater challenge than simply hitting a target. This is where tournament accuracy casting and fly fishing are two very different sides to the one coin. The dry-fly fisher has a target on a moving surface, at a variable distance, across an intermediate moving medium that works, in the main, against the angler, and is possibly protected by trees and bushes above the trout lie or on the back cast. The problem is how to present and, having made an accurate cast, control the fly on the water. Only then do the problems of imitation come into effect.

Charles Ritz put the equation very strongly: 'Technique represents 85 per cent of success. Precise imitation 15 per cent only. The fish reacts above all to presentation and only in a minor degree to the fly.' I am not too sure about the exact percentages but the general balance is about right *for most trout*. The majority of trout do not need a close imitation of the natural fly, just a general impression or a caricature of what they are looking for. Only a small percentage need to be satisfied on some finer aspect of imitation. The most perfect imitation or even one of the Creator's own will fail to rise all but the most gullible of trout if the fly behaves unnaturally on the surface. We are all aware that sometimes a poor cast will catch a fish, and a crazy trout might chase a fly across a couple of yards of water or grab one that scoots sideways as drag takes effect. I confess that some of the trout I rise are not always the ones I am casting to. But on balance the best hope for consistent successful dry-fly fishing is to offer an accurate and natural presentation. Only when that is achieved need there be any worry about the pattern of fly.

If a trout refuses the artificial fly, it's deemed to be selective. But selective about what? Most trout are far more selective about presentation than about the pattern of fly.

The three major problems of presenting the fly are:

1. Drag is imparted to every drifting fly whenever there is any tension between it and part of the leader or fly line. The drag-free drift is achieved if there is no tension on the fly from the line or leader. The natural fly, helpless on the surface, is taken where every whim of current dictates. The artificial must behave in a manner conforming exactly to that of the natural.
2. The leader and fly line are visible to trout to varying degrees. The effects of their presence must be minimised.
3. The fly fisher must remain undetected by the trout.

Much of this chapter deals with these three problems in turn – achieving a drag-free drift, reducing the effects of the line and leader, and stalking trout. The three aspects cannot be tackled separately but must be approached as one, greater, problem. Different presentation techniques answer the individual problems to a greater or lesser extent and it is very much up to the angler on the water to assess which presentation is most suited to the trout in question.

PRESENTATION TECHNIQUES

General Principles

The nearer the trout one can get, without detection, the easier the task ahead.

A River Test carrier. Arthur Oglesby approaches with the cover of the tree
behind him and uses a horizontal cast to avoid the tree branches.

Trout rising steadily during a hatch of fly are reluctant to move beyond a narrow feeding lane to take a fly. This may be because they are lying just below the surface and have only a small window through which to view food. A fly falling too far to one side of the window will not attract interest, except as a light pattern on the mirror. Additionally, a trout close-focusing on surface flies may not be aware of items further afield. The fact that they are feeding with little need of effort may also make them reluctant to move very far.

Casting a fly into the window of a trout may possibly make the fish wary of what it is being offered. It is totally unnatural for a dun to arrive on the surface in such a fashion. With spinners, terrestrials and egg-laying sedges this rule does not apply so much since they reach the surface at any time, and trout rising to any of them may be usefully attacked with a fly in the window. It is better to cast to a trout feeding steadily on duns with a fly presented just inside the mirror so that it drifts naturally into the window.

Avoid overcasting where possible. Whichever presentation technique is used or from whatever angle the trout is approached, the cast should be made so that the minimum amount of leader passes over it. If, when fished across or upstream, the fly is presented slightly to the angler's side of the fish the leader is relatively inconspicuous; if the fly is overcast the fish has the opportunity to see a lot of leader and might decide against the rise. Rippled water may minimise the problems; on a flat calm the effect of the leader is more marked. Never 'line' a trout by allowing the fly line to pass into the trout's window; this is far more serious than sight of the leader.

Limit the amount of false casting to the minimum. When false-cast over a river fly lines, particularly white ones on a sunny day, may reflect the sun as they go back and forth

The moment of the take. Dry-fly fishing on the Oxfolds Beck, a chalk stream in the north of England.

over the surface. Even if the trout one is casting to is not put down, trout elsewhere in the river become aware of the angler's presence. The movement of the rod as it is lifted high into the air may also be detected.

Even if a poor cast is made, do not whip the fly off the water quickly unless it is well out of the trout's view. As the fly is lifted off it is inevitably dragged before it takes to the air. Fish the cast out and withdraw the fly after it has passed from view. The worst thing the fly fisher can do at any time is rip the line off the water after the drift, shattering the surface and sending a shower of droplets over the stream. How much safer it is to lift slowly, or, better still, to roll the line into the air, and then begin false casting.

The need for different lengths of rod for different sizes of river will be obvious but other factors also influence the choice. The longer the rod, the more control can be exerted over the fly line, leader and fly. Shorter

rods are less able to manipulate the line on the surface but they have the advantage when fishing at short range of being less likely to be seen by wary fish.

The more uniform the currents and water behaviour between the angler and the fly, the less likelihood of drag.

The avoidance of drag is best achieved by allowing the fly only a short drift and by frequent casting.

Use any wind to your advantage. It may be that with a strong wind on your back it is possible to reach lies normally out of casting range. The wind can also be used to create an upstream belly in the line or an angle in the leader – important aspects in some presentations in trying to minimise the amount of drag.

Natural presentation today on most rivers is not the wholly drag-free one aimed at in previous generations. For most occasions the drag-free imitation of the upwinged duns

113

and terrestrials is what is required, but in order to represent realistically some aquatic fly behaviour a controlled movement of the fly is necessary. Notwithstanding these occasions, drag-free presentation is the most important tactic in any attempt to make the artificial conform to the appearance and behaviour of most surface flies.

The Straight Drift or Drag-free Presentation

A drag-free float means that the fly is presented at the same speed and along the same path as the current. The problem is to overcome drag on the fly caused by the tension of line or leader. From the fly fisher's viewpoint very slight drag may not be detectable but, rest assured, from the trout's position even the slightest deviation from a natural drift will be very obvious. The intervening currents between the fly and the line at the end of the rod may move at different speeds and eventually any slack line is tightened by the varying water speeds and the fly begins to drag. Most trout demand a drag-free fly and are almost wholly unforgiving when expecting to see a fly that conforms exactly to where the current takes it. The purpose of each of the following presentation techniques is to buy more time before the dreaded drag takes effect. The amount of time may only be a few seconds, or a foot or so of travel on the surface. These precious extra inches of drag-free drift are so important. It seems to be one of those cruel twists of fate that a dry fly only drags when it floats over the trout. Success may be dependent on gaining only a few extra inches of drag-free float.

There are two basic answers to the problem, which in turn offer varying techniques in presenting the fly. Which method of presentation is chosen will depend very much on the circumstances of the lie of the trout, the approach possibilities of the angler, the currents either side of the lie, and the effects of

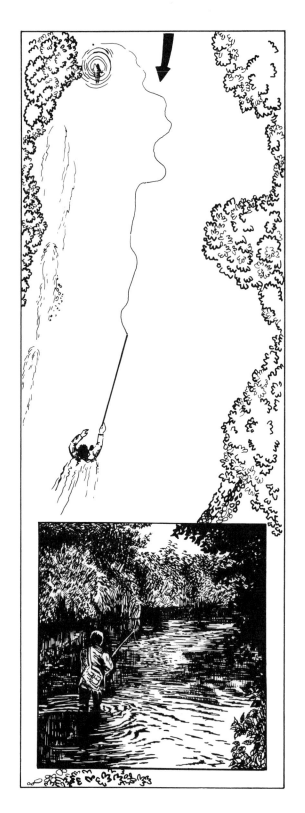

Fig 20 The traditional upstream presentation illustrated here with a curve and slack line and leader to aid a drag-free presentation.

114

The approach directly upstream.

any wind or bright sunlight in aiding or handicapping the presentation.

The standard classic dry-fly cast is the traditional presentation of upstream and across, the actual proportions of how much upstream and how much across varying to suit the circumstances (Fig 20). Depending upon intervening currents it is not long before drag soon affects the fly. This is eliminated in a number of ways.

The first answer is to cast so that the fly line and leader are in a direct line and are influenced by the same currents as the fly. This means that the rod tip must be either directly above or below the fish so that the line and leader are in the same current lane. Because the fly, leader and fly line are carried by the same current they travel at approximately the same speed. The result is no more drag. When casting upstream make sure that only the front couple of feet of leader pass over the fish. Sometimes this alone may be enough to scare the fish but with luck it won't. Cast so that the leader turns over fully in the air

before it hits the water. This allows the fly to drop gently on the surface. Presenting a fly downstream, either through choice or because the circumstances of the lie dictate it, demands a little more skill. Pay out line on to a parallel feeding lane until enough line is out to reach the trout. Pay out an extra two yards. Then cast the fly over the correct feeding lane so that the line and leader straightens out in the air and lands a few feet upstream of the trout (Fig 21). With a bit of practice this can be done so that a wiggle in the leader is also achieved (*see* page 119). Pay out the extra couple of yards by short side-to-side waves of the rod tip. The fly should drift drag-free over the fish.

These presentations work well though they are not without their problems. Even though everything beyond the rod tip is in the same current lane as the fly, the current speed is not necessarily the same. All too often the water where the fly is resting ten yards up or down stream might be much quicker or slower than that at the rod tip. The presentation

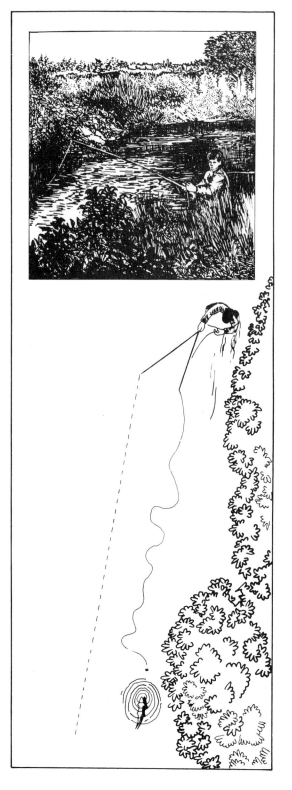

works best where the current speed is uniform for some distance.

If I didn't know better, the ability to cast a good straight line would seem a high priority. It looks neat and is more impressive than a snaking series of bends across the surface. In reality, for the dry fly fisher trying to eliminate drag, it is often the last thing he wants. The skilled caster puts a fly on the water at the end of a series of Ss in the line. Only when the line, leader and fly are in the same current lane, moving at the same speed, is a straight cast of any value.

The second solution is to continue to cast across the currents but to give the line and leader enough extra slack line to absorb the effects of the current as the fly drifts drag-free over the trout. One answer is to mend the fly line and leader to incorporate an *upstream mend* or *curve* so that the currents move the line for a time, absorbing the slack without affecting the fly. The belly is created by mending the line and leader after it has landed on the surface. The curve is created by manipulation of the fly line before it lands on the water. When casting over intermediate fast water the easiest method is to flick the line upstream as soon as it lands on the surface (Fig 22). The current takes longer to give the line a downstream belly and create drag, by which time the fly should have drifted over the trout. Unfortunately, the process of mending the line with the upstream flick also has its drawbacks. Sometimes the fly is also moved, and any slack in the leader may be taken up, which creates immediate drag. Be sure that the fly lands with plenty of slack leader and that the mend is made as soon as the line hits the surface.

When casting the line to create a curve (Fig 23) when it lands on the water, have enough slack line off the reel to cover the distance to the target and sufficient for the upstream curve. As the final forward power stroke of the cast is made, release the slack line. As it shoots out, smoothly and quickly move the rod upstream so that the line rests upstream of the target area but the leader

Fig 21 The downstream presentation.

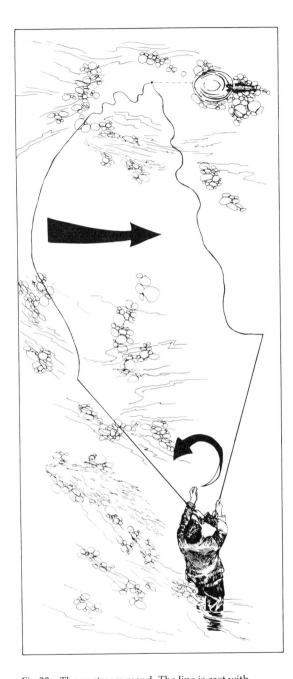

Fig 22 The upstream mend. The line is cast with slack to a position a few yards upstream of the trout. The rod is rolled in a forceful arc in an upstream direction so that it has an upstream belly. The line and fly drift over the trout with the intervening current gradually reducing the belly until drag sets in.

lands facing downstream with the fly on target. There should now be a good upstream curve in the line to aid a drag-free presentation. This offers a longer period of drag-free drift than a typical cross-current cast with an S-cast.

There are other ways of creating curves either side of the line, both of which are most useful for casting directly upstream. The *positive curve* is the curve which for the right-handed angler curls to the left. The *negative curve* curls to the right for the right-handed angler. Figs 24 and 25 illustrate the techniques for both curves. For the positive curve the rod should be held at a 45° angle or lower. When the final forward power stroke is made it should have extra power so that when the rod is stopped or pulled back, as in the diagram, it has enough power in it to catapult round the front of the line and leader. As the rod is stopped an additional tug on the line by the non-casting hand will aid the execution of the curve. The negative curve is more difficult to complete. The rod should be held almost horizontally and the final forward stroke should be angled sloping down from a highish back cast. The object is to cast a wide loop which will land on the surface before it straightens fully, leaving a curve at the end of the line. The angler's attitude should be lazy and laid-back. Release some free line as the final forward stroke is made. One definite aid to creating the negative curve is to exaggerate the separation of the forward and back casts so that they are at least 180 degrees apart. This, of course, may only be practical when the rod is moving in a horizontal plane.

The *S-cast*, or creating slack, in the line and/or leader which can be taken up by the currents before they affect the fly, is an extremely important feature of dry-fly presentation where water in the target area is moving much more slowly than the intervening currents on which the line and leader float. A nice straight line and leader to the fly may look like a good cast and a neat presentation but in reality it is one of the quickest ways of ensuring drag on the fly, unless all the water between the rod tip and the fly is moving at exactly the same speed. Most presentations

Fishing across the current. The cast is finished with an upstream mend or curve to allow a drag-free drift.

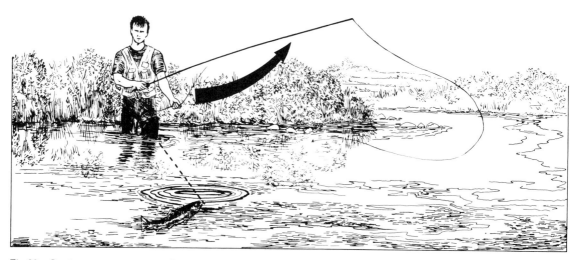

Fig 23   Casting to create a curve. The direction of the cast is made towards the trout. As slack line is released on the forward power stroke the rod is smoothly and quickly moved upstream. The line will rest in a curve upstream of the target area with the fly free to float drag-free over the fish.

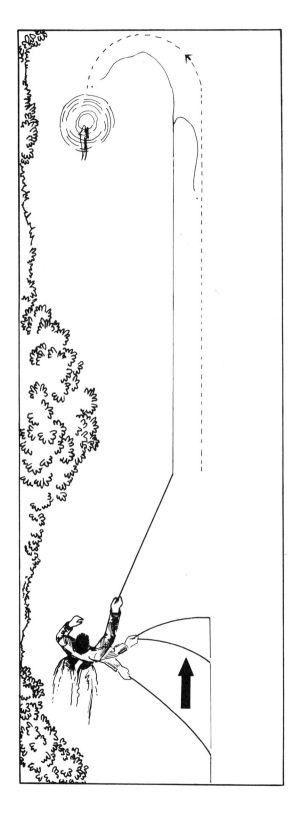

require varying degrees of slack line and leader on the surface. Some situations only require slack in the leader; others also need large S-shaped loops in the fly line. It may not look very attractive but it is necessary to permit a drag-free float. In this technique enough spare line is pulled off the reel so that it would reach to a point some distance upstream of the target area. The final forward cast is pitched a yard in the air above the target. As the line straightens out and the fly is over the dropping zone and the power stroke is completed, immediately release the extra line held by the non-casting hand. Simultaneously, lower the rod tip, waving it smoothly from side to side (Fig 26). With practice, a series of Ss will develop through the line and leader.

The *parachute cast* also creates the same wiggle in the line and leader. Like most of these presentations it can be used in a variety of situations and should not be confined to up or down stream but should be adapted to meet the problem of each situation. False-cast enough line to go upstream of the target, and on the final power stroke stop short of the follow-through, and sharply drop the rod vertically. The cast is checked and the line and leader spring back into loops as they fall to the surface.

Another variation on this theme is the *stop and drop*, which is as above but does not stop on the follow-through. When line speed is built up, a short power stroke drives the line forward. Lean forward with the cast and lower the rod tip. When most of the line is shot, quickly raise the rod tip high. The line will spring back in a series of Ss.

On a similar theme, the *tug cast* (Fig 27) involves tugging back the line with the non-casting hand as the line straightens out. Slack line results, although not as much as with some of the other techniques. Sometimes it is

Fig 24   The positive curve. The rod should be held at 45° or lower. A tight loop should be maintained. The final forward power stroke is very strong with an abrupt stop before the end of the line straightens. The line momentum catapults the front of the line and leader into a left curve for the right-handed angler.

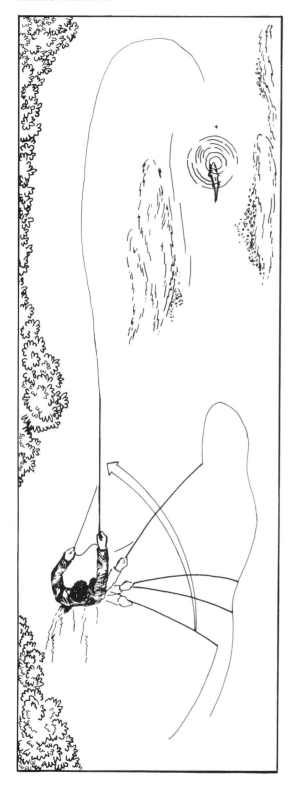

a matter of necessity rather than choice to fish downstream, perhaps to trout which are positioned at the tail of a pool or on the lip of a flat above faster water; for whatever reason, a downstream cast with some slack leader is required to cover the fish. One of the above presentations will work, or the *downstream check* (Fig 28), which combines the attributes of some of the other presentations. The final forward power stroke is made aiming to land the fly on a plane a yard in the air above the target area. As the line straightens out the cast is checked by breaking the follow through and pulling back the rod. The line and leader will land with enough loops to give a drag-free drift over the trout. If the cast is made at an angle across the stream as well, the imaginary target area should be upstream and also beyond the actual lie of the fish so that when the cast is checked it falls on to a current directly above the fish.

These are the basic methods of presenting a fly so that it can float for some distance with the minimum of drag. There are other methods but these are sufficient for most situations. One key to all drag-free floats is: the longer the leader, the more likely a longer drag-free float.

Spring creek devotees in the United States have developed a different method of presenting a dry fly to sipping trout. The problem with such fish is that they rise in a very precise current line and refuse a fly even an inch off the drift. Add the fact that the artificial has to compete with hundreds of naturals during the hatch and the puzzle becomes not just finding a correct imitation but getting it to an exact spot at the right moment.

This method was developed on the Fall River (California). A fly fisherman uses a boat to position himself on the wide flats above rising trout. He holds the rod straight up in the air and strips out line until the fly is hanging in the slow current directly up-

Fig 25 The negative curve. Keep the rod in a near-horizontal position with a slightly higher back cast. Maintain a wide loop with a slow forward stroke so that the line and leader land on the surface before straightening out. This results in a right curve for the right-handed angler.

Fig 26 Creating slack. As the final forward power stroke is made aiming a yard
or more in the air above the target, shoot spare line and drop the rod tip,
simultaneously waving it from side to side. Slack line will lie on the surface to
absorb the effects of a faster current.

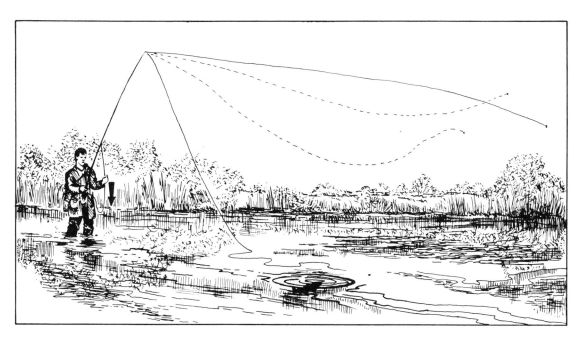

Fig 27 The tug cast. As the final forward power stroke is made aiming a yard or
more in the air above the target and upstream of it, tug the line back with the
non-casting hand as the line straightens out. The line should drop with slack on
the target zone.

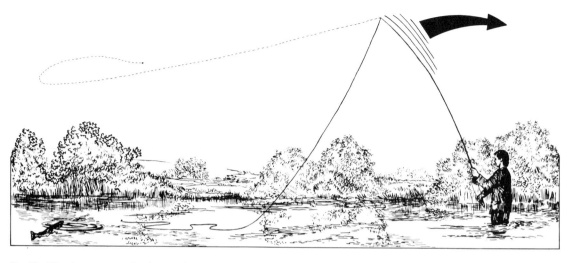

Fig 28 The downstream check. Aim the forward cast a yard or two above the target. As the final power stroke is made, check the follow-through and sharply pull back the rod tip. Loops of line and leader will land upstream of the target zone and allow the fly to drift drag-free over the trout.

stream from the fish. Then, in rhythm with the trout's rises, he drops the rod tip and lets the fly drift right into the feeding area. If the fly isn't taken, the fisherman leads it over to the side, picks his rod back up, repositions the artificial, and repeats the procedure.

Naturally, using a boat is out of the question on any British trout river and on most North American spring creeks, but walking and wading anglers have adapted the method. With ultimate care, creeping in with a very low profile, they'll position themselves thirty or forty feet above a rising trout and 'feed' the fly to a tough fish.

ALTERNATIVE TRICKS AND TACTICS

There are occasions when sedges – and, to a much lesser extent, female spinners – skitter on the surface and a fly fished in a straight drift attracts no interest. What is required is something to imitate the main feature in the natural – its movement. Sometimes the pattern of fly is of minimal importance; it is the activity of the fly on the water that triggers the rise. Any movement must be across or

upstream and certainly not downstream. The best way to achieve this is to present the fly downstream so that the angler controls the fly from an upstream position.

The most suitable patterns to use are long-hackled sedges, Variants or Bivisibles, which rest on the water on their long hackle-fibre points. These float very well and are much easier to manipulate and can be rocked or rolled on the hackles. It is significant that trout seem willing to move further for a fluttering fly. Whether this is out of annoyance, excitement or some triggered feeding mechanism I would not like to say. Some of the techniques mentioned below are also more successful than conventional tactics on slow-moving, less prolific dry-fly water, such as that over deep pools The twiched fly may bring a trout from some depth.

The Induced Rise

This presentation is made when fishing downstream. The cast is made so that the fly lands about a foot upstream of the feeding trout. A gentle twitch is imparted to the fly by moving the rod tip, and the drift is allowed to continue. If there is no response, cast again

This very deep pool prohibited a closer approach. The food lane can just be made out under the far bank. This fly fisher is faced with a difficult cast across and down stream and a short drag-free drift.

and twitch the fly when it is nearer the trout. Almost all sedge movement is upstream or sideways and therefore this presentation is really only possible when fishing downstream. There are a number of variations on this theme, all of which involve movement of the rod to impart movement in the fly. One can cast across the stream to a position slightly above and beyond the trout. When the line lands on the water mend it upstream with a flick of the rod. The fly is drawn towards the angler and settles on to a drift in line with the trout, which has seen it skittering or twitched on to its food lane. There are scores of similar techniques for individual situations.

The Upstream Retrieve

This, the most dramatic presentation of all, is the second part of a downstream cast of a well-hackled sedge pattern, which I refer to in Chapter 6. It can be incorporated as part of any of the downstream presentations men-

tioned above after the lie has been unsuccessfully covered. Avoid letting the fly line drift over the trout. Retrieve the fly by stripping in the line so that the fly moves rapidly upstream leaving a wake. Trout rise to a fly at a speed in direct proportion to the likelihood of the fly escaping, so be prepared.

APPROACH

When deciding the best approach for a rising trout a number of factors influence the type of presentation most suited to the fish and its lie. The type of fly being taken, the intervening currents and those surrounding the lie, the cover above the lie, the freedom for the back cast and the prospects for casting from the bank or wading the stream should all be evaluated before making the first cast. There is some debate whether the upstream or downstream approach is generally more successful, or fishing across the stream with a

An old mill-pool on the River Costa, one of the smallest English chalk streams.

little of an angle either up or down. There is much to commend each approach.

Upstream

Fishing upstream, it is possible to approach a fish much closer because of its rear-view blind spot and its concentration on forward vision. The chances of drag may be slightly less than the alternative approaches. The disadvantages are that the leader or the line may be visible to the fish, and any inadvertent drag will be totally unnatural. The angler should also be aware of the conspicuousness of an approach within the two zones to the rear of a trout that are permanently focused at infinity (*see* Fig 6).

Downstream

Fishing downstream reduces the opportunity of trout being spooked by the line and leader passing overhead. Because of the trout's forward vision it is rarely possible to approach a downstream fish closely unless some intervening obstruction shields you from its view. The fish can be hooked with a minimum amount of slack line to be taken up. With good slack-creating casts the length of a drag-free drift should not be less than when fishing upstream, and may in fact be longer. Any drag imparted is in the upstream direction, which may imitate the sedges at take-off or the egg-laying spinners and sedges. When fishing this way consideration should be given to the marginal effect of the strike being more likely to snatch the fly out of the trout's mouth rather than setting the hook.

Across

Fishing across the stream enables the fly fisher to watch more closely the path of the fly over a lie. Little of the leader is seen by a trout. Unfortunately, drag is soon encountered unless the line is cast with an upstream curve or an upstream mend or with plenty of slack line on the intervening currents. Because of the intervening currents this approach probably offers the shortest drag-free drift.

FLY LINES AND LEADERS

The second aspect of presentation is the question of making the best use of the system that delivers the fly to the trout's nose while minimising its effect of deterring the fish from rising.

Leaders

The leader is an intrinsic part of the delivery system, the final link in the chain between angler and fly. It is certainly as important as and in some ways more important than all the other items of equipment with the exception of the fly itself. To spend a small fortune on a good rod, reel and line but to skimp over the cost of a good leader is sheer folly. A good fly fisher can make do with using an incorrect length of rod with a poor action, the wrong weight of fly line on a battered old reel, but failure is more likely if the wrong leader is used. A leader that is too soft, too stiff, too short or too thick at the tippet is much more likely to produce a failure than an incorrect choice of any item of equipment from the leader butt back. A cheap rod and the best possible leader is much more desirable than all the latest gimmickry in rods and reels coupled to the wrong leader.

The purpose of the leader is twofold. It

Fig 29 Three approaches to presenting a dry fly: upstream and across, across, and downstream and across. Each has its own merits and imperfections.

The calm shallow water of this piece of river necessitates the fly fisher standing some way from the rising trout. A closer approach might alert the fish. Fished across the stream, the fly has almost come to the end of its drift. The fly line is now straight and soon drag will set in.

provides a means of connecting the fly to the bulky fly line and keeping as much distance as practically possible between the two. To this end the leader should appear as near invisible to a trout as possible. Visibility decreases with a reduction in the diameter of the leader. So too does the strength. The tippet is therefore a compromise: the strongest line you can persuade a trout to rise to. Second, the leader presents the fly as an extension of the fly line rolling out on to the water. The taper between butt and tippet is very important. An incorrect taper may result in a failure to straighten out or a general imbalance in the way the fly and leader hit the water.

It is ironic that the good fly fisher can handle and land a fish on the finest tippet, but the best fly fisher can rise the same fish on a bigger tippet. The angler who needs to go down to a finer point because of poor presentation is not as skilful as the guy who can rise them on a stronger and larger-diameter tippet. This is notwithstanding the requirement of large or small flies needing a tippet of an appropriate diameter.

The length of leader should vary according to the size of the stream being fished and the relative calm or turbulence of the surface. In general, the bigger the river the longer the leader that may usefully be used to aid presentation. On a small stream a shorter leader will be more manageable and necessary if only short casts can be made. The shorter the leader, the steeper the taper to turn the fly over well. Bigger rivers or a calm surface require a longer leader. If too long a leader is used there may only be a short amount of fly line beyond the rod tip, which may not be enough to work the rod properly. The leader length must be assessed for each stream. My shortest is seven feet and tapers down to ·0006 inch (6X), about 2lb breaking strain, or occasionally ·0005 inch (7X) or 1–1½lb breaking strain. I have very occasionally used ·0003 inch (8X), about ½lb strength, for very low water conditions on a small brook on which the wild trout rarely reached a pound in

126

weight but could cast a very critical eye over the slow-moving fly. For most river dry-fly fishing in the United Kingdom I rarely need a leader longer than 12 feet from fly line to tippet. I read somewhere that Lee Wulff sometimes uses 30-foot leaders! On rivers where long drag-free drifts are required the longer leader offers a greater facility to make a cast with slack leader or with a curve.

The tippet strength should be determined by two factors: the size of fly and the sharpness of the trout's eyesight. Small flies demand a fine tippet so that the point will pass through the eye of the hook and enable the fly to float naturally. Larger or bushier flies need a stronger tippet to prevent the nylon being weakened in front of the fly in the casting process. If one changes fly size dramatically during the course of the fishing day it is essential to match the change with a suitable tippet.

Traditionally the butt section has been of stiff or hard nylon, which enables the leader to turn over well at the end of the cast. I prefer a leader with a butt of short, flat nylon and the remainder of soft, round nylon. I have tried leaders made entirely from soft nylon but they are more difficult to cast with on windy days. Soft nylon makes it much easier to create the all-important leader wiggle for a drag-free presentation. Stiff nylon has too much resistance to being snaked and is much less able to provide a drag-free float. The diameter of the nylon has a bearing on its flexibility, whether or not it is hard or soft in angling terms. The stiffness of any material varies with the fourth power of its diameter: if the thickness is doubled it becomes sixteen times as stiff. So, the finer the tippet, the easier it is to create slack. A leader tippet which is too short and too stiff will fall in a straight line on the surface and immediately drag the fly. A tippet which is too long and too fine will be difficult to cast with. Casting accuracy is severely impaired and the chances are that it will end up in a heap around the fly.

The butt diameter of hard, round monofila-

The calm flats where, given clear water, trout have a leisurely view of the surface fly. To aid a presentation without sight of the leader this fly fisher has chosen to float a fly downstream.

127

ment might be .02 inches. A hard, round leader butt can actually be five times stiffer than the tip of the fly line. This can hardly aid a smooth presentation. Flat monofilament of 20lb strength has a width of approximately .012 inches. Because of the stiffness factor between lines with different diameters, the flat mono which is only slightly more than half the width of round mono is many times more flexible than the latter. Using flat mono for butts enables a tighter loop to be cast in the line, producing a much better turnover of the leader. There are commercially produced fast-taper knotless leaders which use flat mono for the butt section which extends for up to two-thirds of the total length.

The rate of taper of the leader also influences the presentation. Some knotted leaders have much bigger jumps in line diameter than others. The more gradual the taper, the more steps in reducing the line diameter, the better for producing a smooth turnover and presentation. If you are prepared to tie your own leaders you can be assured of the gradual taper of small steps. The alternative is to trust a bought knotted leader or use the tapered knotless leaders. The disadvantages of knotted leaders are the risk that the knots might be visible to a trout and possible knot failure. The knotless leaders are made from a single piece of tapered nylon. There are no knots to snag or catch surface scum, but the disadvantage is that the taper cannot be altered. When the tippet has been used up another can be tied on, but then it is no longer a knotless leader.

In the last few years some manufacturers have introduced a range of braided leaders. These are not made from a single strand of monofilament as normal leaders are but from a series of finer strands braided together. No strength is lost and the line is considerably more supple than monofilament, which at the butt can be very stiff. One manufacturer correctly compares the two leaders to a steel bar and a steel rope; the strength is still there but the flexibility is far greater. This enables the leader to be presented more smoothly as it rolls out as an extension of the fly line. The tip turns over with ease, but in my experience

the very soft butt makes casting into the wind more difficult. However, the suppleness of the braided leader makes creating slack or a wiggle much easier. The manufacturers also claim that because the leader is not a smooth strand it is less reflective and is less likely to spook fish, although my experience has been that the braided leader is very visible on and below the surface. A leader point of soft mono should be used as the final link to the fly. After some seasons of experimenting with braided leaders, I have come to the conclusion that, on balance, they offer no advantage to the dry-fly fisherman using a correctly tapered leader of an appropriate length. Where I have been required to punch a fly into any sort of breeze the performance has been less than satisfactory. Their cost is two or three times that of normal leaders. In fairness I should add that some dry-fly fishers have found braided leaders excellent, even though others cannot find a good word to say about them.

There is no general agreement about whether it is more advantageous to have a leader tippet that floats or one that sinks. It does seem that when viewed from below a calm surface the floating leader is much more visible than the one that sinks. Some authorities say that it doesn't matter either way; that the trout concentrates on the fly, not the leader. My own experience suggests that on rougher, rippled water you can sometimes get away with murder and have a strong tippet that floats, but for most of my dry-fly fishing and on all calm surfaces the floating tippet is a definite hindrance and I will do everything possible to make the last ten inches of leader sink. A mixture of fuller's earth and glycerine seems to be as effective as any commercially available product.

Fly Lines

The best type of line to present a dry fly delicately under most conditions is the double-tapered line, which will present a fly smoothly at most normal casting distances.

The taper should be gradual so that the line rolls over smoothly. All reputable line manufacturers produce an adequate taper which gradually reduces the weight of line to a fine tip.

The line should be supple and flexible so that the necessary wiggles can be created. Hard lines often only become supple in warm summer weather and are more prone to cracking.

The surface of the line should be smooth so that it shoots through the rod rings with the minimum of friction. In fact, lines should not be ultra-smooth but feel very slightly rough or bumpy. A smooth line has more contact with the rings and therefore creates more friction. Less friction results when only the tops of the bumps touch the rings. I emphasise that this roughness is still relatively smooth and should not be confused with the lumps and bumps one sometimes finds in an imperfect line. Some manufacturers have the ultra-smooth finish, others have the rough texture. One manufacturer who makes both types of line confirmed to me that it is possible to shoot more line with the latter type but it makes more noise as it runs through the rings.

The line should float high on the surface. This ensures maximum visibility for the angler and greater ease in lifting off the line when mending or striking. What should be avoided is an old line which has an end that has begun to sink. This can cause havoc with the timing of the strike and may well become visible to fish.

The colour of lines has been debated for years with the protagonists declaring that different coloured lines have a varied effect upon trout. Unfortunately, the transparent floating fly line has not yet been invented and all lines are opaque. Because no light can pass through them, all lines, whatever the colour, appear dark when viewed from below the surface against the light. Just how dark a white line appears depends on how much light is reflected from the riverbed or weeds below the surface. A line is clearly visible when in the trout's window, whatever its colour. Hopefully the trout you are casting to will never see your fly line in its window, but it may see it in the mirror. The mirror gives a

very distorted reflection of the riverbed, which is usually dark, and the white or light-coloured fly line on the surface is as obvious as the beam of a searchlight penetrating the night sky. It is logical to use a fly line that matches the colour of the image being reflected, usually a dark riverbed and weed. A dark-green or brown line is the answer. The other disadvantage of light-coloured lines is that they reflect the light when being false-cast in the air. On a bright, sunny day these lines catch the sun and flash in the light as they are cast back and forth. On calm, unrippled, clear water trout could well be affected by the false-casting of a light-coloured line on a sunny day. The problem of line visibility is more of a problem on clear chalk streams and on small clear waters. On the recommendation of Richard Walker I have been fishing with near-black or very dark floating fly lines for about four seasons and I feel more confident in using them than white ones, and on calm clear water particularly I am sure my catches have been higher as a result. (The entire white line is dyed except for a tip of two or three feet, which is left undyed so that it remains more visible to the angler.) In some circumstances a clear view of the line is needed by the angler and on balance a light-coloured line or a bright-orange or yellow one is easier to see. But if preventing scaring fish is the main consideration a dark line is much to be preferred.

KNOTS

Two knots link the fly line to the leader and the leader to the fly. For the first of these most anglers use the nail knot or a loop-to-loop link, or one of the more modern alternatives, such as a small plastic connector or a glued splice. Fig 30 illustrates the uni-knot splice. Its greatest virtue is its simplicity, and it is no less effective than any of the others. With braided leaders I use the plastic sleeve provided with the leader and have found this easy and effective.

The improved half-blood knot or improved clinch knot (Fig 31) is the most commonly

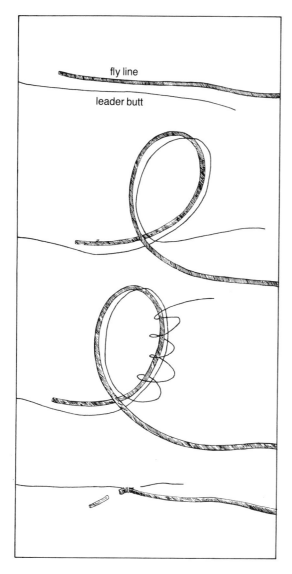

fly line

leader butt

Fig 30 The uni-knot splice.

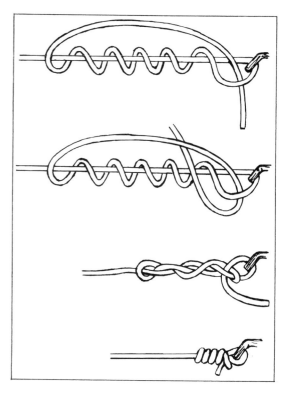

Fig 31 The improved half-blood knot or improved clinch knot.

and needs much less attention to ensure a satisfactory presentation.

It was Eugene V. Connett who wrote in *My Friend the Trout* (1961) that in his fifty years of fishing, the angler's equipment, flies and knowledge had improved a great deal, therefore the odds were shifting in the fly fisher's favour. The irony was that Connett reckoned that after fifty years of fly fishing, the trout were harder than ever to catch.

THE APPROACH

The third hindrance to a successful presentation is an inadequate approach to the river or to individual trout. Wild trout have a strong sense of self-preservation and any unusual or unnatural bankside or water activity may well be sufficient to alert a fish to danger and cause it to melt into a weedbed or send it

used knot for tying on the fly. The main drawback with the knot is that the hook is attached by only one loop of nylon and the bulky knot is in front of the eye. This means that the fly is forever being twisted sideways and must be constantly checked to ensure a good presentation. A better but more demanding knot is the improved turle knot (Fig 32), which holds the fly much more securely, has the bulk of the knot over the head of the fly,

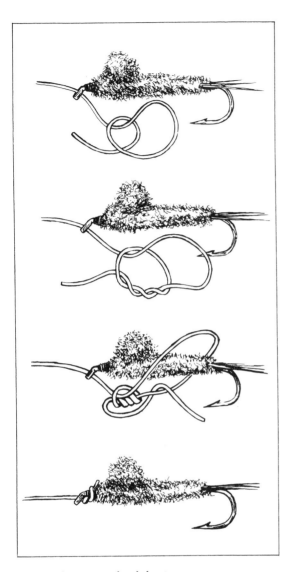

Fig 32   The improved turle knot.

bolting for cover. No fish, other than a friendly stocky, will take a surface fly if it is unaware of an unfamiliar movement on the riverbank. I cautiously use the word 'unfamiliar' to qualify movement. Bankside activity alone may not be a deterrent. I fish a stream where cows come down to the water's edge to drink. Half a dozen of these large black and white creatures moving down the bank do not deter trout from rising. A man walking along the bank will. Remember: if you can

see a trout, the chances are it can see you.

The aim of the approach is to find trout if they are not already betraying their presence by rising and to cast a fly to them whilst remaining undetected. By their very nature some rivers are not conducive to being searched for non-risers; they are too big or the water is too fast or not clear enough. Smaller, calmer and clearer waters are ideal for stalking individual fish. Knowing the general trout lies will give some idea on where trout might be expected. Recognising where to look is the key to stalking non-risers, but the basis for all approaches, the secret of remaining undetected, is *slow movement*.

A logical approach to stalking trout is to begin by understanding how trout comprehend an angler on the bank. By far the best book I have come across on approach is *Stalking Trout*, written by two New Zealanders, Les Hill and Graeme Marshall. It is thoroughly recommended.

Because trout are basically wild, or in the case of stocked fish, on the way to becoming wild, they have developed a strong defence system which works as well against the fly fisher as any other enemies. Trout are by nature timid and fearful. If danger approaches they disappear. Even if simply alerted to a sense of something unusual they will stop feeding.

There is a zone of approximately 45° to the rear at each side of the fish in which the eyes will be permanently focused at infinity, even when the forward vision is close-focusing on surface food (*see* Fig 6). Trout adopt lies that give them quick access to the safety of deep water or the shelter of weeds or under banks. Their visual sensitivity to movement and colour contrast on the bank is very high.

Their hearing is extremely good and they can detect low levels of vibration transmitted from the bank. They are well camouflaged. They are subject to unpredictable movement. For no apparent reason a trout maintaining a position in the stream may turn tail and swim downstream a few yards and adopt another position.

Fortunately there are weaknesses, too, in the

The bankside movement of these cows has no effect on rising trout, whereas an angler on the horizon would put fish down. The angler is using the high bank as cover.

defence system and some of these may be exploited to the fly fisher's advantage.

There is a blind zone immediately behind the trout. By remaining very low one can approach a trout from the rear quite close without detection. Also, when a trout adopts a position near the surface its window is smaller and its view through the window is proportionately restricted.

Their vision into the sun is very poor. When flies on the surface are strongly back-lit they may be invisible. Those that are seen will appear only as silhouettes, with shape and size as the only recognisable features. Colour assessment of flies in the window with bright sunlight directly behind will be close to nil. Fish lying in water lit by bright sunlight will not be able to see very clearly through their window into areas of shade.

Despite their sensitivity to movement it is possible for very slow-moving objects to pass into view without suspicion. The angler must approach extremely slowly. An angler standing perfectly still may not attract any attention at all, even though in full view of trout.

Trout have high awareness levels of contrasting tones but not of similar tones. The implications on the fly fisher's choice of clothing should be obvious.

Some trout behaviour is predictable. They have a known preference for certain lies. They can be expected to feed at the surface at certain times on particular species of fly. Although they can be very selective they are also catholic in their surface feeding. When there is no obvious aquatic fly on which to feed they may rise to almost anything edible.

Brown trout particularly are territorial and

Fig 33   Trout lying just below the surface.

One safe approach to the tail of this pool on the Davidson river, North Carolina, is from well below the lip. Note how low the angler is in relation to trout in the upper pool. There is no way trout can see the angler.

even if temporarily scared they will return to their territory. Some fish may even patrol their territory for food.

Clothing

Sartorial considerations are a prime concern for the fly fisher who wants to get close to his trout. Because of the trout's sensitivity to colour contrast, clothing that does not have similar colour tones to the area behind the angler is likely to be a liability. If the banks have bushes and trees, or if the angler intends to wade the stream against a background of high grass or greenery, it would be advantageous to wear clothes that blend in with the environment. If the banks are open with little cover and the skies are clear and bright some lighter-coloured clothing would be preferable. This should not be bright and gaudy, likely to reflect the sun, but dull and matt. A good stalker has the colour sense of a chameleon.

I invariably wear a cap, not just for protection from the extremes of cold rain and the burning sun but primarily to shade my eyes from bright sunlight, which hinders a view into the water. The biggest aid to stalking trout is a pair of high-quality polarised sunglasses. I would sooner leave one of my fly boxes or my lunch at home than forget these. As one of the many who have to wear spectacles I tolerated the clip-on type of sunglasses for many years. Some years ago I had my prescription incorporated into a pair of polarised lenses and the difference is tremendous.

The choice of footwear is not so important. One is largely governed by whether wading is necessary or not. I make only one comment about waders and it really applies only to the smaller stony streams. On such waters I have stopped wearing studded waders because, unless the approach is made extremely carefully, I think the crunching of the metal studs on stones on the bank or stream bed is a

Roy Shaw playing a trout on the Driffield Beck.

134

vibration that trout will easily pick up. I feel happier wearing any non-studded type.

STALKING

Trout are extremely wary of any unnatural movement in their window. The approach must avoid quick or sudden movements. The effects of quick movement can be minimised if you wear colour tones that blend in with the background. The best time of day to go looking for fish is when the sun is at its highest. The light rays hit the surface at close to ninety degrees and so very little is reflected. When the sun's light strikes the water at a lower angle much more is reflected so the subsurface is not so well lit. The reflected light also produces glare on the surface, which impairs the view into the water. This is reduced when the sun is high in the sky immediately behind the angler.

Use all the available cover on the bankside. The higher the position from which one is able to look down into the water the deeper one's view will penetrate. If one is able to stand behind bushes or peer through branches or shrubbery a better view is obtained than from peering over the bank edge. There may only be a few bushes along the riverbank; do not approach them along the bank but from a wide position away from the river. When the reconnaissance has been made and a fish spotted, the casting position should be gained by the same roundabout route. Background cover can be used to good advantage, too. It is quite possible to stand in front of bushes and trees if your clothing is suitably camouflaged and you move extremely slowly. This approach is made much easier if the fish is lying in bright sunlight and your position is in deep shade. Whether one is stalking or not, it is always advisable to stand in shade rather than sunlight if the choice is available.

Notwithstanding the need to reconnoitre the water from as high a position as possible, the approach to a trout should be as low as possible. The higher the approach, the more likely the angler is to fall within the trout's field of view. Remember, the deeper a fish lies, the wider its window and the more it can see of objects on the banks. The lower the angler's profile, the less likely the chances of being seen by trout. If a fish is rising you don't actually have to see the fish to cast to it. Keep low and out of its view. The only time you need to see the fish is when searching the water for non-risers. The danger is that if you can see them they can see you.

Exploit the weaknesses in trout vision. Make the most use of the trout's blind zone to the rear by wading up from immediately behind. It is possible to approach fairly close to trout just below the surface. But in doing so remember that, although a trout may be lying very close to the surface focusing on flies only a matter of a few inches away, there are two 45° zones to the rear that are permanently focused at infinity. The approach to such trout is best made from immediately behind or opposite or upstream of the fish, where the angler has a better chance of being unnoticed if he moves slowly and is camouflaged. In such a position he will not be in focus, though a sudden movement will alert the fish to danger.

Wading must be done with care. Tell-tale upstream waves, the crunching of boots on stones, or stones dislodged are enough to alert trout to your presence. In shallow or calm water move very slowly. When wading, the angler is lower than when on the bank and therefore more likely to be below a trout's line of vision, whether or not he approaches from a downstream position. When fishing downstream you are far more likely to be below the line of vision when wading than when standing on the bank.

Total concentration is required. At the risk of being repetitive I emphasise again that observational skill is just as important an attribute of a good fly fisher as casting ability or fly-tying expertise. If during most of the day trout are not rising it is the observational skill of finding fish, or at least their lies, that will bring the greatest rewards. When stalking a piece of water it is essential to employ no less than one hundred per cent concentration for the slightest subsurface movement or shadow that betrays a trout's presence. Any-

This angler is in the intimate surroundings of a small overgrown stream. Almost any sort of back cast is impossible and he has resorted to the very short catapult, or bow-and-arrow, cast. The end of the leader is held against the rod tension and released to be projected forwards. Only a short cast is possible and each fish must be carefully stalked.

thing less than total concentration will mean missed fish.

Strangely enough, the item of tackle that we may prize most of all, the rod, may be one of the greatest hindrances to successful stalking and casting. When wading or stalking along the bank we too often give trout prior warning of our presence with the rod sticking out eight or nine feet in front of us. Always keep it low and, better still, keep it pointing behind or to one side, not in front. Stalking or wading with a rod held vertical is a sure way of advertising your presence. Too many rods have a high-gloss finish. The colour of the rod does not matter, but as it is waved about when casting sunlight reflects off the varnish. The answer is to have matt-finished rods, though very few manufacturers produce these. I confess that my own rods are not matt, but they are old and dirty and I guess they have lost much of their reflective qualities. An alternative to casting in the usual manner with a flashing rod tip twelve feet in the air is horizontal casting, with the rod and line parallel to the surface. Keep false casts to a minimum. It is not just the rod that can spell doom for the angler's chances. The reflection off any metal, completely unnatural on a trout stream, alerts the fish. The fly fisherman has to avoid obvious objects, like bright polished reels, metallic badges and those odds and ends we mistakenly hang off our vests, and even rings and metallic watch-bands. The wariest fish watch for any warning sign.

One of the most enjoyable and productive stalking techniques is to operate as a team with another angler. One leads the way, slithering along the banks like a Sioux Indian and climbing through bushes and trees to pinpoint trout for the fishing partner. Not only is this a very productive exercise in terms of fish caught; it can also teach the spotter a great deal about trout behaviour and attitudes to the artificial fly. Watching a fly being cast and recast over a feeding fish, one soon becomes aware that it is the presentation rather than the pattern of fly that is often the determining factor. There is a great thrill in watching a trout being duped by a fly, especially a fish that has proved a reluctant riser and has needed some accurate presentation which could only have been provided by working in a team. I enjoy a pulse-quickening excitement in informing a fishing pal of a trout's progress and if the trout in question is a big one the exhilaration in being the spotter is almost as great as being the guy with the rod. Teamwork pays its dividends in fish caught and in understanding trout reactions to a fly.

With overhanging branches blocking out the light this fly fisher can approach
quite close with careful wading.

Fig 34   When there is no hatch of fly in progress, at the height of summer in
bright sunlight trout will probably be found sheltering in a shaded lie.

A SUNSHINE AND SHADOW STRATEGY

In my early days as a beginner to fly fishing I was taught never to approach the stream with a bright sun on my back. The danger was that I would cast a shadow ahead of me, quite possibly on water I was likely to fish. This, of course, is true and the angler's shadow falling over calm water will scare trout. However, the approach into the sun has a number of drawbacks, whereas having the sun on your back has a number of benefits. Each of these should be weighed for the circumstances of each stream or lie, bearing in mind the position and brightness of the sun. No one approach is suitable for all situations.

Staring into the sun for long periods can be painful, particularly if the sun is also reflected from the surface. It will often cause only half one's attention to be focused on the fly on the water. When fishing into the light there is a strong tendency for everything on the surface to be seen only in silhouette. This applies not only to surface flies but to the water itself, which appears black and white with any signs of gentle rises very hard to see. Because of water glare and reflection it becomes almost impossible to see below the surface. There is little chance of spotting fish. Fishing with the sun behind gives a better chance of seeing into the water. One's line of sight follows the light into the water and any reflected light does not come back in the same direction. A much clearer view of the surface is given and flies, whether the angler's own artificial or the emerging species of natural, are much easier to observe.

Trout do not like bright sunlight. Their eyes cannot accommodate strong light and they may seek shaded areas at such times. Natural flies on the surface are frequently ignored in bright light simply because trout cannot see them on the surface or they have turned their attention away from the source of the light.

Imagine a stream with the sun shining

Fishing the pockets with a short line. The angler is keeping below the trout's line of sight and staying in the shadow of the trees behind him.

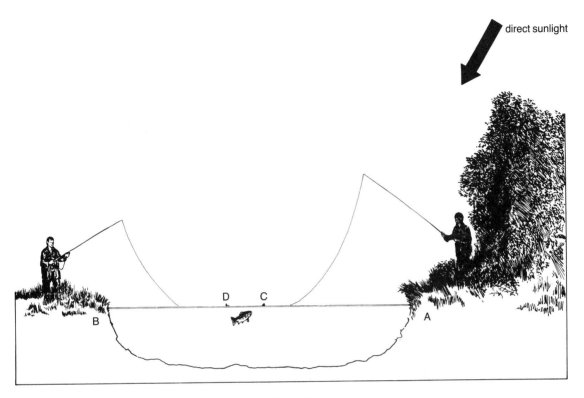

Fig 35 A sunshine and shadow strategy. The angler on bank A remains in the shade of the shrubbery; he is much less likely to be seen by fish than the angler on bank B. Direct bright sunlight may prevent the trout from seeing the fly at C but it will have a good view of the fly at D. In contrast to this situation, if the sun is shining not too brightly the trout may get just an impression of the fly at C and may be unable to make a critical inspection of it. The decision to take the fly at C may be made even though there is a poor view of the light pattern and fly. Close scrutiny is impossible. In not too bright direct light there may be good reason to present the fly at C rather than at D, where a clearer view of the fly will be given.

from bank A and a trout rising in midstream (Fig 35). The old rule would suggest that the angler should approach to cast from bank B to avoid shadows. What is not taken into account is that the trout's eye facing the sun will see very little of the surface whereas it will be using the eye facing bank B for observing the surface for food, and beyond the surface through the window it will be aware of bankside activity. The chances of keeping the fish in ignorance of our presence are best if we fish from bank A where the bright light behind us prevents fish from looking in this direction. Shadows can be minimised by kneeling and keeping low. The approach is even more likely to succeed if we stand in the shade of trees or bushes on our bank and the sun shines above the foliage. Trout vision from bright light into shade is extremely poor. If we cast to position C it is doubtful whether a trout will see much of the fly and it probably has its attention diverted elsewhere. A fly that lands in position D is much more visible to the trout, which will be using its eye on this side to look for surface food. The fly can be seen with the benefit of the light shining on it and it will be seen to the trout's maximum advantage. In bright sunlight these areas of trout attention are important and the fly should be presented in the zone which the trout will be concentrating on, not the one it finds difficulty in seeing.

This means that for an angler who is facing the light, either through choice or physical restriction, the presentation zone should be the area of attention on the near side of the fish. Be aware that a fish may be concentrating on only a relatively small zone to one side and the presentation should be very accurate.

Apart from the shadow problem when casting to position D from bank A the only drawback is covering the fish with the leader. The effect of this is reduced by casting an upstream curve or mending the leader on the surface so that the fly comes into view before the leader.

It may be that a trout has too good a view of the fly and the artificial is revealed for what it is. The answer then may be to cast the fly very slightly towards position C, where a trout will be aware of a surface fly but be unable to make a critical assessment of it other than by moving. If the fish is not being very selective it may rise on the basis of the general impression of surface food.

I spent my years of apprenticeship on small streams. Stalking on such waters is a test for the very best. Stealth and concealment are much more important here than on the larger waters. The slightest error has trout and grayling fleeing in alarm. The fish are relatively small, well camouflaged and difficult to see. You are probably six feet tall, pounding the riverbank in heavy waders, carrying an eight- or nine-foot rod. Don't be surprised if a stream seems empty of fish.

Part Four
Dry-fly Design

The ghosts of Lunn, Halford and Marryat still haunt some of the hallowed English chalk streams in much the same way as the spirits of Gordon, La Branche and Hewitt move across the face of the waters of the Beaverkill and other classic trout streams of the Eastern states of America. Their legacy is our inheritance, which has been enjoyed, analysed and developed further.

Fly tying is evolutionary and most of our dry-fly patterns can be traced back to a basic design of a century or more ago. Over the intervening years a few imaginative and thoughtful individuals have taken major steps forward towards tying a more lifelike imitation. New materials and new designs will continue to develop as long as trout turn up their noses at our offerings. Tomorrow's flies will owe much to today's patterns – our own link in the evolutionary chain.

8 The Art of Deception

Whatever the trend of the times, the trout can be relied upon to upset and confound both the theories and the practice of the fly-dressing fisherman, as, indeed, he has always done; and this is good for the sport, and very good for the soul. Moreover, it is ever to be borne in mind by contemporary fly-dressers and fishermen that, apart from the technical advances and refinements, there is very little that is really new in the arts of fly-making and fly-fishing that was not known to our forebears. Realisation that this is so detracts not a whit from pleasurable interest; rather does the resultant humility clear the vision and prepare the way for fresh endeavour. We look back in order to advance!

W. H. Lawrie, *A Reference Book of English Trout Flies*, 1966

I am convinced that fly fishing is decidedly uncharitable. Most fly fishing makes me more devious, cunning and deceitful. Admittedly, not towards my fellow man, but surely wherever it is directed it must do little, contrary to the homilies of those early writers, for the good of my soul. Fly fishing, and in particular dry-fly fishing, is entirely devoted to deceiving trout into believing something is what it isn't. All the fly fisher's skills are channelled into the ultimate angling deception, rising a trout to a dry fly. What compounds our sin is that we gloat and rejoice in each success and strive towards an even more perfect deception. Surely no other sport or pastime asks a man to stoop so low. Golfers, footballers and tennis players can win with honour, without resort to the shadier sides of man's character.

For the fly fisher with a natural interest in entomology the private lives of different species is fascinating, but for the trout fisher who fishes widely and wants to match the hatch the logistics are frightening. With scores of North American upwingeds, what hope has he of identifying all the species he comes across, or tying a suitable imitation of each emerger, stillborn, dun and spinner, and how does he carry them all at the waterside? This doesn't even scratch the surface when he also has to consider the 700 sedges and scores of assorted stoneflies, midges, and the rest. The British trout fisher finds hatch matching somewhat easier, with less than thirty upwingeds of varying importance and

a mere handful of the almost 200 caddis species worthy of specific imitation. Exact imitation of that number of flies is barely physically possible nor, fortunately, is it a necessity. However intelligent or selective a trout is, it is still pretty dumb to be duped by the artificial fly. The dumbest are those on the clear, calm flats which have the closest look at the fly and fall for it. Those which are risen on rippled surfaces with a poorer view of the fly have an excuse.

The strict hatch matching that anglers have striven for in years past is rapidly diminishing. Three factors are of prime importance. Find a *design of artificial* that adequately represents the features of the natural that trout find important and are triggers to the rise, *match the wing and body colours* and fish the *correct size*. I applaud the move towards simplification in matching a species. It has become more a question of seeing a grey-winged, olive-bodied fly on the water and fishing a pattern called simply a Grey Wing/ Olive Body. What could be more straightforward than ringing the colour and size changes on favourite designs of fly?

Inevitably, the fly tyer must compromise in his attempt to match a natural fly. Man has not yet been able to emulate the Creator. He is always bound by certain limitations, not least a piece of curved metal called a hook. The problem of the trout's view of the hook in the mirror is doubly difficult as not only is the bend visible below the surface but so is its reflection on the undersurface. In the window the double image of the hook disappears but the bend still remains in clear view. Fortunately, trout feeding enthusiastically and even more discriminating fish somehow fail to notice the blatant and obvious bend of metal. Some of the other limitations have been reduced over the years as more suitable materials and innovative fly designs have been introduced. Some of the problems will always remain. It is worth a close look at the problems so that we are in no doubt about the shortcomings of the artificial fly compared with the natural dun.

Advantages of the Natural Fly

1.   It is real.
2.   It is alive and moving. As it emerges it is struggling to free itself from its nymphal skin. Once on the surface there are tiny leg, abdomen and wing movements.
3.   It conforms exactly to the natural drift of surface currents and the effects of wind. All the duns drifting over a lie will conform more or less to the same behaviour pattern.
4.   It conforms exactly to what trout expect in its shape, size, colour, movement, etc.
5.   It rests on the surface supported only by its six legs.
6.   The light pattern in the mirror will be totally natural: only the effects of the feet of the fly will create the pattern.
7.   It is usually on the water in some numbers, thereby accustoming trout to its presence.
8.   It is not attached to a leader.

Disadvantages of the 'Standard' Artificial Fly

1.   It is neither living nor moving except for the effects of a breeze in the hackle fibres.
2.   It is attached to a leader and a fly line, either of which may be visible.
3.   It is affected by drag. Even though imperceptible to the angler, this is detected by trout.
4.   There is the problem of the hook bend breaking the surface and being visible both in the mirror and the window.

Fig 36   A rising trout.

5.   Many patterns have tails that rest unnaturally on the surface.
6.   If tails are not included in the dressing, and even in some patterns with tails, part of the body of the fly may rest on the surface. This is incompatible with the natural dun but necessary for a spent spinner imitation and acceptable for an emerging or stillborn pattern.
7.   There is difficulty in assessing the right number of turns of hackle to produce the correct light pattern in the mirror.
8.   It must be made to stay afloat.

Items 2 and 3 above are problems of presentation and the solutions are examined in Chapter 7. The remainder have to be resolved at the fly vice. Traditionally, we have tried to match the natural with as accurate an imitation as possible, attempting to represent the natural in shape, size, colouring, wing height and light pattern. If we are unable to offer an imitation or we are unsure what natural fly is being taken we offer the most general imitation with the broadest possible appeal. Having looked at the natural fly from the trout's point of view, and come to some understanding about what the fish perceives of surface flies, we can match what the trout sees with the artificial, trying to incorporate in the dressing those aspects which trout can judge as being critical. We know only too well that a failure in any aspect of fly-tying skill or presentation may mean rejection.

THE 'STANDARD' DRY FLY

The 'standard' dry fly, if there is such a thing, has evolved over the last hundred years since the chalk stream anglers of southern England pioneered the task of attempting to copy the natural fly with reasonable accuracy. It consists of a body, usually of natural or synthetic fur, hair, wool, quill or silk, possibly with a rib to strengthen the fly and to represent the segmented abdomen of the natural; a wound hackle to represent the legs and sometimes the wings and to support the body above the surface; hackle-fibre tails to support the rear of the body; possibly wings, usually tied upright in the dun imitation and spent for the spinner imitation.

In Search of the Ideal Hackle

Courtney Williams wrote that 'the difference between a good hackle and a poor one often represents the difference between a full creel and an empty one.' Ideally, the 'standard' fly should rest on the surface only by its hackle and the tips of its hackle-fibre tails, though it is almost inevitable that the hook point will penetrate the surface. A fly dressed with an ideal hackle and tail and well soaked with floatant might balance in such a way. No synthetic material has come close to being able to represent the delicate but supportive legs of the dun. The fibres of a cock hackle are probably the best natural material, although some fur fibres offer other advantages (hair and fur patterns as alternatives to hackled flies are considered on page 176). The hackle fibres must be stiff yet flexible enough to support the weight of the fly, and must be sufficient in number to reproduce a light pattern similar to the one produced by the natural's legs; failure to do so may mean that a selective trout rejects the fly even before it leaves the mirror. It is obvious that only a lightly hackled fly will produce the required effect. Too many turns of hackle will create the wrong light pattern, be too dense to allow the light through as it should, and when wet be harder to dry by false casting, making the fly heavier. The light pattern is the principal

consideration. The second, in the case of a wingless artificial, is that the upper hackle fibres must represent the wings. Therefore the fibres must be of a density and colour to give the impression of wings.

The perfect hackle should have fibres which, when wound on the shank, are of equal length so that the shorter fibres are not wasted, simply adding weight to the fly. Alas, there is no such hackle and inevitably some fibres will be shorter than others; but that is the aim. A good rule of thumb to the length of the most suitable hackle fibres is that, in the case of a wingless pattern where the hackle also represents the wing, the fibres should be about the length of the shank between the start of the bend and the eye. For a winged pattern the fibres need to be slightly shorter so that a clear view of the wing is presented.

The best shape for the individual hackle feather is long and thin. The longer the hackle the more turns can be made with it. If a hackle with only a small proportion of fibres of the correct length is used, two or three hackles may be needed. With the scarcer short-fibred hackle the smaller sizes of fly can be tied.

Very stiff hackles are advocated by most authorities. Fly fishers who recommend softer, more flexible hackles claim that the stiff fibres penetrate the surface film rather than rest on it. The springy, flexible fibres 'give' a little at the resistance of the surface film and do not penetrate it. The danger with the softer fibres is that as the tips bend to lie flat on the surface individually they create a longer light pattern quite uncharacteristic of the tiny dimple of the natural's foot. I feel that somewhere between the two schools of thought lies the middle ground of truth. Some hackle fibres are too soft, offering no support, are lifeless and dull. Others are just too stiff and penetrate the film. What is needed is a hackle with fibres that are well sprung with enough 'give' to prevent the surface penetration, but not at the expense of the fibres' lying flat on the surface. One benefit of a good hackle is that as it balances on the water on its fine tips any breeze or air

Fig 37   A well tied 'standard' dry fly with a stiff-fibred hackle; the natural dun resting on its six legs; a dry fly with a soft-fibred hackle, which allows the body to rest on the surface.

movement may rock it slightly, so simulating life – a difficult attribute to reproduce in a floating fly.

Frank Elder's book, *The Book of the Hackle* (1979), clears away much of the myth and inaccuracies about hackles. The author carefully assesses the number of actual hackle fibres that touch the surface in a given length of hackle. He bases his findings on hackles that have very stiff fibres and are totally dry. For example, Elder suggests that for a size 16 hook a normal length of hackle is about 45mm (1¾ inches), of which the usable length is approximately 36mm. This produces on average 65 fibres of the correct length to be wound round the 360° of shank. The result is one fibre of the correct length per 6°, and as only the bottom 30° of fibres rest on the surface only five hackle-fibre tips touch the water in a 45mm hackle. Even though the fly appears quite bushy, Elder suggests that the number of hackle fibres supporting the fly is surprisingly small. With softer hackles the fibres bend and allow shorter fibres also to come into contact with the surface.

If the firm, springy quality of hackle cannot be found at the right price, one answer is to wind on a slightly longer-fibred hackle and to trim it to the required length. The full 360° may be trimmed or the lower fibres clipped straight in a line just below the point. This will improve floating as more fibres rest on the surface. These flies may be less successful on water where the light pattern is critical but on rough, fast or rippled water where trout have only a fleeting or blurred glimpse of either the light pattern or the actual fly the hackle may be more than adequate. On such waters a well hackled fly with plenty of supportive 'legs' might be necessary to keep the body dry and the fly afloat.

It is strange that in a century or more of specialised dry-fly fishing many of the flies dressed as spinner imitations have a full hackle, which keeps the body clear of the surface in a way uncharacteristic of the spent fly. Apart from the moment when the female spinner lands on the surface, the rear of the abdomen and later, as a spent spinner, its body rests in the film, quite visible to fish both in the mirror and in the window. An accurate spent imitation can be fished without a hackle as the natural's legs are insignificant, and the wings are in the spent position. Alternatively, the underside of the wound hackle can be trimmed in line with the bottom of the body, allowing the body to rest in the film with the horizontal hackle fibres conveying the impression of the spent wings. A fair representation is achieved when the hackle fibres are bunched together to form two spent wings, so that no wound hackle remains. The only drawback is that when the bunches become wet they easily lose shape – but so too may the natural's wings.

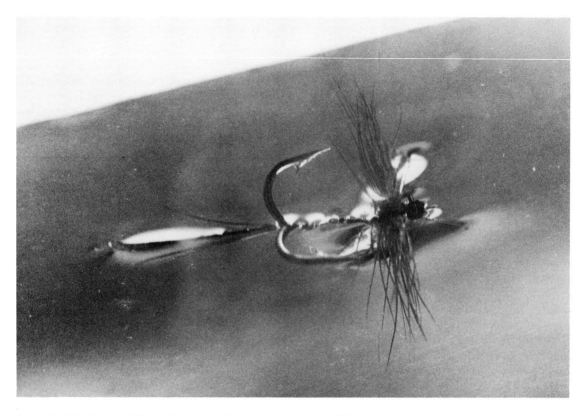

A standard dry fly viewed from below the surface when in the mirror. Weak hackles have sunk into the film, giving no accurate light pattern. The tails are visible with their uncharacteristic light pattern and the body is resting on the surface.

Tails

The purpose of the tail in the 'standard' design of dry fly is to support the rear of the fly on the surface, keeping the body and, if possible, the hook-point from penetrating the film. Too short or too weak a tail will result in the point and bend breaking the surface film and probably the body touching the water. Soft hackles are disastrous and offer no support at all. It is unnatural if the tails penetrate the surface in a floating dun imitation, although some authorities say that the light pattern from the tail fibres is so far away that it does not detract from the fly. It may not be too disastrous if trout are taking the emerging duns. The sunken tail might be mistaken for the nymphal shuck. Some modern emerger patterns are little more than dun imitations

with a tail of Z-lon to copy this shuck. One alternative to the usual cock hackle fibres is to use animal hair such as muskrat or mink whiskers, which are strong and float well. It is better to tie two widely spaced very sparse bunches of fibres than a single large bunch. The fly is better balanced and more stable on the water and the light pattern created by the tails is not as obvious as the single bunch.

The natural dun has its tails pointing upwards and they do not normally come into contact with the water once the dun has cleared itself of the nymphal shuck. They are probably not even seen by a feeding trout. Unfortunately, the tails are necessary to the equilibrium of the artificial 'standard' dressing. The tails of the natural spinner are longer and trout will see them lying flush in the surface film. These should be tied longer and be widely spaced, helping to support the artificial and preventing it from sinking.

The Body

Most fly fishers demand an artificial fly with a body that at least gives a fair impression of the natural it purports to represent. I prefer to dress the abdomen imitation as naturally as possible as I am doubtful about the insignificance of this part of the natural fly. To neglect the abdomen only leaves a greater margin for error, and an accurate representation certainly will not deter a fish from rising to it. As a counter-argument, there is an interesting incident in F. M. Halford's *An Angler's Autobiography* (1903). He and G. S. Marryat found themselves fishing one day with mayflies that had been tied in haste without any bodies. These 'ghosts', as they were dubbed, comprised hackle, wings and tails only. Both men fished the flies and found them as successful as flies with normal bodies. The line of thinking that the experiment produced was not followed through and they reverted to normal patterns simply because to dress a fly in such a way offended their taste.

I suggest that on rough, rippled water, a trout may rise without any sight at all of the fly's body, but on a calm, clear, slow stream, where a leisurely inspection might be made, the presence of a suggestion of an abdomen and thorax may be necessary before a trout is satisfied with the imitation.

If the need to represent adequately the body of the natural dun or spinner is accepted, the main consideration after that of size and shape, colour and translucency is its ability to repel water. A waterlogged fly inevitably sits much lower in the water and eventually the body touches the surface or even sinks. Because of the oils in some natural materials they are generally more water-repellent than synthetic ones. Materials like stripped quill, peacock herl, floss and tying thread may look fine when dry but are totally different when wet. Natural spun fur takes a great deal of beating; the best has the finest fur for dubbing the smallest bodies. Among the many natural furs seal's fur is one of the most popular, but it is in the process of being prohibited. It is easily dyed and remains bright and shiny even when wet. Some of the synthetic materials are effective. Polypropylene dubbing and yarn has a specific gravity of 0.91, less than that of water, and is therefore an excellent floater. Dubbing is not difficult and it floats better than fur and is shiny and translucent. Three fairly recent developments are Antron (very easy to dub), poly yarn and Fly-Rite poly seal, which are very suitable for even the smallest bodies. They are dubbed on in the usual way. A wide range of colours are available to produce very lifelike translucent and durable bodies.

Translucency can be achieved or represented in a number of ways: through the use of thinly dubbed natural fur; a dubbed body over a shiny base of tinsel; shiny dubbing picked out to give a 'fuzzy' body outline; or a wound overbody of transparent PVC. The latter allows the colour to come through but a thin transparent zone surrounds the body, which looks very realistic.

Some of the bulky bodies of peacock herl or floss are a positive hindrance to floating. When wet they absorb moisture like sponges. I find peacock herl a useful body material and I am reluctant to discard it. The answer is to give additional support by tying the pattern with more turns of hackle than is ideal, and also to use fine-wire hooks.

When stripped quill is wound on the shank a segmented appearance representing the natural's segmented abdomen results. If segmentation is required, a rib of fine wire, floss or thread may be used. The rib also acts to strengthen the body, making it more durable in the teeth of an angry trout. The only note of caution when using or tying ribbed flies is to use the lightest possible material. Any sort of wire does little to enhance the floating ability of a fly already laden down with the weight of the hook.

Later in this chapter a section is given over to considering hair and fur alternatives to hackled flies. Some of the benefits highlighted there also relate to their use as body materials.

Wings

After the appearance of the light pattern in the mirror, the second trigger to the rise is the sight of the wing tips whilst the dun is nearing the edge of the mirror. They will become fully visible in the window. Angling practice seems to support the theory that in many instances specific wings need not be incorporated into the dressing; the upper hackle fibres alone are sufficient imitation. However, one cannot doubt that the specific imitation of the wing reduces the margin for error and offers more hope of a successful deception.

I believe it was G. S. Marryat and F. M. Halford who first used slips of quills from opposing wings to represent upright wings. These had the advantage over slips from the same quill, which caused the fly to spin in the air and twist the leader. The revised dressing also cocked better on the surface. Using slips from matched wing quills is now just one of many winging methods, but it is one held in high esteem when specific and highly visible wings are required, as in the case of the Swisher and Richards No-Hackle flies. Now the preferred winging styles in a 'standard' dun imitation are hackle tips, or bunches of hackle fibres, or hackle feathers cut with wing cutters, tied in the upright position. These three are easier to tie than quill slips and are perfectly adequate wing representations. (Although hackle- and feather-fibre wings are now commonplace the concept is not new. Back in 1857, 'Ephemera' (Edward Fitzgibbon) described how to tie wings of bunches of feather fibres.) For spinner imitations hackle tips or bunches of hackle fibres are tied in the spent position.

Quite a number of variations in winging style, utilising different natural and synthetic materials, have been devised. Some of these variations are now so commonplace that they may be considered standard and are listed below.

The *advance wing* is a single wing of bunched animal hair (also called *shaving-brush wing*) or feather fibres or a feather tip or split wings tied slanting forwards over the eye of the hook. One of my favourite patterns, the John Storey, has an advance wing. I am uncertain as to why the unnatural wing style is successful except that the wing is being emphasised or exaggerated to a watching trout. If the required trigger is the sight of the wing, its exaggeration may be advantageous.

The *bunch wing*, or *hackle-fibre wing*, is made from a bunch of feather or hackle fibres and tied in any desired position – advance, upright, spent, or whatever.

The *down wing* is tied at angle over the back or flat across the back, usually to represent caddis or stoneflies.

Fan wings are tied on the larger patterns, often Mayfly or Green Drake imitations. They are generally two small breast feathers tied so that their tips curve outwards.

Hackle-point wings are the tips of cock hackles tied upright or spent.

Hairwings of natural or dyed animal hair are tied in all wing positions.

Rolled wings are made by rolling feather fibres from a single wing feather and are tied slanting back over the body.

Split wings are any pair of wings that are divided without the tips meeting.

Flies dressed to the 'standard' prescription are fished throughout the world wherever trout rise to the natural fly. My guess is that a very high percentage of trout caught on surface flies take artificials of the conventional design. Despite the shortcomings of the 'standard' dry fly it is incredibly successful. From this we must assume that the artificial tails, body, wings (if any) and legs comply with what trout expect to see in a natural fly. The 'standard' fly has its defects and yet convinces all but the canniest of trout. In my view, the reason is simple: any shortcomings are compensated for because they suggest another aspect of the natural's life-cycle which at the time we are not trying to represent. For example, the 'standard' dry fly rests with its tails on the surface and also possibly the rear of its body if there is a weakness in the support of the tail or hackle. I suggest that this shortcoming is ignored because

An accurately proportioned floating fly supporting itself on its hackle points and tail fibres. Even so, when floating on the water, the end of the body may rest on the film.

trout take it for an emerging dun with its nymphal case still clinging to the rear of the abdomen. Other artificials may inadvertently rest with their bodies in the film, or with a wing cocked to one side. How better to represent an emerger or a stillborn? Trout frequently take these artificials which are poor adult dun imitations. My own feelings are that we simply give trout more credit for their diminutive brain than we ought. If it's a confrontation between man and trout there should be no contest.

Angling historians tell us that the dry-fly confrontation began on the West Country rivers fished by George Pulman, whose book *Vade Mecum of Fly-Fishing for Trout* (1841) contains the first unambiguous reference to fishing the dry fly. I find it extremely odd that no one had previously referred specifically to fishing with a floating fly. I am aware that

heavy hooks and the absence of aids to keep a fly dry worked against keeping an artificial afloat. But surely fly fishermen for centuries had been aware that when their flies hit the surface they were frequently taken by trout in the seconds before being submerged and that this was a tactic to be encouraged. In *The Art of Angling or Barker's Delight* (1651) by Thomas Barker fly-dressing materials were discussed with this comment: '. . . and now I work much with Hog's wool, for I find it floateth best and procureth the best sport.' Now why would a fly tyer want to use a material which he finds is an excellent aid to floating and achieves the most success if he intends his flies to be fished subsurface? George Scotcher's book, *The Fly-Fisher's Legacy* (*circa* 1800), suggested that a Black Gnat should be cast to lie on the surface upstream of a rising fish. Reading between the lines, I am sure Barker and fly fishers during the next 190 years knew the value of trying to keep a fly afloat.

Rough and crude these early dry patterns may have been and it was left to a generation of fly fishers to refine the art to its present level. The Test and a few other chalk streams of southern England were the cradle of modern dry-fly design. The baby didn't linger in the cradle; it grew up to spread its seed across the world, maturing and being refined as new methods and materials evolved. Ninety years ago it was the English trout fly fisher who pioneered the methods and patterns; today most of the innovative ideas come from the United States.

The 'standard' dry fly satisfies the needs of most fishermen most of the time. The majority of trout are duped by traditionally designed flies, however unsatisfactory their design may be in theory. However, the trout fly is forever evolving as new synthetic materials are developed. The design of the fly also changes as different aspects of the natural fly are emphasised by different angling authorities. Some have ignored parts of the 'standard' fly and others have seen a need for emphasised wings or accurate body colour.

When confronted with the failure of their conventional flies the greater number of trout fishers accept their failure with good grace and an air of inevitability, knowing that from time to time these things happen. The next time we go fishing we use the same flies with success and happily continue until the next failure, the next wise old trout, the next very selective feeder. Over the years, a few dissatisfied anglers have sought answers to the defects in the 'standard' dry fly and have tried to improve on fly design with the sole purpose of making the artificial appear more like the natural. Most of these men have given much thought to the problem, have studied the difficulties scientifically and have spent time in observation of both trout and flies. Some of their results have been genuinely innovative and effective. It is to these variations that we must turn if the elusive, selective trout are to be caught. Their downfall is seldom a conventional fly; too many have been examined at too close range.

VARIATIONS ON THE DRY-FLY THEME: REPRESENTING THE DUN

Parachute Hackles

The floating fly with a horizontally wound hackle has been around since the 1930s. The shape of the wound hackle and the manner in which this allows the fly to alight gracefully on the surface gave rise to its appropriate designation, 'parachute'. The idea was widely attributed to Alex Martin, who claimed to have patented it, and I have seen samples of his flies from this era with labels attached specifying Patent No. 379343. Until fairly recently I, along with many others, always assumed Martin to have been the inventor of the parachute hackle. However, we are indebted to Jack Heddon, who pointed out in a letter in the correspondence columns of *Trout and Salmon* in December 1981 that the British Patent No. 379343 was granted to an American, William Avery Brush, who applied for the patent in May 1931 and had it granted in August 1932. The first major departure from the 'standard' dressing is attributable to an American.

The hackle was originally wound round a small vertical projection incorporated in the hook but today the hackle is usually wound round the base of the hackle stalk, fine wire, or nylon monofilament. The benefits of the parachute hackle are that a more delicate presentation is achieved as the fly is slowed down by its horizontal hackle as it drops to the surface. The resultant fly on the water is better balanced and floats very well. The spread of the hackle is much more suggestive of the spread legs of the natural dun. However, the main drawback is that the body is situated quite unnaturally below the hackle and rests in or on the surface film and is therefore visible in the mirror and window. It may, of course, be taken for a spinner in such a position, or an emerging dun breaking through the film. A book entitled *Thoughtful Practice with a Dry Fly* (1949), by Arthur Woolley, illustrated a dressing with two parachute hackles, one at either end of the body. This

A parachute-hackled dry fly bearing Alex Martin's patent number.

probably improved the floating quality but did nothing to make a closer representation of the natural dun.

Moving the plane of the hackle from vertical to horizontal was probably the biggest single step towards achieving a closer representation of the natural dun. William Avery Brush started it all off with the hackle on top of the body. A few fly fishers in the 1950s experimented with the next evolutionary step, which was to place the hackle under the body so that the artificial rests on the surface supported only by its hackle fibres, exactly as the natural rests. Now we are getting extremely close to our aim, certainly much closer than with any of the other offerings. Only one major problem remained: the point of the hook still penetrates the surface, albeit only just if a good hackle is used. The answer was to turn the hook upside down and dress the fly with the bend and point uppermost. The first reference I can find to this style of up-side-down parachute fly is in Joscelyn Lane's book *Lake and Loch Fishing for Trout* (1955), in which he refers to an earlier undated article in the *Journal of the Fly-Fishers' Club* written by 'J.H.S.' in conjunction with himself. The book has a line drawing of an upside-down fly with a parachute hackle and the following comments:

The aim has been to produce a pattern which does not penetrate the surface at all and which is really stable in the air and on the water . . . The fly looks very natural, as the body is carried off the water and the tail is dressed well round the head of the hook, with the whisks pointing in the air. . . . They last well if tied with single strip wings, but hackle point wings are not to be recommended.

The concept and original idea came from Lane; the tying of the pattern originated with J.H.S. Two years later, C. F. Walker's *Fly-Tying as an Art* includes a poorly reproduced black-and-white plate captioned 'Some Freaks and Fancies'. There is illustrated J. H. Stothert's (surely the J.H.S. whom Lane refers to) 'Upside-downer', which anticipates by more than twenty years John Goddard and Brian Clarke's patterns on the same theme. Walker does not detail the dressing, which appears to have wings of feather-fibre slips. I can find no other references to the upside-downer; even Walker only mentions it in passing. (The concept of fishing the dry fly with the hook upside down with an ordinary hackle is not an innovation of even this century. It was first mentioned by R. B. Marston in the 1880s.)

The upside-down hook when used in conjunction with a parachute hackle almost completely removes the hook bend and point from the trout's view. Trout are presented with a fly that provides a circular light pattern in the mirror, an excellent head-on profile offering a clear view of the wings as it leaves the mirror and enters the window, and the body and tails are supported above the surface – all of which, in my opinion, produce the most realistic dun imitations yet devised.

The Stalking Fly

The same line of thinking was followed when Hal Janssen produced his Stalking Fly in

151

1973. It is so named because its use was confined to very selective trout that had to be stalked and offered a particularly lifelike imitation. Three variations were devised, two of which are based on the upside-down hook with the parachute hackle under the body. I doubt whether Janssen was aware of Sothert's British pattern as even UK fly tyers seem to have overlooked it, and Janssen arrived at his dressing independently. The wings are of very small whole hackle feathers and are set widely apart in a semi-spent position. The butts of the wing feathers are used for the base of the parachute hackle. One alternative to produce a more durable method of winging is to use hackle-fibre wings. The second option is a no-hackle dressing which uses three bunches of hackle fibres bunched out of the conventional hackle. One bunch acts as an upright wing; the other two are divided as legs on either side of the body in a V-shape.

USD Paraduns

The imitation of the natural dun has reached a peak with the USD paraduns (Fig 38) of John Goddard and Brian Clarke. They are a logical answer to the problem of selective trout in that they are the nearest the fly dresser has come to representing those aspects the trout can see of the dun on the surface. Writing of the USD (upside-down) Paraduns and Poly-spinners, Goddard and Clarke comment in *The Trout and the Fly*:

Our flies have shown that they frequently can offer more: to the trout; to the angler who simply wants to catch it; and to the fly-dressing enthusiast

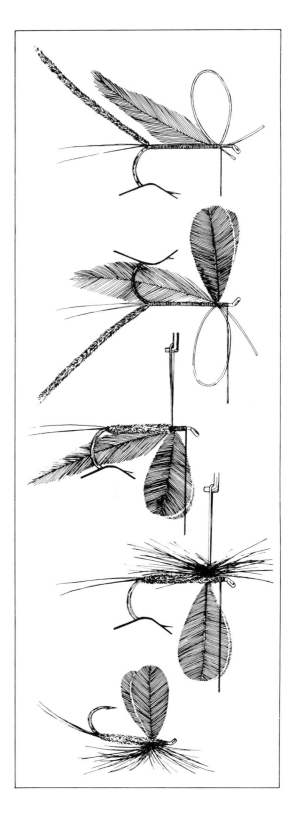

Fig 38 The USD paradun. 1 The various materials to match the chosen species should be tied in. A loop of nylon mono is tied in at the eye. 2 The fly is reversed in the vice and wings cut from two hen hackles with a wing cutter are tied in. 3 Reposition the fly in the vice. Wind on the body materials. Link the mono into a gallows tool. 4 Bind in and wind round a cock hackle as close to the body as possible. Thread the hackle tip through the mono loop and draw the mono tight; the hackle is trapped by the mono. Add a dab of varnish. Allow to dry and trim.

USD Paradun.

USD Paradun from below the surface when in the mirror. This is remarkably like the trout's view of the natural adult dun in the mirror.

who will obtain *his* satisfaction from tying a fly that is as close to the natural as perceived by the trout, that to the best of our knowledge is yet available.

I'll back them all the way. Their USD Paraduns differ from Stothert's and Janssen's dressings in two areas. The first is that their wings are slightly longer and wider than 'standard' wings and are made from the tips of good-quality cock hackles cut out with wing cutters. They are tied to give a pronounced outward curve, which has a stabilising effect, ensuring the fly lands on the water the right way up. The tails are also tied well spread. In the smaller sizes tails are made from bunches of hackle fibres; in the larger sizes two or three muskrat or mink whiskers are used. In each case the tails are tied so that they stick up slightly in the air rather than horizontally. These patterns are more difficult to tie than 'standard' patterns and are not as durable in the sharp teeth of a trout. Therefore they should not necessarily be used in run-of-the-mill dry-fly fishing but confined to fish proving elusive and reluctant

153

A variation on the USD design tied on a Swedish Dry Fly hook and including a bunched wing of white mink tail hair.

to take a 'standard' dressing. No dressing offers 100 per cent success but, notwithstanding the trout's whim, the USD series come closer than any others to it.

Paraduns

Another variation on the parachute theme came from Doug Swisher and Carl Richards with their Paraduns, which have widely spaced tails for good balance, a dubbed natural fur body and a sparse parachute hackle on top of the body around a wing (Fig 39). The preferred wing materials are hen wing tips or bunched and shaped hen hackle fibres. Deer body hair or elk hair are recommended for the body for the larger sizes. The hackle should be about two-thirds the length of the wing so that the latter is not obscured from view. All are tied to represent the newly emerged duns. Because the body rests on the surface a satisfactory light pattern to emulate a fully emerged dun is prevented. The importance of light patterns in both the natural

fly and its imitations are aspects which Swisher and Richards almost totally ignored until they later tied some of their Paraduns with the parachute hackle on the underside of the body. This amendment is only for the purpose of supporting the body above the surface and they make no mention of the need for a light pattern from the legs.

Swisher and Richards also introduced the Paradrake, an imitation of the larger duns. Their extended bodies are made from elk or deer hair with wings also of elk hair or of two shoulder feathers or feather fibres. A further development is the Pontoon Paradrake (Fig 40) for the largest dun imitations. The extended body material is of spun fur wound round an extension of thick nylon monofilament or elk hair. Any of the forementioned wings are used and the parachute hackle is wound either on top of or below the body. An additional item is two forward-projecting hackle stalk butts of the appropriate leg colour, which are tied as the front two legs. They act as pontoons to stabilise the fly

Fig 39   The Paradun.

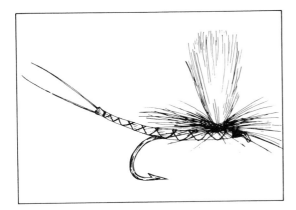

Fig 40   The Pontoon Paradrake.

on the water. The bouyant hollow elk hair helps the fly to float.

William Brush's step in the evolutionary process diverted the fly dressers' line of thought down a very effective road.

Palmered Hackles

Palmered wet flies have been used since fly fishing began. The palmered dry fly has a number of benefits in representing surface flies. Only the hackle fibres touch the water, so keeping the body and any tail clear of the surface. This would appear to be quite a satisfactory solution to the problem of supporting the body except that the light pattern created by the high number of hackle fibres is excessive for an accurate imitation of the dun's light pattern. A sparsely palmered hackle is more satisfactory in this respect.

The palmered hackle is quite an effective imitation of the bulkier shape of some of the sedges. On rougher water, where the chances are a delicate dun imitation would soon be waterlogged, a palmer-style fly could be the answer. They are better floaters if tied with a good hackle, and because of their bulk and light pattern are more easily seen by both the trout and the angler. The palmer hackle can also be used to good effect on flies fished awash in the film to represent the emerging sedges and duns. The blur of the hackle of a pattern fished awash in the film gives a fine impression of the emergent adult leaving its shuck.

The Thorax Fly

Vincent Marinaro devised a useful design of floating fly with the body supported clear of the surface and a widely spaced hackle – which combine to offer a near-natural light pattern – as well as a well placed and highly visible wing. In his original pattern the hackle was positioned in the middle of the shank and two hackles were turned at opposite angles in the shape of an X around the wings. The fly is better balanced than the 'standard' design because the hackle support is in the middle of the body. The widely spaced hackle-fibre tail can be directed at a low angle into the air in the manner of the natural. According to Marinaro, the first to advocate sparce, widely spread tail fibres, 'the tail fibres seldom touch the water, but in the event of a faulty cast or a badly balanced fly the split tails are alway there to act as governors'.

Marinaro believed that the relatively small abdomen on his early Thorax Flies was irrelevant as he maintained that trout have little view of this on the natural dun. What is of greater importance is the emphasised thorax which protrudes beyond the hackle. On an unrippled surface, the thorax of the natural fly is clearly visible in the trout's window and therefore its outline and size – and, depend-

Two Thorax Duns. The first is in Marinaro's early style; the second his later.

ing on surface conditions, probably its colour – are critical or key points when the dun is being inspected. (The first fly tyer to fully recognise the significance of the thorax was Herbert Lock, a Hampshire keeper, who included a pad of dubbing as a thorax on his famous Blue Upright.) Marinaro was later to discard the abdomen to the rear and the thorax in front of the hackle completely.

In Marinaro's opinion, the wing of the dun is the most important aspect and is the main determining factor whether an artificial will be successful. The light pattern is the early trigger that alerts a trout to the presence of surface food, which the trout confirms by sight of the wings as the fly nears the edge of the mirror and enters the window. In the original Thorax Fly the wing is tied upright in the middle of the body. This ensures that the *width* of the wings of the natural fly (which is situated over the middle of the body, although the natural's wings are anchored nearer the head) is adequately represented. The photograph of a natural dun on page 72

clearly shows the wings in a position over the centre of the body, though joined to the body at the thorax. Often the wings of the 'standard' dry fly are tied directly above the thorax and do not have the width to extend over the abdomen. Marinaro positioned his wings so that they would appear in the position of the broadest part of the natural's wings. He also sought to represent the wing width in his choice of winging material. Discarding starling and duck feathers as fragile, and hacklepoint wings as ineffective when wet, he chose to cut and shape the wing from the webby part of broad neck hackles. The wing is cut from the middle of the hackle, so that the base of the stem is fairly thick, and the top of the stalk is fine enough to give some flexibility. These offer the important width Marinaro wanted and maintain their shape with their springy fibres. An alternative is to cut the wings from the tips of duck breast feathers or the small covert feathers at the base of a duck wing.

The method of dressing involves tying the

wings first. In the case of the original pattern they should be tied in the middle of the shank; in the later variation Marinaro placed the wings just forward of the middle. The wings are better tied in individually than together and bound in with figure-of-eight turns of extra-fine tying silk. The wing stalks should be bent back to the rear of the hook under the shank, tied down and cut off. In practice upright wings are essential. Any stiff wings that are slightly split have a tendency to make the fly spin when cast and it becomes impossible to fish with. The tails are two bunches, each of two or three long, stiff spade hackle fibres, which are widely spaced at a slight upward angle. A drop of varnish helps to hold the two bunches apart.

In later life Marinaro amended the body style and considerably reduced the abdomen and thorax. From an original abdomen of spun fur he changed to a single layer of tying silk from the tail to the wing roots. At the roots, spun fur is tied in and wound in a tight ball round the base of the wings. Two hackles are used, one smaller than the other. These are wound in an X shape. The larger hackle is wound along the diagonal that places the upper fibres in front of the wing, and the smaller hackle is tilted so that the upper fibres go behind the wings and the lower fibres in front. The fly rests dipping slightly forward.

The Thorax Fly is a system fly which can be adapted by the choice of colour for the wings, hackle, body and hook size to represent a wide range of upwinged duns. Marinaro suggested that a hackle should be used in such a way that it *supplements and confirms* the color value of the wing, and that means that wing and hackle should be of the same color'.

No-Hackle Flies

Flies without hackles have been fished since fly fishing for trout began. The first English hackle-less flies were recorded in the fifteenth century. One presumes that they were invariably fished subsurface. In the 1960s and 1970s a new series of No-Hackles had an impact on North American fly fishing. Some of the flies were of a design and style remarkably like those of five centuries earlier.

The names of Doug Swisher and Carl Richards are synonymous with this style of dressing dry flies. Their patterns were born out of their experience of fishing for selective trout on limestone and spring-fed streams. In many ways their patterns are a radical approach to persuading trout to rise because they completely abandoned the item in the dry-fly recipe which until that moment had been deemed to be the most critical feature in a floating fly – the hackle. Top-quality cock hackles have been prized and sought after for decades; the demise of the best hackles has been a topical moan wherever pundits pontificate; small fortunes are exchanged for top-class capes and entire books have been given over to their study. If Swisher and Richards are right, angling books will have to be re-written. In the preface to their book *Selective Trout* (1971), Joe Brooks writes that out of the authors' research 'came one of the great dry-fly discoveries of North American fly-fishing history, the "no-hackle dry fly"'. Perhaps all three had forgotten the famous English pattern, the Gold-Ribbed Hare's Ear, which has neither hackle nor (in most dressings) wing. Admittedly, a few fibres are picked out for legs but there isn't a hackle. J. C. Mottram also described a no-hackle olive dun which floats on its dubbed fur body. In 1915 Mottram called them 'Flies of the Future' – how right! Take note: the first No-Hackles intended to float were English, not North American. Having said my patriotic piece, the Gold-Ribbed Hare's Ear, for all its magnificent success, is a one-off dressing and not a system pattern conceived out of observation and experiment. I suspect it simply 'happened' or evolved. Mottram was the prophet, but Swisher and Richards inaugurated the good news and devised a whole new generation of dry flies.

Their patterns are devised specifically for selective trout when the 'standard' design of fly fails to pass a hypercritical inspection. What is required is a 'realistic imitation'. Swisher and Richards feel that trout selectivity increases as the size of natural flies decreases. There are far more tiny upwinged species in North America than in Britain but this generalisation also relates to other aquatic species of fly which are on the water in far greater numbers than the larger species.

They started off at this point:

Many of the standard dressings are so ridiculous that we fishermen, thirty feet away, could easily see our artificial stand out like a sore thumb as it drifted with a group of naturals. Most of you have no doubt had this experience. But *stop and think*: if *you* can tell the difference thirty feet away, the trout three inches away must be having hysterics.'

Of course Swisher and Richards are right; I often chuckle to myself at the sight of my imitation alongside a handful of naturals. But the last laugh isn't always on the trout. Despite their glaring shortcomings when viewed from above through a perfect medium, air, my 'standard' patterns when viewed from below through the air–water interface convince most trout most of the time. But Swisher and Richards are attempting the impossible: to rise all trout all of the time. Even though our 'standard' flies work 95 per cent of the time those selective trout that have the time, the surface conditions and the inclination to nit-pick reject the 'standard' fly for a closer imitation. Swisher and Richards offer the No-Hackle flies as their solution.

They developed their patterns after an exhaustive study of natural as well as artificial flies on the water and in their impressive aquaria. Their studies concluded that the legs of the natural 'play a very insignificant role' in the outline of most upwinged duns. They believe the hackle on the artificial is a ridiculous imitation of the legs of a natural dun. Most hackles are far too bushy and obscure a good view of the body and wings and so become the dominant feature of the artificial, instead of, as in the natural, an insignificant feature. They believe that the overall shape and size as embodied in the wings and body are the trigger features in both natural and artificial and they declared the resulting No-Hackle fly to be far superior to any other dun imitations. Swisher and Richards strongly emphasised their discovery that flies tied with bodies of spun fur or certain dubbed synthetic fibres on 3X fine-wire hooks needed no hackle to float them. When treated with floatant the results were even better.

The salient aspects of the dressing are:

1. The tails are made from stiff cock hackle fibres which are spread very widely to ensure stability on the water. The spread of the fibres is achieved by tying in a small ball of dubbing just in front of the bend, then adding the tail fibres either side of the shank.
2. Natural fur was the original choice for the body material but now polypropylene-based materials are used. These have the advantage of being extremely light with a specific gravity of less than one. Poly yarn and Fly-Rite are easy to dub, translucent, durable and available in a wide range of suitable body colours. The fur is wound on to make the body, then wings are added and a further thorax in front of the wings of the same body fur completes the fly.
3. The original wings were of two matched slips of duck wing quills or small duck shoulder feathers, which are various shades of grey, in an upright V shape, or a single upright bunch of hackle fibres. The duck-wing-quill patterns soon earned the name Sidewinders and are known as this to differentiate between a number of subsequent No-Hackle variations. Other wings include hen hackle tips, shoulder or body feathers. Swisher and Richards believe that cock hackle tips are too narrow to represent the natural's broad wings. Poly II is an excellent winging material as it offers translucency, lightness and a range of colours. In their second book, *Fly Fishing Strategy* (1975), the authors offered a number of variations, one of which is the Double-Wing No-Hackle Sidewinder, which incorporates two sets of wings, the second being a smaller wing quill to represent the hindwings of the natural dun. In addition to being a closer imitation the extra wings help balance the fly. The wing sections may be sprayed with artist's fixative before being tied in. This keeps the fibres together and makes them easier to work with.

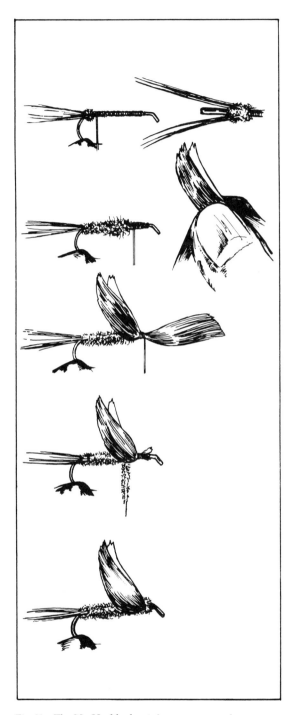

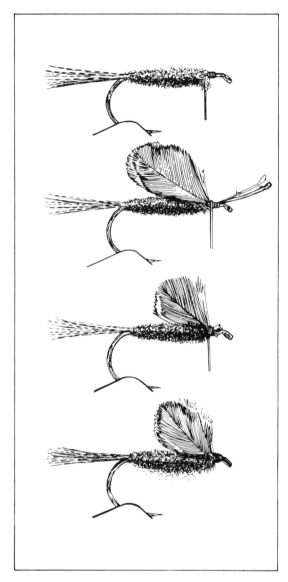

Fig 41 The No-Hackle dun tying sequence using matched sections from a duck's wing feather.

Fig 42 The No-Hackle dun using duck shoulder feather wings.

No-Hackle dun in the mirror. The body rests
unnaturally in the film.

Swisher and Richards's rejection of any
attempt to copy the light pattern created by
the legs of the natural dun is the complete
antithesis of most other authorities. In a
stroke they relegated the imitation of the
natural's legs to insignificance and the light
pattern they create to irrelevance. They maintain that the wings and body are the essential
triggers to the rise. Selective trout need no
light pattern as an initial stimulus.

But does the light pattern play any role in
stimulating a surface-feeding trout? Can the
body unsupported on the surface adequately
represent the natural dun, particularly in the
eyes of *selective* trout? Why should a very
selective trout be satisfied with an accurate
representation of body and wing but miss the
glaring illogic of the body on or in the surface
film? Have fly fishers of the last hundred
years got it wrong or have the selective trout
of Swisher and Richards been rising for the

wrong reasons?

When it comes to representing a natural
dun of average size and larger (hook size 16
upwards), I personally feel that Goddard and
Clarke have produced an imitation that looks
more natural from the trout's point of view. I
have used both types of fly on relatively easy
trout and on selective fish, on both freestone
and chalk streams. I have no hesitation in
confirming that I have found the USD Paraduns far more effective than the No-Hackle
Sidewinders. I am sure the main problem has
been the totally unnatural body on the surface and the absence of a light pattern from
the legs. I have caught many trout on the
No-Hackle flies but the reason for their success is not as Swisher and Richards would
have me believe. I suggest that any artificial
that floats with its body and tails on or in the
surface film is representing a struggling dun,
stillborn or emerger trapped in the film, or
possibly a spinner with its wings in the semi-
spent position. Either of these alternatives
offers an easy mouthful for a trout. There is
no chance of the fly escaping, so why let it
pass by? The fish might be being selective but
the trapped fly is too easy to miss. That, in
my opinion, is the principal reason why
medium and larger No-Hackles work; but for
trout rising to medium-sized duns and proving very hard to deceive, the USD Paraduns
offer a better prospect of success because
they are, at the moment, the closest the fly
fisher can come to representing the natural
dun from the trout's point of view.

However, when trout are rising to minu-
tiae, dimpling on a flat calm river surface,
the No-Hackles can be just the answer to
the problem, when trout seem prepared to
ignore the absence of a light pattern. Perhaps
the light pattern is an insignificant feature
with the tiny natural fly. The stimulus seems
to be the clear view of the body and wings
unobscured by a hackle. The No-Hackles
work well for many trout for the reasons I
have offered, but when confronted with
selective trout the No-Hackles have worked
best in size 16 and smaller when standard
and alternative styles have failed.

Other No-Hackle flies can be found in the

No-Hackle dun resting on the surface.

sections dealing with spinner variations on page 166 and with emerging patterns on page 171.

Comparaduns

Al Caucci and Bob Nastasi produced the Comparadun system of flies (Fig 43) as their closest imitation of the natural dun. This durable pattern is a refinement of the old, rough-water Haystack. The dressing is a No-Hackle fly which comprise a 180° wing of deer's face hair, a body, a thorax in front of the wing of dubbed natural fur, and two widely spaced sparse bunches of stiff hackle or deer hair fibres as tails. The wing is tied in before the body by winding a couple of turns of tying silk round the butts of a bunch of hair and pulling tightly so that the hair flares in a semi-circle. This is secured tightly and the wing fibres bound in an upright position. The authors felt that the wing offered a distinctive silhouette and that its breadth simulated the flapping of the natural's wings before or on the point of take-off. The fly floats very well

and, in my experience, always lands correctly on the water. However, it produces no accurate light pattern and the body rests on the surface very much as a spinner would. Of course the Comparaduns catch trout – even a cigarette end when cast to the right fish at the right time will get a rise. I suspect that the success of the pattern is due to the fact that most trout do not demand a precise imitation of the natural; some are happy to rise to a fly that resembles food. Others are more discerning and need either or both a resemblance of the light pattern and wings. The Comparadun offers a very good wing and body impression but a poor representation of the legs and their light pattern.

Funnelduns

The Funnelduns were devised by Kennet fly fisher Neil Patterson. He recognised the value of the upside-down hook in Goddard and Clarke's USD Paraduns but wanted something easier to tie. He certainly achieved that and other advantages over the 'standard'

Fig 43   Tying the Comparaduns.

Two views of one comparadun on the surface. The upper is viewed on the mirror; the lower through the window. Just one fly is in the photograph; the two images are the result of refraction and the view being through the side and base of an aquarium.

dry fly. The hackle is wound as a 360° collar about a third of the way back from the eye. The fibres are then 'funnelled' forwards over the eye at about 45°. A body of dubbed fur with a thorax between the base of the hackle and the eye is wound on prior to funnelling. Hackle-fibre tails are tied in just a little way round the bend, a dubbed body is added and the tying thread is finished off at the tail. If wings are required, Neil Patterson suggests a bunch of feather fibres tied upright. A V of hackle is cut away on the upper side, which will become the underside when fished. The hackles are longer than normal and because

they are at an angle to the water they do not need to be the stiff top-quality hackles normally sought after. Very ordinary cock hackles can be used. The length for a size 14 hook is a hackle normally used in a size 8 or 10. This means that parts of a cape that would often remain untouched now have a value. Because of the way in which the funnelled hackles make the fly appear longer than a 'standard' fly on the same hook, Neil Patterson advocates using hooks a size smaller than you would normally – for example, if you want a size 14, tie a Funneldun on a number 16 hook.

The side view of a Comparadun on the surface.

The Funnelduns do have aspects in their favour. They hide the hook-point from a trout's view; the wings (if incorporated) and thorax are clearly seen through the cut-away hackle; although the rear of the body rests on the surface an adequate light pattern from the hackle is achieved, but one should be careful that the hackle fibres do not lie too horizontally and create streaks of light rather than the more natural dimples. For all the common sense and ingenuity behind the design, Funnelduns are used by very few dry-fly anglers.

Fore-and-Aft

Another Kennet fly fisher, but of two generations earlier, Horace Brown, is credited with the idea of tying in a second hackle at the rear of the body of the usually wingless 'standard' fly. The benefits are that the body is supported away from the surface and if both hackles are sparsely wound an acceptable light pattern is achieved. It is also a useful design on which to base the imitation of a pair of mating midges or gnats. An all-black fly with two black hackles is sufficiently suggestive of a number of mating species to be successful throughout the summer.

Reverse Hackles

One of the earliest attempts to prevent the hook-point from penetrating the surface and to hide it from a trout's view was to tie in the hackle at the other end of the shank, so reversing the dressing. The hackle is carefully wound to obscure the hook point and to support it above the surface. The tails are tied in over the eye. I have fished with a number of these dressings with modest, but not unusual success. The principal benefit in practice with this design is that they are less easy to foul up on trees and foliage. I fish a couple

163

of heavily overgrown streams and these flies are ideal. They are also admirably suited to fish rising immediately under the far bank. The fly is cast on to the bank grasses and gently twitched off on to the water. There is much less chance of becoming fouled up.

I am aware of the complaint that hooking is more of a problem but I have not found this to be so. I ought to add that I have not fished this style of fly to trout which when rising are barely breaking the surface. These sip rises may make hooking more difficult. One minor irritation in the dressing is that because the tail fibres are tied on top of the shank invariably the rear of the body touches the surface. One way round this which keeps all the body above the water is to tie in stiff hackle fibres or hair fibres on the underside of the shank which will much better support the body. I am aware that the tails of the natural do not touch the water but this is the lesser of two evils and does improve the fly by keeping the body in the air.

Loopwings

This winging style was conceived by San Franciscan fly fisher, André Puyans, in, I believe, the late 1960s. The wings are easy to tie and are of materials normally thrown away, so it scores on two counts before it hits the water. The design is usually with the smaller sizes of fly – I suggest size 14 and below (Fig 44). Six fibres of brown or grey mallard flank or shoulder feather are selected. These should be long enough to form the tails and be looped into a wing shape. They are tied in on top of the shank with the right length showing for the tail. The remainder are doubled over into a loop the size and approximate shape of the wing, and tied in the upright position. The wing is divided in half a dubbing or other needle and bound as two very slightly parted wings. The required body and hackle are added in the usual way. A parachute hackle could be wound round the base of the wing. The wing

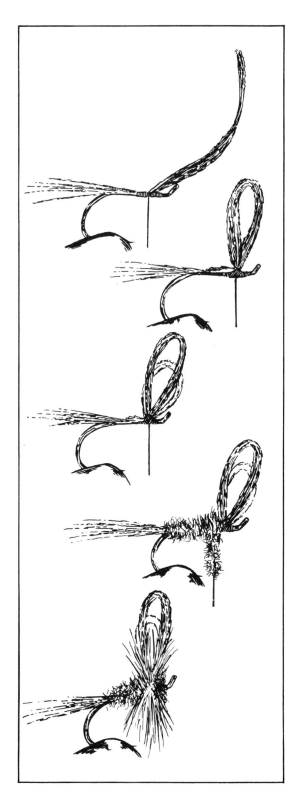

Fig 44   Tying the Loopwing.

materials need not be those suggested above but any colour feather. Often trout simply need the sight of a wing representation before rising and I am convinced that the loopwings offer just such a general impression. This wing outline of an appropriate colour would seem to satisfy all but the most pernickety of fish.

Detached Bodies

A number of fly fishers decry the need to represent the abdomen of the natural fly. Some of those who believe in its importance have devised detached bodies, which are in most instances an appendage to the hook pointing slightly skywards in the manner of the natural dun. Such additions have been added for at least a century. For the most part these appendages are based upon wire, thick nylon monofilament or cork, around which the body materials are wound. Others are of feather fibres or specially made translucent plastic bodies. I confess that for the most part I have found the detached-body patterns of very little value; certainly they have been no better than 'standard' flies. The possible exception to this is on Mayfly or Green Drake patterns, when a larger body is required.

Cul de Canard

No fly tying material has influenced dry-fly design over the last decade as much as the feathers from a duck's preen gland. Although they have been used in parts of Europe for a century it was not until their revival in the 1980s that they achieved a very much wider following. In a short space of time duns and emerger patterns using CDC feathers were being fished throughout the world. The advantages of the feathers are threefold: the oil produced by the ducks makes them highly water repellent; each feather fibre has hundreds of barbules, which makes the fly very buoyant; their appearance from below is highly suggestive of a number of the fly's features – it could be wings, body, legs, or just a blur of them all. They can also be dyed easily for more specific imitation.

Perhaps the source of most modern patterns lies in the simple F Fly devised by Marjan Fratnik and based on earlier imitations. A body of tying thread or a light dubbing is given a wing of one or two CDC feathers. This extremely easy-to-tie pattern is also highly successful.

Which design of upwinged imitation works best on fussy fish will always be a matter of personal opinion. Poll some of the best American fly fishermen on the subject, all of whom cover very selective wild trout on spring creeks, and they make different choices: Bob Jacklin, Parachute; Mike Lawson, No-Hackle; John Mackey, Comparadun; Eric Peper, Thorax Dun; René Harrop, Cul de Canard dun. In Britain John Goddard might go for the USD Paradun; many others would go for shoulder-hackled standards. No fly fisher has an ulterior motive for picking these flies, they just catch more fish for the individuals concerned.

REPRESENTING THE SPINNER

Only for a very short time does the female spinner of most species have its wings erect and at no time does it have all its body clear of the surface. Spinners paying fleeting visits to the surface to deposit eggs attract little trout attention; it is as they lie spent, struggling or trapped in the surface film, that they are easy and enticing targets.

The most obvious aspect to a trout is that the spinner's body lies on or in the surface film, yet so many 'standard' spinner dressings have a fully wound hackle supporting the body above the water. These 'standard' spinner patterns are little more than dun imitations in the appropriate colours with spent instead of upright wings. They take trout because the artificial bears a resemblance to a natural fly and the trout is hungry and into the feeding rhythm and not fussy, and because it is a reasonable imitation of the spinner in the shorter and less attractive period before it is fully spent. The natural spent spinner has its tails, body, wings and legs all flush with the surface. There is no light pattern from the legs and the fly breaks through the film and is clearly seen in the mirror and window. The required imitation is hardly 'dry' in the strictest sense of the word and that is one of the reasons why purists of a narrower code declined to fish it. It does float and is not, so far as this book is concerned, presented below the surface, and thus falls within our consideration.

I would suggest that the following are the key features of the trout's view of the spent spinner and intrinsic components of the artificial:

1. The size and colour of the abdomen and thorax. In a number of species after ovipositing the abdomen is drained of much of the colour and becomes translucent.
2. The wing silhouette and the possible light pattern from the wings as light passes through them.
3. The widely-spaced tails are of minor significance to the trout but are a useful stabilising aid to the fly tyer.

Although, of course, the legs are present, they are of minimal significance and need not be represented. The first two aspects are important and their imitation should be the prime objective.

It should also be remembered that because many of the species do not return to the water until late evening and dusk the effects of the low sun and the dimmer back-light will reduce the effects of the translucency of the abdomen and to a minor extent the completely transparent wings. In low light bodies made from stripped quill or other opaque materials become more acceptable as the translucency of the natural's abdomen is diminished. This will not be true of spinners returning when it is still quite light.

It has been the dun imitation that has attracted most attention from fly tyers looking for improvements to the 'standard' patterns. This is no doubt directly proportional to the amount of time spent fishing duns rather than spinners, which are much more restricted in their appearance. Some of the

more useful, and effective, spinner modifications are detailed below.

No-Hackle Spinners

A number of unhackled spinner styles have been devised, many of which are very similar to the series tied by Doug Swisher and Carl Richards. The spinner equivalents to the Swisher and Richards No-Hackle duns are much more accurate representations of what a trout sees of the fly than their dun imitations. In my view their dun patterns did not meet all the criteria for providing the most natural imitation of the medium and larger duns. However, the No-Hackle spinners are much nearer to what the trout expects to see of the natural spinner. They applied the same basic principles to their spinner imitations

Fig 45   No-Hackle spinner: the hackle-point spent-wing version.

Hen wing spinner.

No-Hackle spinner with light partridge wings.

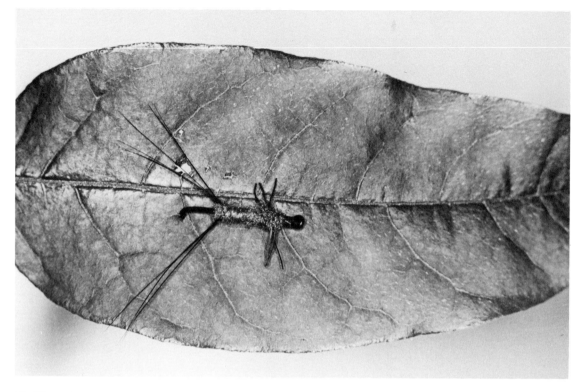

No-Wing spinner.

but this time the results are more natural because the legs of the spinners are insignificant. They have produced four basic types, all of which have dubbed fur, Poly yarn or Fly Rite bodies and widely spaced long-fibred tails separated by a small ball of dubbed body fibres. There is also a small thorax of the body fibres in front of the wings. The first two versions may be tied fully or semi-spent. In each case Swisher and Richards recommend that the surplus wing fibres are clipped, not stripped.

1. The hackle-point spent-wing version (Fig 45) incorporates wide, webby hen wings. They experimented with bunches of hackle fibres and synthetic poly wings but did not believe them to be as effective. Overall they find this No-Hackle spinner variation to be their most successful. Duck wing quill segments are also used for wings and extended-body versions are tied to represent some larger species.

2. The second version is with wings of light partridge breast feathers tied concave side down. The success of these wings is due to the fact that when wet they become very nearly transparent and their speckled appearance gives a fair impression of the heavily veined wings of many species.

3. This is not actually a No-Hackle fly at all, merely Swisher and Richards's version of the 'standard' spinner. No wings are tied but a fully wound hackle is used to represent the newly alighted spinner. Alternatively, the hackle can be trimmed and bound with the tying silk to represent the fully or semi-spent wings.

4. The final variation is truly original and arose when Swisher and Richards came to consider that the near-transparent wings of some spinners will appear invisible from a trout's viewpoint under conditions of low light. A very dull grey-blue sky would render

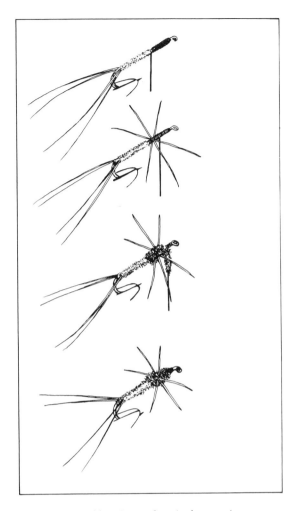

Fig 46   No-Hackle spinner: the wingless version.

stripped hackle stalks or deer hair. The thorax is of the same material as the abdomen but a shade darker. The only problem in fishing the No-Wing spinner in low light is that it is extremely difficult to see – so much so that one has to guestimate the position of the fly and hope that the rise you've just seen is to your fly and strike in hope. The No-Wing and No-Hackle spinners must be well soaked in floatant.

The Clear-Winged Spinner

In 1973 Gary LaFontaine introduced Antron, also known as Sparkle Yarn, to fly-tying. Originally its use in fly-tying was confined to caddis pupae and submerged, egg-laying caddis females. With the yarn filaments both translucent and reflective they accurately represented the air bubbles carried within a translucent sheath on the natural pupa. An additional benefit was that Antron fibres on the surface gather and hold real air bubbles, accentuating the realism.

Antron is also very suitable in the imitation of the spent wings of spinners. All natural spinner wings are translucent and the semi-opaque hackle fibres, feathers and poly-propylene fall well short of an ideal imitation. Another problem is that spinner wings are invariably pleated, not smooth, and those pleats collect tiny air bubbles – so do the Antron filaments. The use of *clear* bunched Antron fibres for the spent wings takes imitation a step closer. The style can be adapted for any upwinged species.

USD Poly-Spinners

From the enquiring minds and the fly vices of Goddard and Clarke come their own interpretation of the best spent spinner imitation (Fig 47). They have broken away from tradition and used upside-down keel hooks or Partridge upside-down hooks in combination with a parachute hackle. The latter is an aspect which I have long maintained is an excellent aid in producing a spinner pattern when the hackle is tied on top of the body, allowing the body to rest on or in the surface

the clear wings of some species invisible; why then try to imitate something that cannot be seen? I suspect that this is true for fish a few feet below the spinners, but that when viewed from a close distance the wings will be visible. (John Goddard and Brian Clarke observed a different phenomenon when spinners are viewed from below at dusk. *See* the Sunset Spinner on page 214). In addition to the body and widely spread tails, the only concession to further imitation is the addition of three legs either side of the body on the larger patterns (Fig 46). This is as much an aid to balance as it is to imitation. The legs are represented by stiff cock hackle fibres,

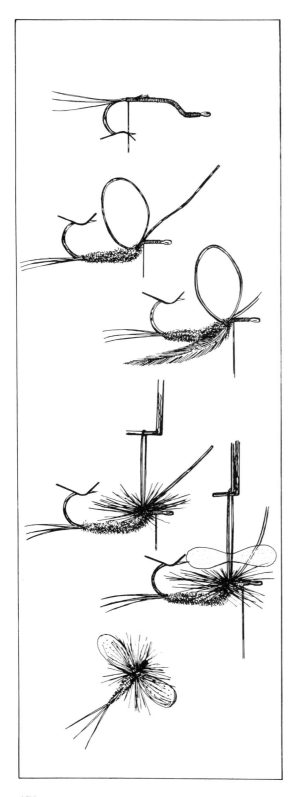

film. Although the parachute hackle represents the legs, this is a minor role; its primary function is to keep the fly afloat and hold the body in the film. The shape of the keel or upside down hook ensures that the body is well down in the film. The third aspect is in some respects an advance on the more traditional winging materials. Goddard and Clarke opted for colourless, totally transparent polythene sheet cut to shape with wing cutters. If the polythene remained as it was the wings would be barely visible but the wings are lightly pierced with a thick but sharp needle. In this way only the tiniest hole is produced in the centre of a larger dimple in the polythene. The effect of this is to create a highly realistic light pattern imitating the heavily veined but transparent wings of the natural. The major drawback with the design is that the wings cause the flies to spin when casting. This may not be a problem on hooks size 14 and smaller, but on larger patterns hackle-point wings are needed.

The method of tying the basic design is as follows. There are other methods of securing a parachute hackle but in this instance a gallows tool is used to support the loop of nylon monofilament used to secure the wings. Tie in two or three mink whiskers for the tail, well spaced and held in position by a dab of varnish. Reverse the hook in the vice. Wind on the body of natural fur to a point where the shank begins to rise. Tie in a loop of nylon half way up the slope and add a little more body fur. Tie in a hackle by the butt round the base of the loop and wind it round the loop now supported by the gallows tool. After winding between two and five turns the tip of the hackle is passed through the loop and held securely until the pre-prepared wings are passed through the loop. The nylon is then pulled tight and the wings can be bound tighter with figure-of-eight turns of tying silk carefully taken through the hackle fibres. Appropriately coloured body materials, tails and hackle can be selected to match various naturals. The USD poly-spinner style

Fig 47   The USD Poly-spinners. See text for tying instructions.

of dressing can be adapted to 'standard' spinner pattern.

REPRESENTING THE EMERGERS AND STILLBORNS

I have already suggested that more trout than we would care to admit actually take many of the 'standard' flies with their tails under the surface, or the waterlogged artificials half submerged, as emerging duns. This failure to represent the floating dun in either dressing or presentation is compensated for because, inadvertently, some other stage of the life-cycle is imitated. In the absence of patterns tied specifically to represent the emergers a quite adequate solution is to fish with the tails and rear of the body below the surface supported by the hackle fibres alone. This is particularly effective when a pattern with an advance wing is used. The wing points vertically in the manner of the newly erected wing of the natural and the body and tails are submerged in the film. Also, I have long thought that one of the reasons for the success of the parachute fly with the body supported in the film by the hackle is that it is likely taken by trout for a floating nymph, stillborn or emerger, and not, as we would like to think, for an adult dun. More enterprising fly tyers have offered the solutions detailed below. In 1963, V. S. Hidy gave his emerging patterns the appropriate name 'Flymphs'. As Hidy's patterns are fished below the surface (albeit only just), they do not fall within the scope of this volume.

Lawrie's Hatching Dun

One of the most prolific but undervalued British angling writers of this century, W. H. Lawrie, devised a system pattern for the hatching dun which can be adapted for any upwinged species. The tail fibres are soft hen fibres; the abdomen and thorax are of natural fur, with the thorax more pronounced. The wings and legs are represented by two different trimmed hackles. The wing hackle should be of the natural's wing colour,

wound on with the lower fibres trimmed level with the shank. The leg hackle should be the approximate colour of the legs or underside of the thorax, and the upper fibres are cut away level with the shank. The fly is fished so that the tail and abdomen sink into the film while the hackles and thorax should be on or above the surface.

Jardine's Emerger

This emerger pattern from Charles Jardine should be fished low on the surface, as though trapped in the film. Appropriate body colours should be selected to match the naturals. Fine-wire down-eye hooks are used. The example illustrated in the colour section has tails of three lemon wood-duck fibres, and the body and abdomen is a dubbed mixture of rabbit and mole's fur. Other suitably coloured materials could be used for different naturals. The emerging wings are two grey mallard slips tied in short and rear-facing on either side of the body at the rear of the thorax. The hackle is lemon wood-duck tied on either side of the thorax.

Swisher and Richards Emergers

Although the stillborns and emergers are listed separately because they represent two different stages – the stillborns are dead and either trapped in the film or floating on the surface; the emergers are still struggling to leave their skins and break through the film – the dressings for both are interchangeable, so fine is the dividing line and the differences between the two.

Swisher and Richards devised a number of emerging patterns, some of which are designed to be fished deep or just below the surface. The ones included here are those suitable for fishing as floaters – what the designers call 'dry emergers'. The colour of the materials should be chosen to match the relevant natural. Extra-fine-wire hooks are used as an aid to floating. Widely spaced cock hackle fibres (tied as for the No-Hackle dun) or a single bunch of feather fibres are tied for the tails. The body is of dubbed natural fur or

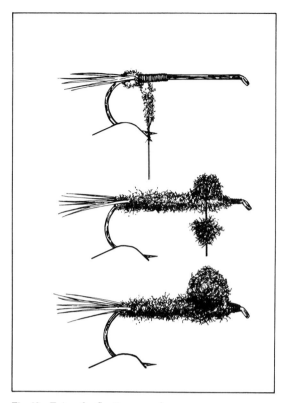

Fig 48   Tying the floating nymph.

from Richard Walker. It was a pattern intended to be fished just below the surface and therefore comes, like Hidy's Flymphs, into the wet category, but I have had some success with the pattern tied in polypropylene materials soaked well in floatant and tied on fine-wire hooks so that they float. An additional aid is to have tails of widely spaced cock hackle fibres with a small ball of body fibres holding them in position. The only snag is that once a fish has been caught on a fly I have the greatest difficulty in getting it to float again until it has fully dried out. Walker's dressing is a nymph pattern which includes a bunch of cock hackle fibres (polypropylene yarn might be a better substitute) to emerge from the top of the thorax. The fibres are tied vertically, and the wing-case material is divided either side of the wing fibres. The colour of the yarn or hackle should match the wing-colour of the natural.

Swisher and Richards are so convinced of the value of the floating nymph that they write in *Fly Fishing Strategy*: 'One of the most universally devastating methods of fishing the rise is with a *high floating nymph*, exactly like a dry fly. We have found in the last few years (by the use of a stomach pump) that more nymphs are taken dry than are winged duns during a hatch.' This is a radical claim indeed, and whilst I would be the first to acknowledge that trout do take floating nymphs and that their imitation is at times, of value, I have never been aware of trout taking more floating nymphs than duns. They offer as their dressing a variation on their familiar theme of a fine-wire hook, widely spaced cock-hackle-fibre tails and a dubbed fur or Fly Rite abdomen. The thorax is the same material of a different colour to match the natural's thorax colour. This is carefully dubbed on in a small amount, exaggerating the thorax only on the upper side of the shank (Fig 48). One option is to include wing-cases of quill segments, feather fibres, or strands of Poly II. No wings or legs are incorporated but if the latter are desired these should be the same as the tail fibres, tied to stick out horizontally to aid floating.

Charles Jardine has produced an interest-

polypropylene-based Fly Rite. The wings are tied in the Sidewinder No-Hackle dun style and made from short feather fibres or short duck quill segments. According to Swisher and Richards, the key to the pattern's success is keeping the wings short, three-quarters of the body length at the most. Other variations are concerned mainly with alternative winging materials and the addition of legs. According to the pattern's creators, hackle tips are a viable alternative wing, although they are prone to collapse when wet. (So what? What's left is a pretty good imitation of a stillborn with wings that have failed to erect.) Legs are represented by a few soft partridge breast or wood duck fibres tied in at the head.

Floating Nymphs

This suggestion for a hatching nymph came

ing floating nymph combining the attributes of the exaggerated thorax with a parachute hackle on top of the body but under the thorax. The body is held in the film by the hackle but the thorax remains above the surface. This is a highly attractive pattern indeed. My stream trials of this have been embarrassingly short because the pattern is new and only came into my hands a few weeks before completion of this book. However, on the three occasions I have used the style of dressing I caught about a dozen fish. I very much doubt whether any of those trout had been concentrating on floating nymphs; some were taking duns, others just were not surface-feeding, but they took this pattern. A trout eyeing it in the film sees something that isn't suddenly going to take to the air. Trout nymphing just below the surface often respond to a floating nymph, the silhouette being the trigger, and this pattern is likely to succeed in such a situation.

The example described here and illustrated in the colour section is suitable as a large dark olive or blue-winged olive imitation. Materials of different colours should be used for other species. The tails are wood duck fibres. The body, which is started slightly round the bend of the shank and tapers from the rear, is the Orvis Antron/hair mix (dark olive). The rib is a few fibres of white synthetic parcel string. This unusual material appears to be quite translucent. The thorax is a ball of dubbed Poly II (Adam's grey), around the base of which is wound a golden olive cock hackle.

Stillborns

The bigger the hatch, the more likely stillborns will be the target of feeding fish. One overcast mild September day on the River Costa, a tiny Yorkshire chalk stream, I encountered a half-hour multiple hatch of sedges, midges and at least three upwinged species. In addition, the surface seemed littered with small black terrestrial flies. Trout

Fig 49 A Swisher and Richards No-Hackle stillborn with a reversed cock hackle to represent the trailing shuck.

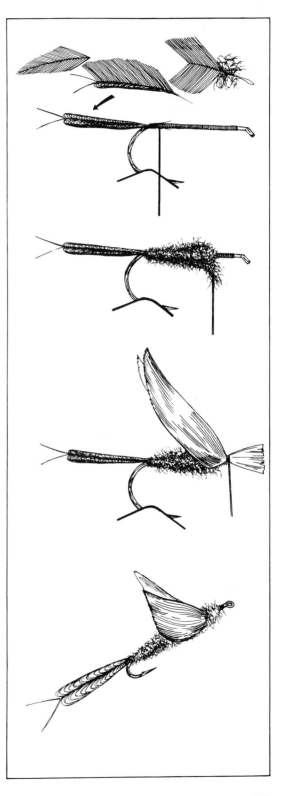

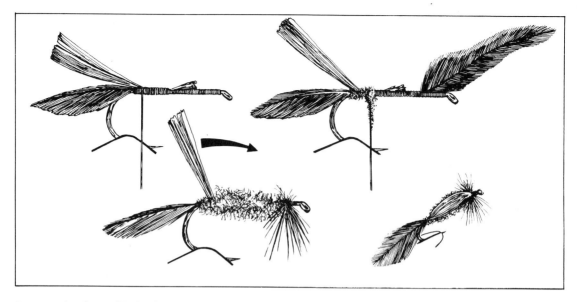

Fig 50   A Swisher and Richards stillborn (trapped wings).

surface-fed throughout the stream and I rose one or two on a tiny pale sedge. A closer examination of the water showed that a high percentage of the very pale upwingeds had failed to erect their wings or were even trapped like spinners with one wing in the spent position. It became clear that most trout were rising to these trapped stillborns in preference to anything else. Here was one food source that wasn't going to escape and trout were making the most of it. I was ill-equipped for the situation but after trimming flat the hackle in line with the body on a Goddard's Last Hope it passed as a makeshift stillborn. For twenty minutes those Costa trout loved it.

The stillborn dressings below are intended as upwinged representations but in the appropriate sizes and materials they are acceptable emerging midge and caddis floaters for river or stillwater use.

Swisher and Richards suggest two basic types, some with wings erect and others wingless to imitate the stillborn with trapped, non-erected wings. Both patterns have a tail appendage to represent the trailing shuck, which is often still attached to the natural stillborn duns, midges and caddis. The desig-

ners of the flies recommend hen hackle tips and Poly II fibres as the best and easiest to obtain for the shuck imitation, although they also experimented with – and found acceptable – body feathers, hair, plastic films and assorted feather and hackle fibres, including a process they call 'reverse-pulled feathers' which is time-consuming but realistic (Fig 49). This is made by taking the centre portion of a hackle feather. All except the top few fibres are pulled back on themselves (reversed) and tied in this position at the rear of the shank. The untouched top fibres should remain in a trailing V shape. The dubbed fur or polypropylene dubbing body is added, making a body and thorax exactly like the No-Hackle Sidewinders. Now the two basic designs differ. The first with upright wings is tied as for the No-Hackle duns with short rear-sloping duck primary wing segments. The second type (Fig 50) is tied with or without upright wings but with a leg imitation of a stiff short-fibred cock hackle wound in the conventional manner with the upper fibres clipped off. The non-erected wing is represented by a section of a feather fibres or wing quill to match the natural's wing colour. This should be tied in at the rear of the body

Swisher and Richards trapped-wing stillborn with trailing shuck.

before dubbing the body material, and brought forward over the back and tied in behind the eye.

I don't pretend to understand the purpose of this flattened wing since it must be all but impossible to see from a trout's angle of view. Swisher and Richards have found the need for the two designs because, although the upright-winged versions are fine, some still-borns without wings ride the current at an angle with the thorax supported higher by the legs.

Trailing Shucks

As well as the stillborn designs mentioned above, other patterns incorporate the empty nymphal skin hanging from the rear of the dun's abdomen. Today we go out of our way to ensure an accurate representation with specialist materials such as Z-lon and stocking mesh, but before this more specific imitation the feather-fibre bunched tail did exactly the same thing.

SEDGE DESIGNS

Sedge design has been much neglected until really only the last twenty years, when more thought has been given to why trout exercise selectivity over the naturals and how those problems can be overcome in fly design.

Most sedge designs were originally based on the palmer-style flies with or without the low-slung roof-shaped wings. One of my favourite patterns, Skues's Little Red Sedge, is typical of many of this design. Many artificials are well hackled and bushy and float high on the water. Those that do not have palmered bodies have many turns of hackle or more than one hackle at the shoulder wound over the wing roots. These are fine under some circumstances and are easy to twitch or skitter on the surface. Any breeze also gives the fly some movement. However, the failure of these patterns sometimes may be put down to the fact that they look as though they will leave the surface at any moment and this might be enough to deter a trout conserving its energy for a more certain mouthful. What might be required is a low-floating pattern which rests with its body on the surface or with its body below the surface

175

supported by a buoyant wing material. One simple design has a natural or synthetic fur body with a single wing of bunched polypropylene yarn. These offer excellent profiles of the ovipositing females.

One of the most significant features of the trout's view of the floating caddis is its light pattern, especially in the case of the active insect rather than one in a static drift. The drawback with most floating imitations is that they appear either as a high-floating pattern held aloft by generous turns of hackle or as a low floater in the film. Until fairly recently no one had come up with an imitation that could represent both types. No one, that is, until Gary LaFontaine. In *Caddisflies* (1981) Gary came up with his Dancing Caddis (*see* Fig 54), which can be fished to represent a wide variety of sedge species and their different positions on the surface and their behaviour. He incorporated into the dressing features to take into account the silhouette and in particular the lateral spread of the wings, which is a feature he discovered to be keyed on by selective trout. The other features are the twin streaks of light created by the wing edges of a skating sedge, the light pattern from the legs, and the insect body for those naturals in the film. As if all this was not enough Gary was aware that the hook-bend below the surface was a pretty good anchor and inhibited the flush fly from skating. The answer was to tie the dressing on an upside-down hook and he finally opted for the Swedish Dry Fly Hook.

To quote Gary LaFontaine: 'The new fly proved very effective with both dead-drift and twitch presentations, eliminating most of the frustrating refusals by choosy trout. In specific instances it worked as well as flush imitations on fish that were feeding selectively on passive females, and it also worked as well as high-riding imitations on fish that were feeding selectively on active females.'

On the creator's own admission the pattern is not a cure-all. Sometimes a much lower-floating pattern or a high-riser rocking on its hackle tips is required; then a more specific imitation is needed. 'The Dancing Caddis, however, is certainly a very consistent all-round producer for selective trout.' The dressing is given in the Sedge section of Chapter 9. The size and colours can be varied to suit the natural on the water.

The Delta-Wing Caddis was devised by Larry Solomon, co-author of *The Caddis and the Angler*. It was the first pattern to specifically represent the low-lying spent or dead females in the film. The delta shape of the spread wings is a key feature for trout feeding on these naturals. The dressing is given in Chapter 9.

The hairwing sedge such as the Elk-Hair Caddis has a natural or synthetic fur body, usually with a palmered short-fibred hackle and a wing of natural hair. Hollow deer hair is suitable for larger patterns and deer face hair for smaller flies. The wing fibres may be pulled down either side of the shank so that the upper half of the shank is masked by the wing.

Most sedge wings follow the example of the natural's roof-shape over the body. One low-floating variation is to use a flat wing in the following way. The appropriate colour of fur is dubbed on for the body and a hackle palmered along its length. All the upper fibres are cut off and the other three sides heavily trimmed. A flat wing of a previously prepared hackle, which is trimmed to an elongated V shape, is tied flat across the back.

At one time dry sedge designs would include only the adult imitations. Now floating pupa imitations are used and are classified as dry flies. Those that I fish are very damp, half within the film, yet floating and visible. I shall mention two designs that I have some experience of. The first is the Superpupa of Scandinavian origins, which I came across in Swedish Lapland where the sedge hatches are extremely important. The pupae in the film were consumed in far greater numbers than the adult sedges. The design is extremely simple: a hackle is palmered along a thorax and abdomen of poly dubbing in two colours. The upper and lower fibres are trimmed away and the imitation lies flush in the film. The second floating pupa comes from the Austrian, Roman

Moser. Both dressings are described in Chapter 9.

HAIR AND FUR ALTERNATIVES

The first question should be: Why have an alternative to feathers? Have they not proved themselves over a century of successful use? The answers lie in the school of thought that contends that the best-quality animal hair is a far better material for making floating flies than even the highest-quality hackle feathers. The best-quality hackles are scarce and expensive, so why, even if the best hackles can be found and afforded, should one settle for only second best? While some adherents to the hair and fur alternatives might admit that, perhaps, the best cock capes could not be matched as the leg support for a dun, they would not concede that about the other 99 per cent of cock capes. Weak, second-rate hackles can be replaced by the excellent qualities of animal hair and fur. Dubbed bodies of hair and fur are commonplace; their qualities have been long renowned. It is replacing the hackle that is the greatest stumbling-block.

Animal hair, particularly that of amphibious mammals, is greatly superior to and more efficient than feathers in its water resistance and water-shedding properties. Unlike hackle fibres, hair fibres are hollow and therefore more buoyant – a desirable property for any material to be used in a floating fly. Hair or fur from an amphibious animal has natural oils to assist the shedding of water. When compared with a feather-hackled fly, both soaked in floatant, the hair and fur pattern is much easier to dry, needs less false casting, and does not absorb water to the same extent.

The strength of much hair and fur is greater than feather fibres, resulting in more support where the material is tied for that purpose, and greater durability. There are few things more frustrating than a trout-catching fly disintegrating; anything that prolongs the life of a fly is a bonus. Because the best hair is stronger than hackle fibre and sufficiently stiff, far fewer fibres are needed to offer the same support. Therefore the correct light pattern can be achieved without the overdressed appearance of many turns of hackle. Better support from fewer fibres means a much daintier, more delicate pattern, a nearer imitation of the frail newly hatched dun. This does not necessarily mean that the finished fly looks neater to the fly tyer – quite the opposite. Very often a high degree of scruffiness is achieved, and as any fisher knows it is the well chewed fly that rises the fish. The greatest problem is in trying to find the most suitable hair and fur of the right colour. Mink and weasel tails offer a wide variety of suitable colours and have a natural sparkle, useful for representing the natural wing, which is very hard and expensive to find in a cock hackle. There is of course no reason why the same materials cannot be used for caddis patterns, with appropriate hair for the wings.

In addition to the benefits of buoyancy and water shedding, hair and fur bodies have the additional attribute of offering a high degree of translucency, an aspect in the abdomen of the natural fly that will be apparent to trout under certain back-lit conditions. The skill in dubbing a fly body is to apply enough hair or fur so that the correct silhouette and reflected colour is achieved but little enough to enable the colour of the underlying tying silk to show through when back-lit or when wet with floatant. The body should be tapered, thickening and more densely wound towards the opaque thorax. Young seal's fur is one of the best natural materials for dubbing as it is bright and shiny, easily dyed, cheap and, at the moment, still obtainable.

Tying in the leg fibres is not as easy as simply winding on a hackle. The first task is to remove the excessively long fibres and underfur from the clump and manipulate the fibres so that the tips are approximately in line. One method of tying is to select the fibres and spread them evenly around the shank, pointing out over the eye. The butt ends are saturated with fixative or varnish, allowed to dry, and trimmed. At this stage the tail and body fur should be tied in. The projecting fibres are drawn back over the eye, ideally with a special looped tool, and bound at right angles to the shank. An upright wing or spent wings can be tied in bunches in a similar manner. For the spinner patterns no leg fibres are needed, merely two spent bunches of hair. A second method involves rolling the fibres round the hook shank as the tying thread (be sure it is a strong one) winds round. As the thread is tightened the fibre tips lift off the shank as legs.

FLUORESCENT MATERIALS

Fluorescent materials emit their own colour strongly in daylight. In ultraviolet light they become very bright and may be seen as a different colour from that in normal daylight conditions. Because the colours are vivid there may be a case for incorporating them in the imitation of those naturals that exhibit key colours – for example orange in the blue-winged olive, crimson in the iron blue. (The aspect of key colours in a natural is also considered on page 96.) Materials that fluoresce these colours could well make a fly more attractive than an ordinary dressing. I do not advocate tying the whole pattern with fluorescent materials but a judicial use of fluorescent tying silk dubbed sparsely, or a tip or rib, might be just enough to prove an extra stimulus. At dusk and dawn and in cloudy weather there is a much higher proportion of ultraviolet rays in the sun's light as other rays are filtered out, so fluorescent materials, particularly reds at dusk and

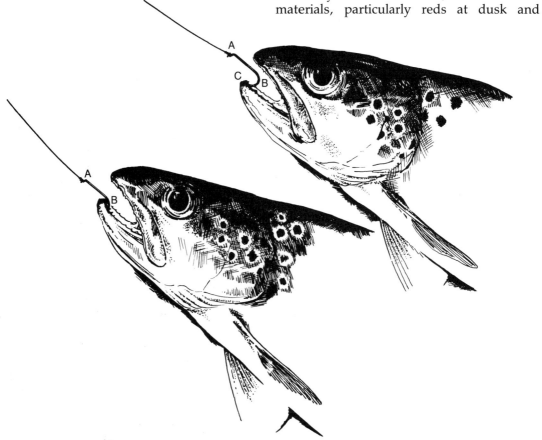

Fig 51 Hook strength is tested when the point does not penetrate fully. Because of the leverage pressure is exerted at point B, where the hook may weaken. If the hook penetrates fully there is much less leverage.

greens at dawn, show up well at these times. The consequences are clear for imitations of the red spinner – female olive spinners, which return to the water in the late evening. Neon-magenta is a useful dusk colour to incorporate in the iron blue dressing, which often includes a tip of red silk.

Fluorescent floss tails provide abundant colour, which the trout can see when viewing the floating fly from below. Fluorescent floss bodies give a varying silhouette density for the fish to view; fluorescent yellows, oranges, blues, reds and pinks all give a dark-grey-to-black silhouette, with Fire Orange giving the blackest. Long fluorescent floss tails on dry flies, because of the abundant colour they emit, can in fact be classed as bodies, thereby moving the hook-point to the middle of the fly and offering a more positive hooking position. I have not had a great deal of experience of using fluorescent materials in dry-fly patterns; nor, it seems, have many others. Britain's leading authority on fluorescents in fly dressing is probably Tom Saville and I am grateful for his advice in writing this section. He has had considerable success with fluorescent materials in all sorts of flies and feels that there is a great deal of scope for further experiment with their use in dry flies, particularly for dusk use.

HOOKS

Following the train of thought that suggests

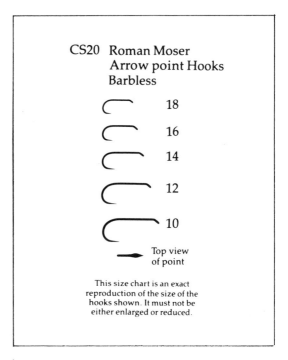

Fig 53   The Partridge Roman Moser Arrowpoint hooks CS20.

that the nearer an item of equipment is to the trout the more important it is, hook quality should be at the top of the list of priorities. Quality can be summed up as a strength-to-weight ratio (maximum strength for minimum weight), hook penetration and leverage. It would also simplify matters if hook manufacturers world-wide would standardise on sizes. At the moment the designation 'size 14' means absolutely nothing unless the manufacturer's blurb is studied to see what shank length and gape are offered. One maker's long-shank size 16 is another's standard-length size 12 with a narrow gape. Surely the millions of trout anglers across the world deserve better treatment. For this reason hook sizes in books of fly patterns and in Chapter 9 of this book serve as a guide only.

The strength of a hook is not very often fully tested by the weight of the fish in the course of most dry-fly fishing, unless you are fortunate enough to fish streams where real whoppers are ready risers. More likely the strength is tested because the hook has failed

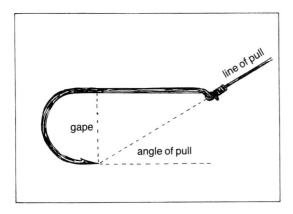

Fig 52   The angle of pull.

to penetrate the flesh and has only achieved a very shallow penetration on some hard part of the mouth. The weakest part of the hook is the top of the bend, which under pressure along the line A–C (Fig 51), and meeting resistance at C, may weaken and widen and allow the fish to escape. If the hook penetrates fully the pressure is along the line A–B and because there is little leverage there is only a slim chance of breaking the hook.

The weight of the hook is a critical factor in the ability of the dressed fly to float. The lighter the hook the better for floating. Unfortunately, the strength of a hook generally diminishes with decreasing weight. One of the best hooks is the Captain Hamilton Dry Fly range (Partridge). These are 4X fine wire, or 6X for the featherweight range, which are claimed to be the lightest on the market. I have not used the featherweight hooks but the 4X hooks have never let me down.

Effective hooking depends upon two factors: gape and shank length. The wider the gape the better the chances of pricking the trout's flesh as the mouth closes on the fly. Thereafter the ease of penetration of the hook is usually increased as the gape narrows. Much depends upon the ratio between the gape and shank length. (Shank length in these terms means effective shank length – the length in front of the hook-point, which is the only part of the shank to exert leverage.) Penetration improves as the angle of pull decreases (Fig 52), and the narrower the gape the more closely the point is aligned with the direction of pull. Imagine a very long-shanked lure hook and the direction of pull from the leader; penetration is easy because the long shank reduces the angle of pull. Imagine, again, a very short-shanked wide-gape dry-fly hook; the angle of pull is in-

creased and penetration is minimal. Penetration is increased by narrowing the gape or lengthening the shank. With the exception of small hooks which need a wide gape to ensure initial pricking, a ratio of effective shank to gape of about $1\frac{1}{2}:1$ is considered to be the ideal for most dry flies. But the longer shank needed for some longer-bodied flies gives even better penetration.

If hooking quality is determined by the angle of pull, this angle must be influenced by the angle of the eye and whether the hook is up-eyed or down-eyed. There has long been a tradition of tying dry flies with up-eyed hooks. However, penetration is marginally improved if a down-eyed hook is used as this reduces the angle of pull.

I will not enter the controversy as to whether barbless hooks should be used, save to comment that I have used de-barbed hooks intermittently for a few seasons and I do not think I have lost any more fish during the course of bringing them to the net than I have when using barbed hooks; indeed, it seems likely that barbless hooks give better initial penetration. I kill only a small percentage of the trout I catch and if the use of barbless hooks increases the survival rate of released fish a general move in this direction by as many anglers as possible must be a good thing. A recent innovation devised by an Austrian, Roman Moser, and the hook manufacturers Partridge eliminates the barb but incorporates an arrowpoint, which takes a stronger hold than the simple barbless point and possibly as good a hold as a barbed hook (Fig 53). If, like me, you prefer to release the vast majority of the trout you catch, the Partridge CS20 or CS27 hooks should provide good penetration and a strong hold combined with the benefits of simple release.

9 Natural and Artificial Dry Flies

The imitation may be
   Impressionist,
   Cubist,
   Futurist,
   Post-impressionist,
   Pre-Raphaelite, or
   Caricature.
The commonest is Caricature.
It therefore catches most fish.

G. E. M. Skues, *Flyfishers' Club Journal*, spring 1916

The two most influential factors on whether trout are caught are the angler on one end of the line and the fly on the other. The first is the most important because there is little that will compensate for poor technique, the wrong presentation or tactics, an ignorance of trout behaviour, or poor watercraft. A skilled fly fisher with but three or four patterns will catch more fish than a bungling fool equipped with every one of the flies in this chapter. There is no substitute for a fly fisher's knowledge of trout and their behaviour and the skills of fly fishing. Being fully equipped means applying an extensive knowledge *and* being prepared to offer a broad selection of floating flies.

Adams

When Ray Bergman wrote his book, *Trout*, in 1938, few would have believed that it would remain in print until the present day. A whole generation grew up on it. Its simple title summed up all the American angler ever needed to know about fly fishing for the species. Not only has Bergman's writing withstood the test of time but some of his patterns still float proudly on streams on both sides of the Atlantic. Bergman's contribution was that he popularised so many good flies. Though he is closely associated with the Adams, he didn't invent it – that was done by Leonard Halladay in 1922.

The Adams is a useful general pattern and catches trout when a wide variety of up-winged duns are on the water. *The Fisherman's Handbook of Trout Flies* by Donald Du Bois lists eighteen variations and I give the original dressing below. I doubt whether there has been a more successful American dry fly.

Hook 14–16
Tying silk Grey
Tail Grizzle hackle fibres
Body Grey or blue-grey dubbed wool or fur
Wings Two grizzle hackles tied upright. A spent wing version is also tied.
Hackle Red grizzle cock wound with a grizzle cock

Amber Spinner

The two dressings overleaf represent the amber-bodied spinners of the pale watery and spurwings and are also effective blue-winged olive imitations. Roger Fogg informed me that his pattern below is best fished on the smooth glides below broken water and is particularly useful as an early-morning and evening fly from late April until July. Not surprisingly, Thomas Clegg, author of *The Truth about Fluorescents*, incorporates some fluorescent materials in his dressing. It is likely that these materials are particularly effective in the early-morning and evening light. Both are also good grayling flies.

Amber Spinner (Roger Fogg)
Hook   12–16
Tying silk   Amber
Tail   Cree cock hackle fibres
Body   Amber seal's fur
Rib   Amber tying silk or marabou floss
Hackle   Generous turns of cree cock hackle with the upper and lower fibres trimmed off so the remainder give the impression of spent wings

Amber Spinner (Thomas Clegg)
Hook   14
Tying silk   White
Body   Orange DFM floss
Rib   Brown Naples silk
Wing   Six lengths of grey DFM floss, equally divided and tied spent or slightly forward
Hackle   Two cock hackles, dyed light blue-grey

Ants (Hymenoptera)
For some reason trout seem to find ants particularly attractive. It can't be their size, surely; they hardly seem big enough to bother about. It was left to E. R. Hewitt to suggest that it is the tartness of their taste that appeals. He put forward the theory that the taste of their formic acid content is strongly attractive, and, being a chap to put his mouth where his money is, he ate some to prove it. This must be one of the most pointless angling experiments I can imagine. Hewitt assumed trout to have the same degree of taste that humans enjoy, and that because a taste is tart it is pleasurable to trout. Other fly fishers have followed Hewitt's example only to find ants tasteless. I am an angler who likes to put theories into practice but I stop short at tasting flies to see if trout might like them. Mayflies, caddis, caterpillars, dragonflies are all available – why did Hewitt stop at ants?

The principal reason why trout eat ants is that they are both available and abundant. Warm weather tempts them from their sheltered haunts on to open ground and vegetation. Wind or no wind, they seem to find their way on to the surface. Apart from a variety of colours – red, brown and black – two 'types' of ant are encountered: winged and wingless. The wingless fall or are blown off vegetation. Once on the surface they neither float nor sink. Because of their weight and leg-support they actually rest in the surface film supported by their spread legs. As a result they are difficult for the fly fisher to detect. One clue might come from the quiet dimple or sip rise forms on calm water.

At about 40 million years old, they are one of creation's oldest members and they live in a highly ordered society of different roles. Only a minority have wings, which they possess for the sole purposes of mating and dispersal. In relatively high humidity the winged ants take to the air to mate and on such occasions the air seems full of them. I have only experienced this once, when I appeared to be the honeymoon hotel as mating pairs copulated all around me. The male dies shortly afterwards. Inevitably, some winged ants also end up on the water. Some hold their wings in the upright position rather like a dun; others have them fully spent, and these are the most difficult to detect.

The commonest species are black but brown and red ants are also found. I have come across only the black species either on the wing or being taken by trout. In common with the manner in which I fish most terrestrial patterns, they are used when ants are on the water or when I fail to discover what trout are actually rising to or when they are not surface-feeding at all. When they are rising with the slightest of sips, barely causing as much as a ripple, it can often be to ants. Ernest Schwiebert once wrote an article in which he revealed his forty (!) favourite ant imitations. He must fish for some ultra-selective trout. The critical feature in any imitation should be a bulge for the abdomen and thorax with a thin waist. The natural's body is entirely opaque.

McMurray Ant
This excellent pattern came from Ed Sutryn of McMurray, Pennsylvania. I first read of it in *Fishing Dry Flies for Trout* by Art Lee, who had experienced fantastic success with the fly. It

was variously described as 'one helluva fly', 'absolute dynamite', and 'the deadliest pattern . . . ever to shake hands with a leader'. I can vouch for the pattern's attraction to fish, particularly in the smaller sizes. The very week I read about the pattern I called at the Orvis shop in New York and bought the necessary materials. Within a matter of days I was catching trout on the McMurray Ant from both freestone and chalk streams back in the United Kingdom. Even the most selective of trout have fallen for it. Orvis in the UK will order the materials, or the ants are available from The Hatch, DeBruce Road, Livingston Manor, NY 12758, USA.

Hook 14–22 (size 20–22 should be on straight-eye hooks)
Tying silk Black
Body Two small cylinders of balsa wood affixed to a strand of nylon monofilament and black varnished
Hackle Black cock, clipped top and bottom and tied in the middle of the body

Aphis

This winged, green, very small terrestrial species is occasionally blown on the water during June and July and if this happens in sufficient numbers then trout will feed upon

McMurray Ant.

them. Even when they are not in evidence I have found that a small green-bodied fly will catch trout that are proving reluctant to rise. I suspect that the artificial is mistaken for one of a range of terrestrials that sometimes end up on the surface.

Aphis (John Roberts)
Hook 14–16
Tying silk Pale green
Tail Blue-dun cock hackle fibres tied short
Body Light green floss
Hackle Blue-dun cock

Autumn Dun or August Dun (*Ecdyonurus dispar*)

The distribution of this species is restricted to parts of northern England, South Wales and the West Country, where it inhabits stony-bedded rivers and occasionally stony lake margins. In addition to emerging on the water surface the mature nymphs are, on occasion, observed crawling on sticks, stones or other objects projecting out of the water so that emergence takes place out of the water. The large adults appear between June and October, with the most prolific period being July and August.

Both male and female duns and spinners are almost identical to the late March brown. The duns particularly are difficult to tell apart, with only a close examination of the wing veins confirming the identification. Therefore an imitation of the late March brown or March brown will suffice.

The male spinners swarm over water, usually during the afternoon period. The mated female spinner then rests on an object above the water and oviposits underwater on the substratum.

The male dun has two dark grey tails. The wings are grey with black veins. The upper side of the abdomen is yellow-olive with dark brown bands on the sides. The legs are long and are dark brown-olive. The female dun has similar tails, light fawn wings with black veins. The upper side of the abdomen is yellow-olive or pale olive-brown.

The dun can be represented by the March brown imitations.

August Dun Spinner (G. E. M. Skues)
Hook 16
Tying silk Hot orange
Tail Honey-dun hackle fibres
Body Orange seal's fur
Hackle Natural red cock

Barton Bug
Roy Darlington devised this pattern for some very selective Itchen trout feeding on emerging medium olives. It should be fished so that the rear half of the fly is submerged and the front half floating, supported by the thorax and hackle. The tails are exaggerated to represent the shuck being left just below the surface. Donald Overfield relates in *50 Favourite Dry Flies* how during the pattern's first outing in 1971, when trout were carefully selecting only those emerging duns, its creator took six trout in a 150-yard stretch.

Hook 12–14
Tying silk Primrose
Tail Long fur fibres from a rabbit's neck
Body Hare's ear fur dressed thinly with a slight thorax
Rib Fine oval gold tinsel
Hackle High-quality short-fibred blue-dun cock

Beacon Beige
The original Beige pattern, of which this is a derivative, was devised in 1917 as an olive dun imitation for West Country rivers. I have no doubt that the fly has been improved by the professional fly-tyer, Peter Deane, when he included an additional dark red hackle wound through the original Plymouth Rock. It is an excellent olive copy wherever it is fished.

Hook 14–16
Tying silk Light brown
Tail Plymouth Rock cock hackle fibres
Body Well marked stripped peacock eye quill
Hackle Plymouth Rock cock with a red Indian gamecock wound through

Beetles (Coleoptera)
There are no natural aquatic beetles that can be satisfactorily represented by the dry-fly fisher but scores of varieties of terrestrial beetles fall or are blown on the water surface. Since the earliest lists of fly dressings were published the beetle imitation has been recognised for its fish-attracting qualities. More than a quarter of a million species exist world-wide, with over 4,000 species in Britain. Individually, even the common species would be tedious to copy but as many have undersides coloured shades of black, brown or orange only a handful of patterns are necessary. They vary in size, from the barely visible on the surface to fingernail size. The largest often seem to fall on the surface upside down and drift along helplessly waving their legs in the air. Most have a shiny back covering the whole of the abdomen. It is the imitation of the silhouette of the back that is often the key factor in a successful imitation.

The use of all terrestrial patterns is usually limited to times when there are no aquatic flies on the water or something a little out of the ordinary is required. A beetle imitation could be just the answer to a potentially blank period of a hot summer afternoon. Generally speaking I would prefer to fish a beetle pattern a few inches below the surface, for which purpose I know of no better pattern than Eric's Beetle. I have used this as a floater on a number of occasions, with mixed results.

Eric's Beetle
Hook 10–12
Tying silk Black
Body An underbody of yellow wool with bronze peacock herl wound over leaving the wool exposed as a butt at the rear
Hackle Two turns of black cock or hen

Deerhair Beetle
Hook 10–12
Tying silk Black monocord
Body Black or natural deerhair. Encircle the hook shank with hair, rib and secure. Trim at the eye. Pull forward back over the body the hairs extending beyond the bend and secure

at a point mid-body. Pick out three hairs each side for legs, separate them and bind in. The remaining deerhair is tied in behind the eye. The legs are trimmed and the back varnished.

Bivisibles

This series of flies is one of the oldest American dry flies. They came from the vice of E. R. Hewitt in 1898, who devised them because he needed highly visible and buoyant patterns for the fast water on some of the big North American rivers. Hewitt said that the Bivisible 'seems to attract trout when there are no hatches on the water'. This still holds good today. In addition to the dressing below it is possible to adapt any existing pattern into the Bivisible style by the addition of a white cock hackle in front of the usual hackle, which should be palmered down the body.

These dressings are known as the Black Bivisible or Brown Bivisible, etc., depending upon the hackle colour.

Hook 10–12
Tying silk To match the hackle colour
Tail Two small hackle tips (black, brown, grizzle or badger to match the body hackle)
Body Palmered cock hackle as for the tail
Hackle White cock

Black Gnat

The commonest British species is *Bibio Johannis* but many other similar Diptera may also be found on the surface. The mating pairs which fall on the water can be represented by any of the patterns listed with the inclusion of a second hackle at the rear in the fore and aft style.

Black Gnat (Freddie Rice)

Hook 12
Tying silk Black
Body Black silk
Rib (optional) Fine silver wire
Wing Approximately 12 light-blue-dun hackle fibres tied at about 35 degrees over the body
Hackle Black cock or starling breast feather

Blue-winged Olive (*Ephemerella ignita*)

This is one of the commonest and most easily recognisable of all the upwinged flies. This medium-to-large fly has large, dark blue-grey wings which slope back very slightly over the body and make the fly a fairly easy one to identify, even at a distance. It is the only British olive species with three tails. They are widespread throughout the United Kingdom on all types of running water and on some larger lakes. The adults appear from April until November although hatches may be scarce at either end of this period. During 1961 Oliver Kite recorded the adults appearing during every month of the year in southern England. No doubt some of these were little more than isolated examples but it illustrates that emergence times are at best only approximations and not fixed rules, and that adults of a number of species should not be ruled out during any month. The duns emerge mainly during the afternoons and evenings, and the spinners swarm mainly in the late evening, but should be expected at any time of day. This is one of the few species of which the male spinners also fall on the water, and are therefore of interest to trout and fly fishers. C. F. Walker records that, in his experience, the duns sometimes have difficulty breaking free of the nymphal shuck, so becoming easy prey for trout. If the duns are on the water and trout are feeding, but seem to be ignoring the duns, it could be that the struggling emergent adult is the target. Over the years angling writers have stressed how easy the identification of the species is, and also how difficult they can, on occasion, be to imitate. The answer might be that those rising trout earlier writers referred to were not taking the emerged and drying duns but the emerging fly or stillborns trapped in the film. One of the different emerging patterns might be the answer.

An accurate description of the adults is given below but it has been noted that the female dun's body darkens from olive-green to rusty-brown towards the end of the season. J. R. Harris also observed that in neutral or acidic waters the colour of the duns is subdued and they are often smaller.

The male dun has three dark grey tails with brownish rings. The wings are dark blue-grey and the abdomen is orange-brown or olive-brown, of which the last segment is yellow. The legs are olive-brown.

The female dun has light grey-brown tails with dark brown rings. The wings are as for the male and the abdomen is greenish-olive changing to rusty-brown later in the season. The legs are dark olive.

The male spinner has fawn tails with black rings. The wings are transparent with light brown veins and the abdomen is dark or deep brown. The legs are pale brown.

The female spinner, also known as the sherry spinner, has olive-grey tails with light brown rings. The wings are transparent with pale brown veins, and abdomen colouring can vary between olive-brown to sherry-red. The legs are pale brown. The mated female spinner carries a distinctive small green egg-sac at the rear of the abdomen.

In addition to the patterns below the Orange Quill is an excellent late-evening imitation of the duns, despite being superficially more akin to the spinners. It is probable that trout optics make more of the late-evening light combining with the orange body and hackle than we can understand, and perhaps the Orange Quill is really taken for a spinner.

Blue-winged Olive Dun (David Jacques)
Hook 14
Tying silk Orange
Tail Dark olive cock fibres
Body Dirty-olive ostrich herl overlaid with olive PVC
Wings Coot, set upright
Hackle Dark olive cock

Blue-winged Olive Dun (Jim Nice)
Hook 12–14
Tail Blue dun or olive cock fibres
Body Front half, blue fluorescent floss; then the whole body, including the front half, covered with lime-green fluorescent floss
Hackle Blue dun or olive cock

Blue-winged Olive (a North American version)
Hook 12–14
Tying silk Black or olive
Tail Dark dun cock hackle fibres
Body Dark olive thread or dyed olive rabbit fur
Wing Grey duck wing quills
Hackle Dark dun cock

Sherry Spinner (Freddie Rice)
Hook 14
Tying silk Light yellow
Tail Natural buff-barred cree fibres or the same dyed light olive
Tip Light yellow rayon floss
Body One dark and one light moose-mane hair, the lighter dyed olive-brown or shades of sherry through to pinkish-red, wound together to give the impression of a segmented body
Wing Pale ginger cock hackle fibres wound on bunched in the spent position
Hackle Natural light red gamecock

Caenis
The caenis is the smallest of the upwinged flies in Britain and is easy to identify by its cream body, broad whitish wings and three tails. Their wing shape has also led to the adoption of the alternative name Broadwing. Because of the difficulty the fly fisher often has in satisfactorily representing the adult caenis, the designation 'angler's curse' has been found to be a more appropriate name. Of the six species, three are confined to rivers. Of the remaining species, two are very similar and to be found on stillwater, while the other is even smaller, fairly uncommon, and only appears at dawn. The family is widespread throughout the country, preferring slow-moving rivers and lakes. The most prolific hatches appear on stillwaters. The nymphs are of the burrowing type and so require a river or lake bed of mud or silt.

The adults appear during the early mornings or evenings between May and September. Trout seem to prefer the spinners, which are considerably whiter than the duns. The males have much longer tails than the females. As adults, the species has the shortest lifespan of all Ephemeropterans; from emerging as a dun to dying as a spent spinner a mere ninety minutes may elapse. This means that the fly fisher should be aware that towards the end of a hatch the spinners may be returning to the water. Copying the natural at the fly vice does not present too many problems except that of size. Often hook size of 16 or 18 are satisfactory but occasionally a much smaller fly is demanded. Alas, tying on size 24 or 26 hook is beyond me. Another difficulty lies in the fact that frequently the fall of female spinners can be so great that it may be only sheer chance that a trout selects the artificial. Having dressed a pattern on a small hook and persuaded a trout to select your fly, the next problems are hooking the fish and playing it safely to the net. Few naturals are more aptly named.

Caenis Dun (Frank Sawyer)
Hook 18–20
Tying silk Special midge thread
Tail Short cream cock fibres
Body Mole's fur abdomen and a thorax of stripped black ostrich herl, shiny side uppermost
Hackle Three turns of a very small dark blue hackle

Caenis Dun (J. R. Harris)
Hook 16
Tying silk Brown
Tail Cream cock fibres
Body Cream-coloured herl or floss silk
Hackle Pale cream-coloured cock or henny cock tied in by the butt with some of the downy fibres still on the hackle stem, and wound slightly towards the tail, taking up about one third of the shank

Caenis Spinner (Stuart Canham)
Hook 18
Tying silk Special midge thread
Tail Three white cock hackle fibres
Body White polythene abdomen and a thorax of a single turn of brown turkey herl or brown condor substitute
Wings White hen hackles cut out with a wing cutter and tied spent
Hackle White cock trimmed along the bottom edge

Calf's Tail Emerger
This is a fine emerger pattern from Danish angler Mogens Espersen. It doubles as both a dun and a sedge emerger even though the white wing never appears on a natural fly. The deer hair thorax provides good floatability.

Hook 12–14
Tying silk Medium brown wound over the rear two-thirds of the shank
Tail Light badger saddle fibres tied well into the bend and spread
Body Mixed fur from a hare's mask, spun on a dubbing loop, tied into the bend and tapering to the rear
Wing White calf's tail
Thorax Deer hair spun and clipped muddler-style to cover the front third of the shank

Caterpillars
In my experience of finding caterpillars on or in the vicinity of a river they have been of two types. The first is a smaller type about half an inch long which descend from tree branches on slender gossamer threads. In a breeze or a sudden gust these may be blown on to nearby water. I have never attempted to represent these with an artificial fly; the result would be something like a maggot. The second type is larger, varying in colour and degrees of hairiness. These too must venture near water and be sometimes blown on to the surface from overhanging trees and bankside vegetation. I confess that my imitation of these caterpillars is a slow-sinking pattern. This floating pattern came from Richard Walker.

Hook Longshank 10
Tying silk To match body colour
Underbody Varnished polythene foam
Overbody Dyed black, brown, white or green ostrich herl over the wet varnish
Rib Crimson or buff silk soaked in diluted

Durofix adhesive and allowed to dry

Coachman

Just how and when the first dressing of this name came about no one knows. It seems likely that it was named after the occupation of its inventor. The earliest reference to this name came in Thomas Salter's *The Angler's Guide* of 1814, which says: 'There is a fly very much used at Watford, in Herts, called Harding's Fly, or the Coachman's; the merits of such flies experience will teach how to appreciate.' Over the last 175 years the Coachman in its many variations has probably become the most widely used trout fly across the world, whether as a small dry fly, a wet fly, a sea-trout lure or a bucktail lure. As a floating fly it is very nondescript, possibly passing for a moth or a sedge. Best of all the variations I have found to be the hackle-point dressing from Dave Collyer. This has caught trout that have refused to look at many other patterns and it would be pushing hard to enter a list of my six best-ever dry flies.

Coachman
Hook   10–16
Tying silk   Black or brown
Body   Bronze peacock herl
Wing   White duck or swan fibres
Hackle   Natural light red cock

A wingless version can be tied with a white cock hackle and a shorter natural red cock in front, or wound together. The Grayling Coachman has an additional red wool tag and a wing of bunched white hackle fibres set upright or slanting over the body.

Hackle-point Coachman (Dave Collyer)
Hook   10–14
Tying silk   Red spinner
Body   Bronze or green peacock herl wound over wet varnish for durability
Wing   White cock hackle points tied semi-spent
Hackle   Ginger or natural red cock with the underside trimmed flat in line with the hook-point

Royal Coachman

According to an article in *Esquire* in 1956, Preston Jennings confirmed that this is truly an all-American variation which started off as a wet fly when a New York fly tyer needed a more durable Coachman and included a few turns of red floss in the middle of the body. Surprisingly enough, there is an American natural fly of which the Royal Coachman is a fair imitation. The transition to dry fly is probably the work of Theodore Gordon.

Hook   10–16
Tying silk   Black or brown
Tail   Golden pheasant tippets
Body   Peacock herl at each end of the body for a short length only; red floss in the middle
Wing   White duck or swan
Hackle   Light red game

Cranefly (Tipulidae)

Most of the craneflies or daddy-long-legs are terrestrial but a few species are semi-aquatic, living as larvae in muddy lake margins. It is as a stillwater fly that the cranefly is of most value, where dry and wet patterns can be deadly. For the river fisher, the dry Daddy-Long-Legs is very much an occasional pattern, for use in mid-to-late summer when the adults, which are poor, ungainly fliers, are sometimes blown on to the water. The natural insect has six legs, but in dressings that have legs of knotted pheasant tail fibres it is better to tie in more than this as they invariably break off when a fish is being played. The pattern below has black nylon monofilament legs, which are much more durable.

Culard

Hans van Klinken originally tied this with a longer wing as a sedge pattern. He ended up shortening the wings and producing an extremely good emerger.

Hook   4× fine, longshank 18
Tying silk   Black
Body   Dark grey or dark blue dun synthetic dubbing
Rib   Extra-fine gold wire or yellow silk in six turns, wound the opposite way to the body

Wing Four cul de canard feathers, pulled together and trimmed half-way along the body length
Hackle Two turns of a very small dark blue dun cock (dry) or starling body feather for the emerger

Daddy-long-legs (Geoffrey Bucknall)
Hook Longshank 10
Body Brown floss
Legs Strong knotted black or grey nylon monofilament
Hackle Ginger cock
Wing Ginger cock hackle-tips tied spent

Dark Kyll
Hans Weilenmann devised this large dark olive imitation in one of the thorax styles of tying.

Hook 12
Tying silk Brown
Wing Single upright wing of wood-duck breast fibres or subs
Tail Four moose body hairs, split by a small amount of dubbing
Body Dark brown Partridge SLF dubbing along the whole body length
Hackle Natural red cock wound in open turns over the thorax area and trimmed flush with the body of the fly

Dark Olive (*Baetis atrebatinus*)
This upwinged species is relatively rare beyond some southern and south-western counties and a few northern streams. It has a preference for alkaline water. Most authorities suggest that the medium-sized adults begin to appear in May and continue through to October, possibly in two generations. On at least one tributary of the Yorkshire Rye they are quite common in April, with hatches large enough to interest trout during the late morning and early afternoon.

The male dun has a dark olive-brown abdomen of which the last segment of the underside is yellowish. The wings are grey and the two tails dark olive-grey. The female dun is similar except that the tails are greyer.

The female spinner has transparent wings, grey-olive tails with faint red rings. The upper abdomen is dark reddish-brown with paler rings and the lower abdomen is light olive.

In addition to the pattern below the duns can be adequately represented by any general olive imitation, or large dark olive patterns tied on a size 14, or a similar-sized Kite's Imperial.

Dark Olive (Thomas Clegg)
Hook 14
Tying silk Olive
Tail Dark olive-dyed cock hackle fibres
Body Dubbed dark olive wool
Rib Electron-white fluorescent floss
Hackle Slate-blue and dark brown-olive cock hackles wound together

Dogsbody
In 1924, Harry Powell, a Welsh fly dresser of high repute, created this, his best-known and most popular pattern. It is a general nondescript fly that rises trout throughout the season on waters the length of the country. The body colour variations are as endless as there are dogs. The original was camel-coloured but various shades of brown seem to work.

Hook 12–14
Tying silk Brown
Tail Pheasant tail fibres
Body Camel-coloured dog's fur spun on brown silk
Rib (optional) Oval gold tinsel
Hackle Plymouth Rock followed by a second natural red cock, or wound together

Dusky Yellowstreak (*Heptagenia lateralis*)
This is a fairly localised species, confined to stony upland rivers of the South West, Wales, the north of England and Scotland. The medium-sized adults appear between May and September, when quite large hatches can occur. It is interesting to note that according to one entomological authority emergence can take place on a stone beneath the surface of the water as well as on the surface. The duns are of drab appearance with heavily veined dark grey wings, a dark grey-brown body and two grey tails. The female spinner

has transparent wings with brownish veins along the leading edge. The upper abdomen is brown-olive with reddish rings and the lower abdomen drab olive with the last three segments orange-brown. The tails are brown. A distinguishing feature of both duns and spinners is the yellow streak on each side of the front of the thorax.

I have been unable to find any dressing specifically tied for either the dun or spinner but I would suggest that any darkish fly such as a size 14 iron blue might suffice for the dun, and a Pheasant Tail Spinner for the female spinner.

February Red (*Taeniopteryx nebulosa, Brachyptera risi*)

The second of these species of stoneflies is widespread throughout Britain on stony-bedded rivers and streams. The adults appear from March to July. The first species is common in parts of the north of England, Scotland, Wales and the west of England and prefers to inhabit the vegetation of slower-moving rivers. The adults appear between February and April. Both species are similar in appearance. They are between 7 and 11mm in length. The female is larger than the male, with longer red-brown wings with two dark bands. The back of the body is reddish-brown but the underside is orangey. Most imitations are fished wet but the following floating pattern has been devised to represent the female as she returns to the surface to lay her eggs.

Hook 14
Body Claret dyed peacock quill
Wing (optional) Two dark brown grizzle cock hackle tips tied flat over the back
Hackle Rusty blue-dun cock

The F Fly

This pattern of Marjan Fratnik's started the revival in interest in cul de canard feathers. It is a general nondescript dun imitation that works well on both slow-moving and faster waters. It can be tied without any body materials but if you want to match an individual species more closely, a lightly dubbed body

can be added. It is a very useful fly to have, especially when traditional imitations fail. It is also exceptionally easy to tie.

Hook 12–20
Tying silk Black or grey
Body Tying thread or very sparse muskrat under-fur
Hackle and wing The hackle and wing are combined: one small cul de canard feather for size 18–20; two for size 16; three for larger flies, and all trimmed to shape

Ginger Quill

Never let the age of a pattern put you off from using it. This dressing has survived at least a hundred years of imitating the pale watery and lighter olive duns. Early dressings included upright wings, but more recent dressings omit these in favour of an optional blue-dun hackle in front of the ginger.

Hook 14
Tying silk Brown
Tail Ginger cock hackle fibres
Body Natural or lightly dyed well marked peacock quill
Hackle Ginger cock

Goddard's Last Hope

In recent years few fly fishers have influenced the British trout-fishing scene as much as John Goddard. His excellent book *Trout Fly Recognition* enabled trout fishers to learn much more about the flies they were imitating and become more thoughtful anglers. This pattern is his imitation of the pale watery dun. It is also effective when other small flies, including the caenis, are on the surface. The original dressing called for a condor herl body, but as a protected species this should be replaced by heron herl. Light coloured herls are used early season and dark grey from mid-June onwards.

Hook Fine wire 16–18
Tying silk Pale yellow
Tail At least six of the hackle fibres
Body Pale yellow silk overlaid with buff

heron herl or Norwegian goose breast feather fibres
Hackles   Short-fibred dark honey-dun cock

Gold-ribbed Hare's Ear
Whether this fly is fished as a floater or a nymph, it is one of the best ever general patterns to be devised. It is an excellent medium olive or dark olive copy and rises trout whenever olives are hatching. It was originally tied without a hackle with the body fibres picked out for legs. Halford added wings, which are now no longer incorporated. Later Halford was to discard the fly, probably because it was just too nondescript for his liking, but he believed it to be the most killing pattern of his time for the southern chalk streams. It is probably taken for an emerging dun rather than the upright-winged and fully emerged adult.

Hook   14–16
Tying silk   Yellow
Tail (optional)   Three long body strands
Body   Dubbed dark fur from the base of a hare's ear
Rib   Flat gold tinsel
Legs   Body fibres picked out
Hackle (optional for use without legs)   Rusty blue-dun cock

Gordon
Theodore Gordon, the father of American dry-fly fishing, was influenced greatly by Halford, whose patterns inspired Gordon to copy North American naturals. Few dry-fly fishers across the North American continent would refuse space in a fly-box for either the Gordon or Quill Gordon. Various dressings have appeared in print, largely because Gordon regarded his Quill Gordon as a pivotal pattern to represent a number of naturals by slight amendments to the dressing. To quote Gordon: 'I can vary them to suit.'

Gordon
Hook   12–14
Tail   Speckled mandarin flank fibres (brown mallard as a substitute)
Body   Gold floss silk

Rib   Gold tinsel
Wing   Bunched speckled mandarin flank fibres
Hackle   Badger cock

Quill Gordon
Hook   12–14
Tail   Three summer-duck feather fibres (brown mandarin)
Body   Dark stripped bi-coloured quill for spring use; lighter-coloured quill for summer use
Wing   Summer-duck feather fibres set up-right (brownish olive mallard fibres as a substitute)
Hackle   Smoke-grey cock, or dark blue-dun (spring); or a pale honey-dun (summer)

Grasshoppers
Grasshoppers on the ranchlands of the western United States reach plague proportions, devastating crops in some years. The only thing that stops them is wet weather which festers fungus and bacteria that decimate the hoards. This in some way explains the relative unimportance of hoppers on United Kingdom waters. Fishing an imitation is a very important feature on all western rivers from July until October, where big trout succumb to the many hopper patterns devised. Some imitations are as large as a size 6 or a 4X longshank.

Some of the best hopper fishing comes just before the second cutting of the hay, when it is over waist high. That makes the hoppers jump where the wind catches them. Trout line up against the windward bank where on blustery days every gust dumps dozens of hoppers on to the water. Often these fish only feed when the naturals are blown on to the surface; the artificials won't work during the quiet gaps.

I wouldn't advocate such large imitations on any British water, but there may well be a case for trying an imitation in a smaller size on a windy late-summer day. There is a general concensus that a key element in triggering a reaction from trout is the legs and that the hopper size is critical. On the flats the best patterns are the low floaters without any hackle. They should be fished very close to the bank where a killing tactic is to cast the hopper onto the bank and gently pull it onto the surface with a plop. Twitching the pattern also can stimulate a response. The first pattern below is from Taff Price, who obviously has found the need for a United Kingdom dressing.

Hook Longshank Mayfly 12
Tying silk Green
Body Spun and clipped deer hair coloured green with an indelible pen
Wing Dyed green swan tied roof-like at the sides of the body, not quite meeting at the top
Legs Two cock pheasant tail fibres tied in behind the head and parallel to the body
Head Bronze ostrich herl

Joe's Hopper
Hook Longshank 4–16
Tying silk Black
Tail Red hair or feather fibres
Body Yellow chenille or poly yarn with a palmered brown hackle trimmed short
Wing Two matched mottled turkey wing quill sections either side of the body
Hackle Generous turns of mixed brown and grizzle cock hackles

Hybrid Hopper
This pattern combines a number of important features found in other dressings.
Hook Longshank to match the natural
Tying silk Brown or yellow
Tail Red deer hair
Body Yellow wool or poly yarn with a clipped palmered brown or grizzle hackle
Wing Mottled turkey wing quill segments treated with artist's fixative tied either side of the body or in a V shape
Overwing Yellow deer hair
Hackle (optional) Rear-sloping natural deer hair about half the body length
Legs Two brown grizzle saddle hackles knotted in one or two places to imitate the natural legs; they should be tied in before the head at either side of the body
Head Natural deer hair spun and trimmed

to shape

Greenwell's Glory
When this was first devised by Canon Greenwell and James Wright in 1854 it was as a winged wet fly for the Tweed. It has also produced nymph, spider wet-fly and dry-fly dressings based on the original materials. Its popularity is entirely due to its success as an excellent general imitation of all the olives. The shades of the materials and hook sizes can be varied to represent the different olives. It is truly an all-season pattern.

Hook 12–16
Tying silk Yellow
Tail Greenwell cock hackle fibres
Body Waxed yellow silk
Rib Fine gold wire
Wing (optional) Starling tied upright
Hackle Greenwell cock (black centre with ginger outer)

An alternative wingless dressing uses a furnace cock for the tail and hackle and includes a medium blue-dun hackle in front of the furnace.

Grey Duster
Few patterns can have achieved the popularity of this excellent dry fly. As a general utility fly it probably has no peers. The smaller sizes are a useful caenis imitation, the medium sizes a general dun and stonefly copy, and the larger sizes a good Mayfly pattern. The medium-sized version is often subject to the inclusion of a parachute hackle, which in my opinion works even better.

Hook 10–16
Tying silk Grey
Tail (optional) Badger cock hackle fibres
Body Blue-grey rabbit's fur
Hackle Badger cock

Grey Fox
This classic North American pattern has been rising fish on both sides of the Atlantic for over fifty years. It was devised by Preston Jennings, author of *A Book of Trout Flies*.

When an angling friend of Jennings, Art Flick, wrote *A Streamside Guide* in 1947 he included his own variant, which is tied with longer than normal hackles.

Hook 10–14
Tying silk Yellow
Tail Honey-dun or ginger cock hackle fibres
Body Light ginger or cream-coloured quill
Hackles Three – dark ginger, light ginger and grizzle cock

Griffith's Gnat
This is a hatching midge pattern devised for rivers and is designed to be fished half submerged. It originated from George Griffiths, the founder of the fishing conservation group Trout Unlimited. It is highly recommended by Ernest Schwiebert as a catcher of fish when conventional flies fail. Schweibert wrote that 'it provides a color mix, silhouette and light patterns on the surface film not found with other midge imitations'. It is an excellent pattern for smutting trout even when it is not the true smut they are taking.

When fished in the film the palmered hackle gives an excellent impression of the transient stage twixt pupa and adult, when trout find them so attractive.

Hook Light wire 16–28
Body Peacock herl
Hackle Palmered grizzle

Grizzle Mink
Any fly that catches forty Kennet trout in a single session is deserving of a mention in any book on dry-fly fishing. The Grizzle Mink did just that for Stewart Canham. It was devised by Neil Patterson, who wanted a general pattern that fulfilled his requirements for a scruffy dressing that looked as though it had some life about it. Neatness counts for very little in this dressing. It has already proved itself on European and North American rivers and could easily become a truly international fly.

Hook 14–18
Tying silk Brown

Cecil Pugh playing a trout on the River Ure.

Tail   A bunch of grizzle whisks
Body   Dun-coloured mink fur charged with longish hairs, some of which should stick out through the rib – do not trim
Rib   Fine gold wire
Hackle   Red cock wound through grizzle for the early season; ginger cock wound through grizzle during summer

H & L Variant

This popular American attractor pattern is subtle enough to work well on the calmer waters in addition to being an excellent riffle-bouncer.

Hook   10–14
Tail   White calf tail
Body   Stripped peacock quill wound over the rear half of a pre-lacquered shank; peacock herl on the front half
Wing   White calf tail
Hackle   Furnace or brown cock

Hair Spider (Al Troth)

This is an excellent high floating spider for skating across rough water. The deer hair is a useful aid to floating – much more so than any feather hackle. The fly can be skated by movement of the rod tip or allowed to rock in the wind. It is a fascinating way of fishing the faster riffles.

Hook   12
Tying silk   Nymo yellow
Tail   Natural deer flank hair tied a little longer than the body length
Body   Roots of the tail fibres wound with tying thread
Hackle   Natural deer flank hair laid along the shank protruding over the eye. Wind the thread four or five times round to secure, and clip the butts short. Unwind a couple of turns of thread and spin the hair round the shank and pull tight. Hold back the fibres at 90 degrees and bind in.

Halo Emerger

Gary LaFontaine devised this emerging pattern to imitate the aura of light around the shed skin of the nymph. It is fished with the rear below the surface, and the thorax on the surface.

Hook   10–14 fine wire
Tag   Clear Antron fibres wrapped down the shank
Tail   Coloured marabou
Abdomen   Thinly dubbed seal's fur
Thorax   Dubbed seal's fur
Halo   Large-cell closed foam on each side of the thorax
Spike   Fluorescent dyed orange deer hair extending out over the eye

Hawthorn Fly (*Bibio marci*)

This is one of the most important terrestrial flies of interest to the British fly fisher. It is widely distributed throughout the country. In late April and May it is not uncommon to see the flat-winged adults blown on the surface and when this happens it is not long before trout take advantage of them. The fly is easily identified by its large black hairy body with a pair of long black hindlegs which trail distinctively when in flight.

Hawthorn Fly (Taff Price)
Hook   Wide-gape 10–12
Tying silk   Black
Body   Shiny black rayon floss
Rib   Fine silver wire
Legs   Two knotted black pheasant tail fibres trailing to the rear
Thorax   Black seal's fur
Wing   Grey duck tied flat across the back
Hackle   Black cock

Hawthorn Fly (Preben Torp Jacobsen)
Hook   12
Tying silk   Brown
Body   Black condor herls (or heron substitute) twisted on the silk
Hackle   Two black cock hackles
Legs   Two black condor herls tips (or heron substitute) tied in just behind the hackles so that they trail to the rear and downwards

Hendrickson

The Light and Dark Hendricksons are American patterns devised originally by Roy Steenrod to represent the important upwinged dun *Ephemerella subvaria*, unknown in the United Kingdom. The naturals have a wide colour variation and consequently a number of dressings bearing the same name have been devised. The two listed are also both useful general patterns for British waters.

Dark Hendrickson
Hook   12–14
Tail   Squirrel-tail fur or dark blue-dun hackle fibres
Body   Dark blue-grey fur
Wing   Mandarin duck speckled flank fibres set upright
Hackle   Dark blue-dun cock

Light Hendrickson
Hook   12–14
Tail   Squirrel tail fur
Body   Cream-coloured fox belly fur
Wing   Mandarin duck speckled flank fibres set upright
Hackle   Light blue-dun cock

Houghton Ruby
The Houghton water of the River Test is some of the best trout fishing anywhere in the world. One of the club's keepers, William Lunn, devised a number of dressings for Test trout, some of which are still used today on waters much further afield. The Houghton Ruby is an excellent imitation of the female iron blue spinner as it alights on the surface before crawling below to deposit its eggs. I have caught many fish with this fly, from rivers far removed from its birthplace.

Hook   12–14
Tying silk   Crimson
Tail   Three fibres of a white cock hackle
Body   Rhode Island Red cock hackle stalk dyed crimson
Wing   Two light blue-dun hackle tips tied spent or semi-spent
Hackle   Rhode Island Red cock

Humpy
The Humpy or Goofus Bug in its various guises is a popular and important pattern on the Western rivers of North America. It is fished in a wide range of sizes. It takes its name from the hump on the back of the body made by the bulky deer hair. I offer no explanation as to what trout mistake the larger sizes for but in its more moderate sizes the Humpy has the overall shape of a stillborn sedge or upwinged dun that has been unable to erect its wings and free itself of the trailing nymphal shuck.

Hook   6–20
Tying silk   Black, brown, red or yellow
Tail   Deer body hair (see below)
Body and wing   Deer body hair laid along the shank with the tips sticking out at the rear. A second section of deer body hair is tied in, long enough to form the body and wings. The second section is bound down and overlaid with generous turns of the tying silk along the body. Take the first hair fibres used to form the tail and pull them over the underbody and bind in well behind the eye. The fibres over the eye should be pulled back and bound in as a single upright or a split wing.
Hackle   Mixed grizzle and brown cock

Royal Humpy
This variation was devised by Jack Dennis in 1972 and has since become an extremely popular and successful attractor pattern on fast water

Hook   8–18
Tying silk   Red, yellow or green monocord
Tail   Dark moose hair
Body   Light grey natural deer hair as a back over the wound tying thread
Wing   White calf tail tied in an upright V
Hackle   Generous turns of blue dun, badger, grizzle, brown or cree wound either side of the wing

Iron Blue (*Baetis niger, B. muticus*)
With the exception of parts of the south-east the iron blue is a widespread and fairly common British fly. The wide distribution is probably helped by the fact that both alkaline and acidic waters are tolerated and that *B. niger* prefers a weedy environment while

B. muticus inhabits smaller, stony-bottomed rivers and streams. There are no obvious visual differences and the species can be considered as one for fly-fishing purposes.

The smallish adults are easily recognised by their grey-black wings and dark bodies and two tails. They can appear at any time between April and November, with two main periods of May and September–October. They often appear on cold blustery days when no other duns emerge. Both duns and spinners can appear on the water at almost any time of day. In common with other *Baetis* species the female spinners deposit their eggs by crawling down vegetation and debris to the riverbed. During one July day when the spinners were returning to the water I was wading a northern stream. I became preoccupied with a rising fish and had not moved from my position in the water for about ten minutes. I happened to look down and was amazed to find no less than twenty-six female spinners above and below the waterline crawling down my waders.

The male dun has a grey-black abdomen and grey-black or blue-black wings. The two tails are olive-grey or grey-black.

The female dun has a dark brown-olive abdomen and wings similar to or slightly paler than the male's. The tails are dark grey.

The female spinner, also known as the little claret spinner, has transparent, colourless wings and a dark claret-brown abdomen, of which the underside is paler. The tails are grey.

The male spinner, which is also sometimes found on the surface after mating, has transparent, colourless wings and a white abdomen with the final three segments browny-orange. The two tails are pale grey.

Iron Blue Dun (Pat Russell)

Hook 16
Tying silk Crimson
Tail Dark slate-blue cock hackle fibres
Body Dark heron herl showing a tiny tip of neon-magenta silk at the tail
Hackle Dark slate-blue cock; two short-fibred hackles wound from half-way down the body to the head

Iron Blue Dun (Frank Sawyer)

Hook 14–16
Tying silk Purple
Tail White cock hackle fibres
Body Pheasant tail herls
Hackle Light purple cock

Iron Blue Spinner (female) (Richard Walker)

Hook 14–16
Tying silk Crimson
Tail Six to eight long fine white goat or rabbit guard hairs
Abdomen Mixed magenta and chestnut-dyed lamb's wool (1 : 2)
Rib Crimson silk
Thorax Sepia lamb's wool
Wing Dyed slate-coloured bunches of fine hair tied spent

Itchen Olive

One of the best attributes of this pattern is that it is a system fly, rather like the Quill Gordon, in that by a slight variation of the colour shades different species can be represented. It was devised by Gordon Mackie to represent the paler duns. Its creator comments:

'. . . it was found that while trout rose every evening to pale duns, such as the small spurwing and pale evening duns, they were seldom tempted by any of the standard patterns. The Itchen Olive was an immediate success, and has accounted for hundreds of fish which would "not look at anything" . . . It can be varied to represent other species, such as the medium olive, just by using different silks. Many natural flies are similar in appearance – more so than most anglers realise – so that the Itchen Olive is essentially a general-purpose fly. The fly should float high on the surface.'

Hook 14
Tying silk Primrose
Tail Four or five stiff pale grey spade hackle fibres
Body Thinly dubbed medium-grey seal's fur
Rib Tying silk
Hackle Three or four turns of a light grey

cock hackle, stiff and springy

Jassid

Vincent Marinaro placed great emphasis on the effectiveness of terrestrial patterns. The Jassid was one particular dressing that he found to be effective for the leafhoppers common on many American rivers in mid-summer. It also serves as a useful general terrestrial imitation in the United Kingdom. Marinaro suggested that any colour tying silk and any colour hackle were suitable but the black materials given below are the most popular. The keys to the pattern's success are its size and silhouette. It is particularly effective whenever trout are surface-feeding on tiny flies and works better than most for fish dimpling on flat calm water.

Hook 16–22
Tying silk Black
Body Black silk
Wing Jungle cock nail substitute tied flat to give an oval silhouette (varnished drake mallard neck feather is a substitute)
Hackle Two or three very short-fibred black hackles palmered along the body with the upper fibres trimmed away

John Storey

This is one of my favourite half-dozen dry flies. It is of North Country origins, devised by John Storey, a keeper on the River Rye near Helmsley. The original wing slanted back over the body, but in 1935 when Storey's grandson, Arthur, the present river keeper, was a boy trying to tie the fly he could only manage to tie them forward-sloping. The new style was created. It is a pattern that I fish with great confidence on all sorts of rivers and streams. As a general utility fly it is hard to improve on.

Hook Down-eyed 12–16
Tying silk Black
Body Copper-coloured peacock herl
Wing A small whole mallard breast feather tied in a bunch forward-sloping over the eye
Hackle Rhode Island Red cock

Kite's Imperial

Oliver Kite was a skilled author, fly fisher and amateur entomologist who died whilst fishing the Test in 1968 at the early age of 48. In 1962 he devised this pattern, which he possibly based on an earlier unnamed Welsh dressing. It is an excellent general pattern as well as being a more specific imitation of the large spring olive and dark olive duns. This is another of the few dressings that have tempted some fly fishers into restricting themselves to one pattern.

Hook 12–16
Tying silk Purple
Tail Grey or brown hackle fibres in the early season; honey-dun fibres later
Abdomen Natural heron herl
Rib Gold wire
Thorax Heron herl doubled and redoubled
Hackle Honey-dun cock (light ginger is a more obtainable alternative)

Klinkhamer Special

This is quite probably the best fast-water fly to be devised for decades. Hans van Klinken originally tied it for grayling but it also excels for trout in riffles, streams and pocket waters. It is a much poorer fly on slow-moving water. It has become a fly I am never without because it can be easily seen by both angler and fish, and fishes in the film, that major trout feeding area. The body hangs tantalisingly below the surface, supported by the parachute hackle. Who knows what trout take it for – it just looks a worthwhile mouthful.

Hook Partridge K12ST curved shank 10–12
Tying silk Grey micro thread
Body Fly-Rite light tan poly dubbing, or dark tan or rusty olive
Wing White poly yarn
Thorax Three strands of peacock herl
Hackle Blue dun (preferred), chestnut brown or light ginger cock

Large Dark Olive or Large Spring Olive
(*Baetis rhodani*)
This important upwinged fly is probably the

earliest fly of the season to hatch in any numbers and can appear any time from late February to May and intermittently through the year, with a second generation occurring on some rivers in early autumn. It is common throughout the country, with a preference for faster-flowing water. Many rivers experience prolific hatches on even the most unlikely days. Because they are an early-season fly, often emerging on cold, damp days, the medium-to-large-sized duns frequently remain on the water for quite a while waiting for their wings to dry. Consequently they become an attractive target for trout. The female spinner returns to deposit her eggs below the surface.

The male dun has an olive-brown or olive-green abdomen with a darker underside. The wings are pale grey with pale brown veins and the two tails dull grey. The legs are light olive with olive-grey forelegs.

The female dun has a slightly darker body and similar wings to the male. The legs are pale olive-green and the tails medium-grey.

The female spinner, which is also known as the large red spinner, has transparent wings with brown veins. The abdomen is dark mahogany with a pale olive underside. The two tails are dark olive-grey with red-brown rings, and the legs are dark brown-olive.

Kite's Imperial, Dogsbody, Greenwell's Glory and other general olive imitations of the correct size will rise fish when the fly is

Large dark olive dun (male) (*Baetis rhodani*).

198

on the water.

Large Dark Olive Dun (Freddie Rice)
Hook   12–14
Tying silk   Olive
Tail   Light blue-dun hackle fibres
Body   Generous layers of tying silk covered with white moose-mane hairs dyed dark mahogany, browny-olive or dark grey-olive, lighter in late spring and autumn
Wing   Paired slips of pale starling primaries
Hackle   Medium-olive cock

Large Dark Olive Dun (Preben Torp Jacobsen)
Hook   12–14
Tying silk   Amber
Tail   Ginger cock fibres
Body   Two natural and two olive-dyed heron herls twisted together
Hackle   Three – medium-sized pale olive and a small ginger cock wound together, with a large rusty-dun at the head

Large Spurwing (*Centroptilum pennulatum*)
This is a medium-to-large species which has a very small spur on the hindwing. They have a localised distribution in the south of England and parts of the north, Scotland and South Wales. The nymphs inhabit weedbeds on the slow-moving stretches of rivers. The duns appear between late May and September and have the unusual and distinctive feature of spreading their wings when at rest.

The male dun has a pale brown or grey-olive abdomen of which the upper side of the last three segments are amber. The wings are dark blue-grey. The legs are pale olive-brown and the two tails grey.

The female dun has a pale olive-grey abdomen and dark blue-grey wings. The upper parts of the legs are olive and grey-white lower down. The tails are grey.

The female, also known as the large amber spinner, has an amber upper abdomen with an olive-white underside with grey rings. The transparent wings have pale olive veins. The legs are olive-grey and the tails pale grey.

In addition to the dressing below also see Pink Spinner, Goddard's Last Hope, Tup's Indispensable and Grey Duster for suitable imitations.

Large Spurwing (John Goddard)
Hook   14
Tying silk   Cream
Tail   Pale blue-dun cock fibres
Body   Cream seal's fur
Wing   Pale starling split in a V-shape
Hackle   Pale olive cock

Late March Brown (*Ecdyonurus venosus*)
The late or false March brown is very similar in its nymph and dun stages to the true March brown, with which it has often been confused. The absence of older patterns to represent this species is because the two were thought to be one species until a few years ago. So alike are they that the same artificials can adequately copy both species and suitable dressings will be found in the March brown section. The late March brown is much commoner than the March brown and the large adults appear from April to October in two generations. The mature nymphs are known to crawl ashore to make the transition to duns on rocks and stones. It follows then that trout have little or no opportunity to take the duns and it is only when the female spinner returns to the water that surface feeding on them is possible. Even then the female spinner is known to sometimes deposit her eggs by resting on stones or vegetation and submerging the rear of the abdomen below the surface and releasing the eggs. There is little chance here for trout to feed on them. This no doubt explains why, over the years, it is the subsurface March brown patterns that have succeeded and few adult patterns have been devised.

A description of the late March brown duns will be found in the March brown section. The female spinner, or great red spinner, is slightly larger than the March brown spinner and has a redder body and is similar to the female spinner of the Autumn or August dun. A suitable imitation can be found under that heading.

Leckford Professor

A number of floating flies with reverse hackles have been tried but few have ever established themselves with a wide following. One to come close is this pattern, devised by Ernest Mott, a Test river keeper. It is still widely used on its home waters. The main advantage is that the hackle hides the bend of the hook. I have used the fly on a number of occasions on rain-fed streams with reasonable success. I feel the attitude of the fly on the water can be improved by the addition of a few red cock fibres as a tail.

Hook   12–14
Tying silk   Brown
Body   Dark hare's ear fur
Rib   Fine flat gold tinsel
Hackle   A bright red cock and a white cock tied in at the rear of the body

Light Ollie

Preben Torp Jacobsen devised this fly in 1963 for his home Danish waters but it is effective wherever the large and medium olives appear. Jacobsen also ties a darker version with darker hackles. The dressing was named in 1971 as a tribute to the English angling writer, Oliver Kite, a friend of its creator.

Hook   12–16
Tying silk   Primrose
Tail   Buff Orpington hackle fibres
Body   Four heron herls dyed in picric acid and twisted round the tying silk
Rib   Fine silver wire
Body hackle   Natural blue-dun (henny cock) palmered along the body
Head hackle   Light honey-dun cock (like a Metz sandy brown)

Lunn's Particular

William Lunn introduced this pattern as a copy of the medium olive and large dark olive spinners. It is an excellent pattern on all types of rivers.

Hook   14–16
Tying silk   Crimson

Tail   Rhode Island Red hackle fibres
Body   Hackle stalk of a Rhode Island Red hackle
Wings   Two medium-blue cock hackle points tied spent
Hackle   Rhode Island Red cock

March Brown (*Rithrogena germanica*)

This species is less common than was once popularly supposed, with anglers and entomologists confusing it with the much commoner late March brown. Both species are so similar that so far as the fly fisher's need to imitate the nymphs and duns goes there is no difference. The March brown has a localised distribution on fast-flowing rivers in parts of Wales, the north of England and Scotland, and in parts of the West Country. The large adults appear around midday and early afternoon during March and early April. The hatches may be quite prolific but often the duns are ignored in preference to the nymph and emerging dun. They are most commonly seen emerging at the tail of fast, broken water.

The male dun has a dark brown abdomen with straw-coloured rings. The wings are mottled pale fawn with heavy dark-brown veining. Both the male and female duns have a patch clear of veining in the middle of the forewings. The legs are pale brown and the two tails dark brown-grey.

The female dun abdomen is a duller brown, and the wings are darker than the male's. The two tails are dark brown and the legs are pale olive with darker forelegs.

The female spinner, also known as the great red spinner, has transparent wings with dark veins. The abdomen is dark red-brown with straw-coloured rings. The tails are brown and the legs various shades of olive. Neither spinner proves of much value to the fly fisher.

March Brown Dun (Taff Price)
Hook   12
Tying silk   Primrose
Tail   Cree hackle fibres
Body   Mixed hare's ear and yellow seal's fur
Rib   Yellow silk

Wing Dark hen pheasant wing quill slips set upright
Hackle Cree cock

March Brown Hatching Dun
(W. H. Lawrie)
Hook 12–14
Tying silk Yellow or orange
Tail Three short cock pheasant tail fibres
Body Medium hare's ear fur
Rib Fine gold wire
Thorax Sepia seal's fur
Wing hackle Dark partridge feather with the lower fibres cut away
Leg hackle Dark red cock hackle with the upper fibres cut away

Mayfly (Green Drake) (*Ephemera danica, E. vulgata*)
Surely a big hatch of Mayfly duns or a fall of spinners is one of the most exhilarating sights the fly fisher can wish to encounter on his river. Sadly, in these days of diminishing fly life, the sight is becoming rarer and a river with a good hatch of these, the largest of the upwinged flies, should be highly valued. Words cannot adequately describe the excitement of being on a stream with the duns hatching in their thousands, the air thick with them and every trout, grayling, chub and dace in the river rising with abandon, gorging themselves on a rare banquet. If your casting arm has never turned to jelly with the excitement of so many fish revealing themselves, find such a stream and be prepared to discover just how intoxicating fly fishing can be.

The Mayfly time has been known as the 'duffer's fortnight' because trout can sometimes be easily duped with a suitable imitation. This may be true after some days of steady hatches but in the early days of a hatch taking a fish on an artificial can be difficult. The only difficulty during the middle of the most prolific period when there are clouds of duns or falling spinners is persuading a trout to rise to yours and not one of the wide choice of naturals.

The two species are widespread and a third species, *E. lineata*, is very much rarer. The differences between the species are insignificant for both fish and fisherman. Because they are the largest of the upwinged flies they are easy to recognise. They begin to appear in May and can be prolific until the end of June, with less numerous hatches thereafter. Fewer flies hatch as the summer progresses, with sometimes the occasional dun hatching as late as October. The nymphs are of the burrowing kind and need a muddy or sandy riverbed. *E. vulgata* has a preference for emerging at dawn and dusk, and *E. danica* can be expected at any time during the day but usually in the afternoons. The female spinners, which are also known as the grey drake or spent gnat, return to the water most often in the early evening. Both the male and female spinners are taken, sometimes more voraciously than the duns. John Goddard wrote in a letter to me that 'It is a fallacy to suppose that the natural spinners always float on the surface with both wings flat on the surface on all waters that I fish. I would say that 65 per cent float along with one wing vertical.' To this end he devised his Poly-May Spinner, which floats with one wing on the surface and the other cocked in the air.

The male dun has a greyish white abdomen with brown markings. The wings are grey tinged with yellow and have heavy brown veining. The legs are dark brown and the three tails dark grey.

The female dun has a yellowy-cream abdomen with brown markings. The wings are grey with a blue-green tinge and heavy black veining. The legs are creamy-olive and the three tails dark grey.

The male spinner has a creamy-white abdomen with the last three segments brownish. The wings are transparent with a brown tint and heavy brownish veins. The legs are dark brown-olive with the forelegs black-brown and the tails dark brown.

The female spinner has a pale cream abdomen, of which the last three segments are brown streaked. The wings are transparent with a blue tint and brown veins. The legs are dark olive-brown and the three tails dark brown.

I have listed rather more patterns than for

The true Mayfly dun (*Ephemera danica*).

other natural flies. This is a reflection on the great number of dressings.

Straddlebug
Hook   Longshank 10–12
Tying silk   Brown
Tip   Very fine oval gold tinsel
Tail   Two or three black cock hackle fibres
Body   Natural raffia
Rib   Brown tying silk
Hackle   Orange cock followed by a brown speckled summer-duck feather
Head   Bronze peacock herl

Poly May Dun (John Goddard)
Hook   Wide gape 10–12
Tying silk   Primrose
Tail and wings   Natural calf's tail hair dyed gold laid along the shank and tied in an upright split V shape. The rear fibres should extend beyond the shank to represent the shuck of the natural
Body   Cream-coloured polypropylene yarn wound over the underbody up to and around the wings
Hackle   Three or four turns of a black cock hackle either side of the wing roots

Green Drake (a North American pattern)
Hook   10–12
Tying silk   Olive or yellow
Tail   Moose fibres
Body   Olive poly yarn ribbed with yellow floss, or olive dyed rabbit fur
Wing   Goose or dark duck wing quills
Hackle   Olive dyed grizzle cock

Lively Mayfly No. 1
This and the following dressing originated with Chauncy Lively and have been amended by Charles Jardine, who comments that they are the only Mayfly dressings he

uses and that he has known them to be taken even in preference to the naturals. These two dressings helped the English team to victory on the River Test section of the 1987 World Championship.

Hook   Light wire down-eye 10
Tying silk   Yellow
Tail   Three pheasant tail fibres
Extended body   Light deer hair (10–15 fibres) or moose main
Rear hackle   Grizzle cock tied around the junction of the 'hook and extended body
Body/thorax   Cream/yellow Poly II or Orvis Antron/hare blend
Wing   Wood duck fibres bunched and separated by figure-of-eight turns of silk
Body hackle   Grizzle cock palmered to the head. It is essential to clip a V shape through the body hackle underneath to provide the correct silhouette.

Lively Mayfly No. 2
This has the same tails, extended body and body/thorax as for No. 1.

Wing   Wood duck tied upright slanting back towards the tail with some 10–15 turns around the base to provide ample support for the parachute hackle
Hackle   Golden olive and grizzle cock wound together in parachute style round the base of the wing

Deerstalker
This is a spinner imitation devised by Neil Patterson with which I have had great success.

Hook   Longshank 10
Tying silk   Brown
Tail   Pheasant tail fibres about twice the body-length
Body   White deer hair laid along the shank with the tips sticking out beyond the bend

John Goddard's Mayfly spinner imitation with a tilt to one side to imitate the position of some naturals on the surface.

Rib Generous turns of tying silk and silver wire

Hackle Black cock wound where the thorax should be. This is trimmed leaving the fibres very short indeed. A second natural red hackle is wound through the remainder of the black hackle and bound into two bunches for spent wings.

Poly May Spinner (John Goddard)

Hook Wide gape 10–12

Tying silk Black

Tail Three to five long black cock fibres or black nylon monofilament

Body White polypropylene yarn

Wing Mixed black and natural off-white calf's tail tied in a very wide V shape so that when the fly lands on the water it tilts on one wing

Hackle Three or four turns either side of the wing roots of relatively short-fibred black cock hackle.

Medium Olive (*Baetis vernus, B. tenax, B. buceratus*)

Baetis vernus and *B. tenax* are widely distributed on alkaline waters, with a definite preference for the chalk streams, where they appear in abundance and are an important fly. The nymphs live amongst weeds. There are usually two generations of the medium-sized adults. The first appears in May and June, and the second generation in July and August, continuing irregularly and in fewer numbers until November. Their most likely appearance is in the late morning and early afternoon, with the female spinners returning from early evening onwards.

The male dun has a yellow-olive abdomen with a paler underside. The wings are medium grey. The two tails are grey and the legs are medium olive.

The female dun has a medium-olive abdomen with a pale yellow-olive underside. The wings and tails are as for the male and the legs are pale olive.

The female spinner, also known as the red spinner (although not always red), has an abdomen that may vary between yellow-brown and reddish-brown. The wings are transparent with light-brown veins. The two tails are off-white and the legs are grey-olive. Suitable dun and spinner imitations are listed under other olives. See under Greenwell's Glory, Gold-ribbed Hare's ear, Barton Bug, Misty Blue Dun or olives in the index.

Midges

Midges on running water do not take on the same significance as on stillwater, where they are a very important part of the diet. They are very much less important on our rivers. The larvae prefer the slow-moving stretches and can tolerate very low oxygen levels. Despite the opening remark, there is good reason to believe that they probably appear on our rivers much more than we generally accept. Sometimes autopsies reveal plenty of pupae, probably taken as they ascend to the surface, and I suspect that much of the time we think trout are taking small smuts from the surface the target may well be midges. Certainly midge fishing in the United States has developed into a very fine art. Ed Koch's book *Fishing the Midge* is the standard work. The first dressing comes from that source. Another suitable imitation can be found under Griffith's Gnat.

Adult Midge (Richard Walker)

Hook 16

Body Dyed green or black feather fibres tied with a slightly bigger thorax

Rib White hackle stalk

Wing Two short white cock hackle points

Hackle Long-fibred green or black cock

Low-floating Midge (Datus Proper)

Hook 14–18

Tying silk To match body colour

Abdomen Thinly dubbed fur

Wings Two small hackle-fibre points in a V over the abdomen

Hackle Two or three turns of cock hackle and bunched spent

Thorax Dubbed fur either side and over the wing and hackle roots.

Moths

The adult moth as it skitters across the surface as dusk or night falls can be too tempting a sight for trout to pass by. Even under what appears to man as darkness trout are much better equipped to see food on the surface. Most terrestrial moths appear as dusk falls and some end up on the water. On a number of occasions a moth imitation fished on the last few casts of the evening has caught trout. The natural moths vary in size and colour from white to grey to brown, with various shades in between. I usually fish a white pattern because it is much easier to see in the failing light.

White Moth
Hook   12–14
Tying silk   White
Body   White floss silk or white wool
Rib   Silver wire over the wool body
Wing   White duck tied semi-spent
Hackle   Creamy-white cock

Spruce Moth
This is a terrestrial species unique to North America, where it produces spectacular 'hatches' on northern waters. The moths infest pine trees along riverbanks. They have absolutely no reason to be on the water, but on warm days, between 9 a.m. and noon and again between 6 and 9 p.m., they fly to the surface. Their wings get wet, trapping the insect and they flutter along helplessly. Hundreds litter the surface and trout gorge on them.

The populations of spruce moths are cyclical. Sometimes they disappear from a forest; then the infestation grows until it hits a three year peak. That's when the telephone lines buzz in the West and dry fly fanatics concentrate on the hot areas for six to eight weeks because there's no better surface action.

Hook   12–14
Tying silk   White
Body   Cream mink dubbed to make a substantial body
Hackle   Light ginger palmered over the body and clipped
Wing   Light elk hair flared flat over the back
Head   Spun light elk hair clipped round

Muddle-May
This is an excellent, highly buoyant imitation of an adult dun, devised by Al Beatty.

Hook   12–24
Tying silk   To match the body colour
Tails   Moose body hair or Micro-fibetts
Body   Dubbed fur or wound tying thread
Wings   Wonder wings to match the natural
Hackle   Deer hair to match the natural
Head   Spun deer hair to match the natural

No. 3 Para
Pat Russell, the creator of this parachute-style nondescript dressing, writes that he knows of no better fly (other than his Enigma) for rising uncooperative trout.

Hook   14–16
Tying silk   Scarlet
Tail   Rhode Island Red hackle fibres
Body   Rhode Island Red hackle stalk and silk
Hackle   Barred badger and cream cock in parachute style

Olives
This general heading of olives includes all the olive species. For specific dressings see under the appropriate sections. General olive dressings can be found under Dogsbody, Kite's Imperial, Greenwell's Glory, Gold-Ribbed Hare's Ear and Rough Olive.

Olive Quill
Hook   12–16
Tying silk   Yellow
Tail   Medium-olive cock fibres
Body   Peacock quill dyed olive
Wing   (optional)   Medium starling wing feather set upright
Hackle   Medium-olive cock

Olive Upright (*Rithrogena semicolorata*)
This medium-to-large species is quite common in parts of the north, West Country, Wales and Scotland. The nymphs are the stone-clinging type, preferring faster-flowing rivers. The adults usually appear in the evenings or dawn between April and July but may continue into September. On a cool day the

duns hatch during the afternoon. The female spinners have a reputation for being unpopular with trout.

The duns, which are similar to the blue-winged olives, have a grey-olive body and dark blue-grey wings. The legs are pale olive-brown and the two tails are grey-brown. The spinners are also known as the Yellow Upright. The female has an olive-yellow abdomen of which the underside is creamy-olive. The wings are transparent with brown veins. The legs are pale olive and the two tails pale buff with faint red-brown rings. A Pheasant Tail with a rusty-dun hackle has been recommended as a spinner imitation.

Olive Upright Dun

Hook   12–14
Tying silk   Yellow
Tail   Light to medium-olive cock fibres
Body   Peacock quill dyed olive
Hackle   Light to medium-olive cock

Orange Quill

G. E. M. Skues popularised this dressing for the duns of the blue-winged olive although contemporary authorities believe it is more likely taken for the female spinner. It is a very good evening pattern and as an end-of-season fly I have found it to be very effective. An alternative dressing to the one below has a pale starling wing and a natural light-red cock hackle or medium-ginger cock hackle.

Hook   12–14
Tying silk   Orange
Tail   Orange hackle fibres
Body   Stripped quill dyed pale orange
Wing   Rusty-dun hackle points
Hackle   Orange cock

Orange Spinner

This is a blue-winged olive spinner imitation from G. E. M. Skues.

Hook   12–14
Tying silk   Orange
Tail   Honey-dun cock fibres
Body   Medium-olive seal's fur
Rib   Fine gold wire

Hackle   Rusty-dun or blue-dun cock

Pale Evening Dun (*Procloëon bifidum*)
In years past the pale evening dun was grouped together with the pale wateries and few specific dressings were tied. Identification is relatively straightforward as it is the only British river species of upwinged dun that has no hindwings. The medium-sized male dun also has distinctive dull yellow eyes. They are the palest of all the duns, with pale grey wings and a straw-coloured abdomen of which the underside is even paler. The two tails are olive-grey and the legs pale olive, becoming greyer towards the feet. The spinner returns to the river only after dark and is of doubtful value to the fly fisher.

They are widely distributed but localised on slow-moving alkaline water. They are most prolific during the evenings of July and August. John Goddard points out that often they hatch at the same time as the blue-winged olives and trout sometimes show a preference for the pale evening duns. Imitations of the pale watery are adequate.

Pale Watery (*Baetis fuscatus*)
This is common in alkaline rivers in the south-east, parts of Wales and the north. The nymphs are agile darters, living among weedbeds. The smallish adults appear in the afternoons between May and October and the spinners return mainly in the evenings.

The male dun has a pale grey-olive abdomen of which the final two segments are pale yellow. The wings are medium or pale grey. The legs are light olive and the two tails grey. The male has yellow eyes.

The female dun has a similar abdomen but the last two segments are yellow-olive. The wings are also pale grey. The legs are pale olive and the tails grey.

The female spinner, also known as the golden spinner, has a medium golden-brown abdomen with the last three segments darker. The wings are transparent. The tails are grey-white and the legs pale watery.

For other patterns see Enigma, Goddard's Last Hope, Tup's Indispensable.

Pale Watery Dun (Richard Walker)
Hook 16
Tying silk Primrose
Tail Honey-dun or cream cock hackle fibres
Body Swan secondary herl tinted palest greenish-grey with a few turns of tying silk built up and exposed at the rear. A drop of clear cellulose should be added to the tip to give an amber tint.
Wing (optional) Honey-dun hackle fibres set upright, or bleached starling wing
Hackle Honey-dun or deeply tinted cream cock

Palmers

There is probably no older style of dressing a fly than with palmer-style hackles down the length of the body. With regard to the floating fly the hackles down the body give the impression of the legs of a natural dun or sedge. By varying the body and hackle colours there is little doubt that a wide variety of natural flies can be represented. The modern fly fisher probably passes the palmer style by in favour of what he believes is a rather more accurate imitation. They can be fished as high-floaters balancing on their hackle tips or awash in the film as emergers. The colour permutations are endless but I have listed two proven patterns below. The first is a black pattern that can represent any number of beetles and terrestrial insects, or a black sedge. The Mottled Palmer is a good imitation of the grannom or any mottled-winged sedge.

Mottled Palmer (Roger Fogg)

Hook 10–14
Tying silk Black
Tip Green fluorescent silk
Body Twisted mottled turkey tail fibres wound along the body, or hare's ear fur
Rib Oval gold tinsel
Body hackle Palmered coch-y-bondhu or Greenwell cock
Shoulder hackle Dark brown cock

Parody

This is one of my favourite patterns for late-season trout and autumn grayling. I have no idea what trout take it for, but scores of them have been duped by it.

Hook 14
Tying silk Primrose
Tag Yellow wool or floss
Body Mixed orange and claret seal's fur (2 : 1)
Rib Fine gold tinsel
Hackle Grizzle cock

Pensioners

This series of flies has served me and a number of my fishing acquaintances very well indeed on both chalk streams and northern freestone rivers. They are a parachute-style series devised by Peter Mackenzie-Philps for an elderly angler who needed a highly visible dry fly. The black version usefully represents any dark aquatic or terrestrial fly, and the light version is best when olives are on the water.

Black Pensioner

Hook 12–14
Tying silk Black
Tail Black cock fibres
Body Black-dyed cock pheasant centre tail fibres
Rib Fine gold wire
Wing White mink tail hair tied upright
Hackle Black cock in parachute style

Light Pensioner

Hook 12–14
Tying silk Olive
Tail Greenwell cock fibres
Body Hare's fur
Rib Fine gold wire
Wing White mink tail hair tied upright
Hackle Greenwell cock in parachute style

Pepper's Own

I like this fly very much indeed even though I have fished it for only three or four seasons. It was devised by Tony Pepper for trout and grayling in Yorkshire rivers and is now fished throughout the country with great success.

Hook 12–14

Tying silk   Purple
Tail   Three strands of cock pheasant centre tail herl about twice the body length
Body   Wound strands of cock pheasant centre tail herl
Rib   Red silk
Hackle   Red cock with honey grizzle cock in front

Pheasant Tail

In *The New Illustrated Dictionary of Trout Flies* I wrote: 'The floating Pheasant Tail is one of the best dry flies ever devised.' Far from retracting that today I would endorse it even more. Few, if any, patterns have consistently caught so many fish for me throughout the season under a variety of conditions. As a general imitative pattern only a handful of others come close to it. It is probably taken for a spinner of the blue-winged olive, medium olive, pale watery, and iron blue. Originally, when it was devised by Payne Collier in about 1901, it did not have wings but later variations include spent wings to represent spinners more accurately.

Hook   12–14
Tying silk   Light brown
Tail   Honey-dun cock fibres
Body   Cock pheasant tail fibres
Rib   Gold wire
Hackle   Honey-dun cock (alternatives used are bright blue or rusty-dun)

Pheasant Tail Spinner (M. Riesco)
Hook   12–14
Tail   Blue-dun hackle fibres
Body   Cock pheasant tail fibres
Wing   Light blue-dun cock hackle tips tied spent
Hackle   Golden-dun cock

Rat-faced Macdougall
This highly buoyant North American pattern is ideal for faster broken water.

Hook   10–12
Tail   Deer hair or ginger cock fibres
Body   Spun and clipped deer hair
Wing   Two grizzle hackle points set upright

Hackle   Ginger cock

Red Quill
This is one of the old patterns that was originally fished wet but made the successful transition to the surface. It is attributed to Thomas Rushworth, who was thought to have devised the fly in about 1803. Different authorities suggest that it represents different naturals, both the blue-winged olive and claret dun being mentioned. In addition to the dressing below, recent variations include replacing the wing with a bunch of pale blue cock hackle fibres set upright, or omitting the wing and replacing the hackle with a pale blue-dun cock hackle.

Hook   14
Tail   Bright natural red cock fibres
Body   Peacock quill dyed reddish-brown
Wing   Medium starling wing
Hackle   Bright natural red cock

Rough Olive
All the olives can be imitated by a rough olive by varying the hook size and the shades of the materials used.

Rough Olive (M. Riesco)
Hook   12–14
Tail   Blue-dun fibres
Body   Olive seal's fur
Rib   Fine gold wire
Hackle   Olive-dyed badger cock

Rough Olive (Roger Woolley)
Hook   12–14
Tail   Dark olive cock fibres
Body   Olive-dyed heron herl
Rib   Fine gold wire
Wing   Dark starling or hen blackbird wing quill
Hackle   Dark olive cock hackle

Salmon Fly
This is a recommended pattern for the large stonefly (*Pteronarcys californica*) of the western United States. The body and wing hair colours can be altered to suit regional variations. This pattern can be, and should be, altered to

fit the 'mood of the day'. When the day is warm and the female insects are active, fluttering and swimming vigorously after dropping their eggs, the heavily hackled fly rides high and it can be twitched and skated. On an overcast, cool day, when lethargic females drift quietly with the currents, the hackles should be trimmed with scissors so that the fly sits flush on the surface.

Hook Longshank 4–12
Tying silk Black monocord
Tail Dark elk hair
Body Rusty orange poly yarn palmered with brown cock hackles
Wing Dark elk hair
Hackle Three brown and one grizzle hackles mixed

Sanctuary

Dr Thomas Sanctuary devised this trout and grayling fly, possibly in the 1880s. He was a friend of H. S. Hall and G. S. Marryat, who taught Halford to tie flies. The absence of wings, which were almost compulsory in Halford's day, inclines me to think that the dressing is of later origin. It is an excellent late-season pattern.

Hook 14
Tying silk Primrose
Body Dark hare's ear fur
Rib Flat gold tinsel
Hackle Coch-y-bondhu

Sedge Flies (*Trichoptera*)

The comprehensive list given in Table F provides most of the information the fly fisher needs to know about the general appearance and times of emergence of the commonest British river species. Listed below are the artificial patterns for use wherever trout feed on adult caddis.

Black Sedge (T. B. Thomas)

Hook 10–14
Tying silk Black
Body Black wool or chenille
Wing Black moose hair tied flat and clipped square

Hackle Black cock tied in reverse so that it slopes forward

Caperer (William Lunn)

Hook 12–14
Body Four or five strands of dark turkey tail fibres with a centre band of two swan fibres dyed yellow (goose is a substitute)
Wing Coot's wing dyed chocolate-brown
Hackle Medium Rhode Island Red cock with a black cock in front, or wound together

Cinnamon Sedge (Richard Walker)

Hook Longshank 10
Tying silk Hot orange
Tip Yellow fluorescent floss
Body Buff ostrich herl
Wing Barred buff cock hackle fibres
Hackle Ginger or natural red cock

Dancing Caddis (Gary LaFontaine)

This pattern (Fig 54) can be tied in different colours and size to match the natural. The pattern below is the brown and yellow version.
Hook Swedish Dry Fly hook
Body Yellow fur (with a brownish tinge)
Wing Speckled brown deer hair
Hackle Light brown cock

A simplified version for the larger sizes is now recommended. This is tied on up-eye fine-wire Atlantic salmon hooks, sizes 6–10. No hackle is used; the body is of dubbed synthetic or natural fur; the wing of elk or deer hair is tied on the underside of the hook, as the fly floats upside down. The butts are clipped and left slightly long at the sides.

Elk-hair Caddis

(originally developed by Al Troth)
Hook 12–18
Tying silk To match the body
Body Mixed dyed natural or synthetic fur to produce the required colour and palmered with a brown or ginger cock
Wing Fine grey or tan deer or elk hair tied around the body but not on the underside
Head Clipped wing butts
Hackle None

Fig 54 Tying the Dancing Caddis. See text for materials.

F Sedge
A number of sedge pupa and adult imitations have appeared using cul de canard feathers. This was one of the originals from Marjan Fratnik.

Hook 12–14 standard or slightly long shank
Tying silk Brown
Body Very fine beige dubbing tied slim, or coloured to match the natural
Hackle Palmered natural red cock
Wing Two cul de canard feathers tied slightly longer than the hook

Grannom (Pat Russell)
Hook 14
Tying silk Green
Tip Fluorescent green wool
Body Natural heron herl
Wing Blue-dun cock fibres clipped level with the bend
Hackle Ginger cock

Great Red Sedge (Dave Collyer)
Hook 10–12
Tying silk Brown
Tail Red cock fibres
Body Grey mole's fur with a palmered dark red cock hackle
Rib Gold wire
Wing Brown speckled hen's wing
Hackle Dark red cock

Hairwing Caddis
By varying the wing and body colours different species can be represented. This is an excellent pattern to imitate a fluttering adult.

Hook 12–18
Tying silk Black
Body Natural or synthetic fur
Wing Deer body hair or mink tail guard hair
Hackle Generous turns of a cock hackle over the wing roots

Henryville Special

Originally an old unnamed English pattern, this was adopted by the Pennsylvanian anglers of the 1920s and is now used extensively wherever sedges appear. Doug Swisher and Carl Richards wrote: 'It is the greatest hackle pattern we have ever used and can be fished drag-free, skittered, or even wet and dragging.'

Hook 12–18
Tying silk Grey
Body Olive silk with a palmered grizzle hackle
Wing Two grey duck wing quill sections over wood duck fibres
Hackle Natural brown cock wound over the wing roots

Little Red Sedge (G. E. M. Skues)

This is my all-time favourite sedge pattern. I am tempted to fish it almost regardless of which species of sedge is emerging.

Hook 12–14
Tying silk Hot orange
Body Darkest hare's fur with a palmered short-fibred red cock hackle
Rib Fine gold wire
Wing Landrail wing (red-brown partridge tail is a substitute), bunched and rolled and sloping well back over the tail
Hackle Five or six turns of deep-red cock in front of the wings (longer-fibred than body hackle)

Red Sedge (Richard Walker)

Hook Longshank or standard 10–12
Tip or tag Orange fluorescent wool
Body Clipped chestnut ostrich herl or chestnut pheasant tail fibres
Wing Natural red cock fibres, or red cree, or cuckoo cock, clipped level with the bend
Hackle Two long-fibred natural red cock hackles

Silhouette Caddis

This is Finland's Juha Vainio's answer for the newly emerged sedge. It emphasises the lighter colouring most species display on emerging. The Antron body and snowshoe hair wing make a very translucent imitation.

Hook Tiemco 2302 10–14
Tying silk Yellow
Body Yellow Antron dubbing
Body hackle Short-fibred sandy dun cock, upper body fibres cut away
Wing Snowshoe hare foot hair, not too dense
Head hackle Dark blue dun cock wound sparsely over the thorax
Thorax Antron/Hare blend

Spent Partridge Caddis (Mike and Sheralee Lawson)

This is an excellent imitation of many small spent sedge species. It is fished in the film, where its silhouette is its principal attribute.

Hook 14–22
Body Olive fur
Wing Mottled fibres of a brown partridge feather
Hackle Brown cock fibres palmered over the head and optionally clipped flat on the top and bottom
Head Peacock herl

Squirrel Sedge (Lars-Åke Olsson)

Hook Partridge E1A 8–16
Tying silk Brown
Body Reddish-brown squirrel fur (subs hare's ear or mask) spun on a spinning block
Hackle Natural red cock palmered with the upper fibres cut away and the lower section with V cut out
Wing Reddish-brown squirrel tail, tied in behind the eye with points over the eye, folded back over the eye and large head secured with a whip-finish behind the thread

Swimming Caddis Pupa

Roman Moser fishes this as a floating or sub-surface caddis pupa. He reverses the usual light body, darker thorax combination after considering the success of gold or brass bead pupa imitations close to the stream bed. He fishes this by quartering upstream. By feeding more line he creates a bow in the line. At

211

each feeding mend the fly skitters slightly and so it is fished out in a series of short downstream jerks.

Hook Partridge CS27GRS, 10–18
Tying silk Yellow
Abdomen Orange carpet wool mixed with SLF (Synthetic Living Fibres) to give a sparkle effect
Legs Two turns of light brown cock hackle, second or third grade. When the fly is fished, trim away the lower fibres
Thorax Golden Yellow SLF tied fairly bulky

Voljc Sedge

Dr Bozidar Voljc of Slovenia devised this highly realistic sedge wing using mottled natural feathers. The wings are made by gluing them, underside down, on a non-elastic stocking mesh held tight on a frame. The feathers are then singly cut out and trimmed to shape. The pattern below is a cinnamon sedge.

Hook 12–16
Tying silk Black
Body Palmered dark ginger cock with the upper fibres cut away
Wing Natural game feathers or waterfowl feathers prepared as above and tied in a tight V, extending beyond the body
Hackle Dark ginger cock

Small Dark Olive (*Baetis scambus*)

This is a very widely distributed species with a preference for alkaline water. It is particularly important on the chalk streams. As the name suggests, the adults are very small and appear throughout the season, as early as February and as late as November, with their most prolific period in the afternoons between May and August. In common with other *Baetis* species, the female spinners often crawl below the surface to lay their eggs. After oviposition they are unable to break back through the surface film and lay there trapped in the spent position, where they are an attractive target for trout.

The male dun has a pale grey-green olive abdomen, with the last two segments yellow-ish. The wings are medium-to-dark grey. The legs are pale yellow-olive and the two tails are grey.

The female dun is very similar to the male except that the body is grey-olive.

The female spinner, also known as the small red spinner, varies in the abdomen colour between dark brown tinged with olive to mahogany-brown. The wings are transparent with blackish veins. The legs are olive-brown and the two tails greyish-white.

In addition to the pattern below general olive patterns and smaller versions of the dark olive are effective imitations.

Small Dark Olive Hatching Special
(Terry Griffiths)
A pattern to represent the emerging dun in the surface film.

Hook 16–18
Tail Very short blue-dun fibres
Body A short body of mole's fur
Rib Fine gold thread
Hackle Rhode Island Red cock with a blue-dun in front

Small Spurwings (*Centroptilum luteolum*)

The small to medium-sized small spurwing dun is very similar to the pale watery and small dark olive duns but has a tiny spur-shaped hindwing which is almost invisible to the naked eye. Needless to say, patterns imitating either of the two forementioned species will be adequate. This species is widely distributed except in Wales, with a preference for alkaline rivers, where the nymphs inhabit weedbeds. They appear between May and September but are most prolific in June. The female spinner is also known as the little amber spinner because of the body colour when spent. The body varies between yellow-brown and light amber before fading and the underside is creamy-yellow with the last two segments light amber. The wings are transparent and the two tails pale olive-white. Sometimes the male spinner is found on the water. It has a white translucent body of which the last three segments and thorax are a lighter brown.

Smuts (*Simulium*)

The first pattern listed is from Danish fly fisherman, Preben Torp Jacobsen, who devised it to represent the smut hanging in the surface unable to hatch. The second pattern is an adult imitation from John Goddard, who has found it 'phenomenally successful'. The fly is tied small on the front half of a wide-gape hook so that a small silhouette is presented. Without resort to the tiny sizes a reasonable hook-hold can be established.

Reed Smut (Preben Torp Jacobsen)
Hook   16–18
Tying silk   Black
Body   Black condor herl tied fairly short (black heron is a substitute)
Hackle   Long-stemmed short-fibred black cock tied in parachute style in the middle of the body

Goddard Smut (John Goddard)
Hook   Wide gape 18
Tying silk   Black
Body   Black ostrich herl with a very short flue (taken from near the tip of the feather) wound on the front half of the shank
Hackle   Short-fibred good-quality black cock (three or four turns)

Sparkle Dun

A popular pattern from Western America for the smaller duns, devised by Craig Matthews and John Juracek. It is a Comparadun with an additional tail.

Hook   14–20
Tying silk   To match the body colour
Tail   Sparkle Poly or Z-lon to match the trailing empty shuck
Body   Natural or blended fur
Wing   Fine deer hair tied in Comparadun style

Sparkle Parachute

This is a Paradun with a tail of Z-lon, and is an amendment by Wayne Luallen of the Sparkle Dun tied by Craig Matthews, using the tail material introduced by John Betts – quite a pedigree. Like many other parachute patterns, this is an emerger but made more complete by the imitation of the trailing nymphal shuck.

Hook   14–22
Tying silk   To match the body colour
Shuck   Z-lon in brown (usually)
Body   Natural muskrat or bleached and/or dyed blended fur
Wing   White turkey body feather dyed to match the natural
Hackle   High quality cock to match the natural

Stoneflies (Plecoptera)

Details of the life cycle can be found on page 65. More specific information about different species and artificial patterns in addition to the general imitation listed below will be found under February Red, Salmon fly and Yellow Sally.

Adult Stonefly (John Veniard)
Hook   14
Tying silk   Yellow
Body   Mixed hare's ear and yellow seal's fur
Rib   Yellow silk
Wing   Four dark blue-dun hackle tips tied flat over the back, or hen pheasant wing
Hackle   Dark grizzle cock

Sturdy's Fancy

I make no apology for including this first-class grayling fly because I have caught scores of trout with it. Sturdy devised the pattern for evening use when spinners are on the water. Reg Righyni included a rib of crimson tying silk and the hint of red suggested by this would not be out of place when red spinners (female olive spinners) are about. The white hackle is a fair representation of the transparent wings of a spinner.

Hook   14–16
Tying silk   Crimson
Tag   Red wool
Body   Peacock herl
Rib (optional)   Crimson tying silk
Hackle   White cock

Sunset Spinner and Dun

A red sunset can pose its problems for the fly fisher. Anything on the surface, and particularly anything translucent such as a spent spinner's abdomen and wings, takes on a reddish glow. Charles Jardine devised the dun and spinner dressings below to represent a wide range of species. The variation between species is unimportant; it is the size and the reddish tinge that are the key factors. The spinner dressing is given first.

Hook 14–18
Tying silk Maroon
Tail Nylon paintbrush bristles (Artists' Daler oil No. 8 or 10) widely spaced
Body Rust/orange Poly II 50 per cent, red-brown Poly II 40 per cent, red Burgess body gloss or Antron 10 per cent. Well mixed and blended
Wings Two good-quality blue-dun cock hackles wound together through the thorax and clipped in a V format top and bottom

The pattern for the dun is as for the spinner except that the wing is dark-blue-dyed turkey body feather fibres tied centrally and upright. The light blue-dun cock hackle is wound in parachute style round the base of the wing.

Super Grizzly

John Goddard devised this general all-season pattern for the Kennet. I quote from *The Trout and the Fly*: 'The new fly *is* good: it is exceptionally effective, and has proved itself to be a killer on rivers, lakes and mountain streams. It is intended as a general representation of any of the darker-bodied upwinged flies.'

Hook 14–16
Tying silk Hot orange
Tail Pale red dun cock fibres or muskrat whiskers for calm water
Body Three natural heron herls
Hackle Grizzle and red cock tied back to back

Treacle Parkin

I suspect that this is mainly fished as a grayling fly but it is also an excellent trout pattern on the waters I fish in the north of England. It probably developed as a variation of the Red Tag, which differs only in the colour of the wool tag. Another successful variation for grayling is to replace the orange or yellow tag with one of fluorescent arc-chrome wool.

Hook 14–16
Tag Orange or yellow wool
Body Peacock herl
Hackle Natural red gamecock

Tup's Indispensable

How R. S. Austin came to discover that the urine-stained wool from the private parts of a ram would make an excellent body dubbing one can only speculate. It is likely that he was aware of the reference in Alexander Mackintosh's book, *The Driffield Angler* (1806), which mentioned the fine wool from around a ram's testicles as a body material. The actual materials used for Austin's pattern remained a secret long after his death so that his daughter had a monopoly in the supply of the flies. Needless to say, no one guessed the unlikely source of the wool. Austin tied it to represent the female olive spinners, commonly referred to as red spinners, but it is better as an imitation of the female spinners of the pale watery and small spurwing. The original dressing is followed by a modern version.

Hook 16
Tying silk Yellow
Tail Yellow-spangled lightish blue cock fibres
Tip Small tip of tying silk
Body Mixed white fur from a ram's testicles, lemon-coloured spaniel fur, cream seal's fur and a small amount of yellow mohair. The last item was later replaced by crimson seal's fur on Skues's suggestion.
Hackle Yellow-spangled lightish blue cock

Usual

This very popular North American emerger pattern was devised by Fran Betters on the Ausable River. Much of its success is due to the crinkly, reflective, translucent and water repellent wing and trailing shuck made from the foot fur from a snowshoe hare.

Hook   12–18
Tying silk   To match the body colour
Tail   A small bunch of hair from the foot of the snowshoe hare
Body   Dubbed underfur from the snowshoe hare
Wing   Single upright post wing of the same material as the tail

Variants

Dr William Baigent was one of the first north country dry-fly fishers in the early 1890s. He devised his series of variants which had longer than normal hackle fibres. What should be understood is that the hackles were therefore less stiff. They spread more readily when balanced on the surface and consequently supported the fly better. The wings should be smallish and thinly tied, sloping forwards over the eye. Asked what the Baigent Brown was tied to represent, Baigent replied: 'It is not tied to represent any fly, it is tied to catch trout.' Most variants have longer hackles than normal; all are for floating high on faster water. Also see H & L Variant.

Baigent's Brown

Hook   14
Body   Yellow floss
Wing   Hen pheasant wing
Hackle   Long-fibred stiff furnace cock

Cream Variant (Art Flick)

Hook   Shortshank 12
Tying silk   Yellow
Tail   Long stiff cream cock hackle fibres
Body   Stripped cream hackle stalk which should be soaked well in water before use
Hackle   Long-fibred cream cock

Wickham's Fancy

This has been a popular pattern since at least the 1880s and possibly earlier. It is fished both as a floater and as a wet fly. The floater is best in the smaller sizes and is useful when trout are smutting and proving difficult to catch. It also sometimes works well in a caenis hatch.

Hook   14–16
Tying silk   Brown
Tail   Guinea-fowl dyed reddish-brown or ginger hackle fibres
Body   Flat gold tinsel with a palmered ginger-red cock
Rib   Fine gold wire
Wing   Medium starling wing set upright and split
Hackle   Ginger-red cock

Wulffs

The Wulff series of flies has gained a world-wide reputation over the last fifty years. They were tied because Lee Wulff thought that some of the standard patterns of the 1930s didn't offer much to a hungry trout and so he designed these meatier alternatives. The variations are many because 'the series is a category of flies rather than a particular pattern or patterns'. Lee Wulff comments further that in many reference books the wings slant forwards. This was not his intention. He wrote in a letter to me 'that is a sign of a fly-tyer who is either careless or unable to make them stand vertically'.

Grey Wulff

Hook   8–16
Tail   Natural bucktail fibres
Body   Grey rabbit fur or angora wool
Wing   Brown bucktail tied upright or split
Hackle   Blue-dun cock

Royal Wulff

Tail   Brown bucktail
Body   Peacock herl with a broad centre band of red floss silk
Wing   White bucktail upright or split
Hackle   Two chocolate-brown cock hackles

White Wulff

Tail   White bucktail
Body   Creamy-white wool
Wing   White bucktail tied upright or bunched
Hackle   One or two badger cock hackles

Were Wulff

This is a Bill Blackburn and Gary LaFontaine

variation on the Wulff theme. They combined the best attributes of the Adams, Hare's Ear and Royal Wulff.

Tail Brown deer hair
Body Dubbed dark hare's ear fur
Wing White bucktail split and tied upright
Hackle Mixed brown and grizzle cock hackles

Yellow Sally (*Isoperla grammatica*)

This is the easiest of the British stoneflies to recognise because of its distinctive yellow body and flat yellow-green wings. The medium-sized adult appears between April and August on lowland rivers with a stony or sandy riverbed. They are widely distributed except in parts of the Midlands and East Anglia, and are common on limestone streams. The first pattern is a UK dressing; the second is a North American imitation.

Yellow Sally

Hook 14
Tying silk Primrose
Tail Greenish-yellow cock fibres
Body Drab light-green dubbed wool
Hackle Greenish-yellow cock

Yellow Sally

Hook 14–18
Tying silk White
Body Dubbed fluorescent chartreuse wool with a palmered cream or grizzle cock hackle extending three-quarters of the body length. The upper fibres of the rear half of the hackle are trimmed away.
Wing Light elk hair tied in at the rear of the full palmered hackle so that it extends from halfway along the back to beyond the bend.

An Afterthought

'Fish, of course, have their own ways of getting even with fishermen . . .

'Our conceit, if we have any, and none are entirely immune, must always be moderated by a sense of humility. Then, in compensation, comes the day when we take a two-pounder from an impossible position under a willow and a three-pounder which needed a fly dropped between two weed beds in a space no larger than a cup of tea, where conflicting currents provided instant drag, and we begin to imagine we are not so bad as we thought we were. We even begin to pontificate about the right fly, the length of leader, the need to cast the curve, and before we are aware of it consider, or even begin to write, authoritative articles for the magazines. This, if we are not careful, is where the rot sets in and we come to regard ourselves as reasonably skilful. The cure for that illusion, for it is an illusion, is a couple of splendidly blank days.'

Conrad Voss Bark, *A Fly on the Water*, 1986

Bibliography

Arbona, Fred L. Jr, *Mayflies, the Angler, and the Trout* (Winchester, 1980).

Brooks, Charles E., *The Trout and the Stream* (Winchester, 1974).

Caucci, Al, and Nastasi, Bob, *Hatches* (Comparahatch, 1975).

Dunne, J. W., *Sunshine and the Dry Fly* (Black, 1924).

Edmunds, G. F. Jr, Jensen, S. L., and Berner, L., *The Mayflies of North and Central America* (University of Minnesota Press, Minneapolis, 1978).

Elliott, J. M., and Humpesch, U. H., *A Key to the Adults of the British Ephemeroptera* (Freshwater Biological Association, 1983).

Fox, Charles K., *Rising Trout* (1967).

Fox, Charles K., *This Wonderful World of Trout* (Freshet, 1971).

Frost, W. E., and Brown, M. E., *The Trout* (Collins, 1967).

Gingrich, Arnold, *The Fishing in Print* (Winchester, 1974).

Goddard, John, *Trout Fly Recognition* (Black, 1966).

Goddard, John, and Clarke, Brian, *The Trout and the Fly* (Benn, 1980).

Halford, F. M., *Dry-Fly Fishing in Theory and Practice* (Sampson Low, 1889).

Halford, F. M., *Modern Development of the Dry Fly* (Routledge, 1910).

Halford, F. M., *The Dry-Fly Man's Handbook* (Routledge, 1913).

Harding, E. W., *The Flyfisher and the Trout's Point of View* (Seely, 1931).

Harris, J. R., *An Angler's Entomology* (Collins, 1950).

Hewitt, E. R., *A Trout and Salmon Fisherman for Seventy-Five Years* (Scribner, 1950).

Hill, Les, and Marshall, Graeme, *Stalking Trout* (Halcyon Press, SeTo Publishing, 1985).

Humphreys, Joe, *Trout Tactics* (Stackpole Books, 1981).

Hynes, H. B. N., *A Key to the Adults and Nymphs of the British Stoneflies* (Freshwater Biological Association, 1977).

Hynes, H. B. N., *The Ecology of Running Waters* (University of Toronto Press, 1970).

Jacques, David, *Fisherman's Fly and Other Studies* (Black, 1965).

Jennings, Preston J., *A Book of Trout Flies* (Derrydale, 1935).

Jorgensen, Poul, *Modern Trout Flies* (Winchester, 1975, 1979).

La Branche, George, M. L., *The Dry Fly and Fast Water* (Scribner, 1914).

LaFontaine, Gary, *Caddisflies* (Winchester, 1981).

LaFontaine, Gary, *The Dry Fly* (Greycliffe, 1990).

Lawrie, W. H., *All-Fur Flies and How to Dress Them* (Pelham, 1967).

Lawrie, W. H., *Modern Trout Flies* (Macdonald, 1972).

Lee, Art, *Fishing Dry Flies for Trout* (Atheneum, 1983).

Lively, Chauncy, *Chauncy Lively's Fly Box* (Stackpole, 1980).

Macan, T. T., *A Key to the Adults of the British Trichoptera* (Freshwater Biological Association, 1973).

Marinaro, Vincent, *A Modern Dry-Fly Code* (Crown, 1950, 1970).

Marinaro, Vincent, *In the Ring of the Rise* (Crown, 1976).

Migel, J. Michael (ed.), *The Masters on the Dry Fly* (Lippincott, 1977).

Mottram, J. C., *Fly-Fishing: Some New Arts and Mysteries* (The Field, 1915, 1921).

Overfield, Donald, *50 Favourite Dry Flies*, n.d.

Proper, Datus C., *What the Trout Said* (Knopf, 1982).

Roberts, John, *A Guide to River Trout Flies* (Crowood, 1990).

Roberts, John, *The New Illustrated Dictionary of Trout Flies* (Allen & Unwin, 1986).

Schweibert, Ernest G. Jr., *Matching the Hatch* (Macmillan, 1955).

Schweibert, Ernest G. Jr, *Trout* (Dutton, 1978).

Solomon, Larry, and Leiser, Eric, *The Caddis and the Angler* (Stackpole, 1977).

Sosin, Mark, and Clark, John, *Through the Fish's Eye* (Harper & Row, 1973).

Swisher, Doug, and Richards, Carl, *Selective Trout* (Winchester, 1971).

Swisher, Doug, and Richards, Carl, *Fly Fishing Strategy* (Winchester, 1975).

Swisher, Doug, and Richards, Carl, *Tying the Swisher/Richards Flies* (Stackpole, 1980).

Walker, C. F., *Brown Trout and the Dry Fly* (Seeley Service, 1955).

Walker, C. F., *Fly-Tying as an Art* (Jenkins, 1957).

Walker, Richard, *Fly Dressing Innovations* (Benn, 1974).

Wright, Leonard M. Jr., *Fishing the Dry Fly as a Living Insect* (Dutton, 1972).

Wright, Leonard M. Jr, *Fly Fishing Heresies* (1975).

Wright, Leonard, M. Jr, *The Ways of Trout* (Winchester, 1985).

Index

Note: bold numerals denote page numbers of illustrations.